Lives People Live

WILEY SERIES ON METHODS IN PSYCHOTHERAPY

Series Editor
Boris Semeonoff
Department of Psychology
University of Edinburgh

Jungian Psychotherapy
A Study in Analytical Psychology
Michael Fordham

Lives People Live
A Textbook of Transactional Analysis
Mavis Klein

Further titles in preparation

Lives People Live

A Textbook of Transactional Analysis

MAVIS KLEIN

JOHN WILEY & SONS

Chichester · New York · Brisbane · Toronto

British Library Cataloguing in Publication Data:

Klein, Mavis
    Lives people live. — (Wiley series on methods
    in psychotherapy).
    1. Transactional analysis
    I. Title
    158   RC489.T7   79–40737

    ISBN 0 471 27648 0
    ISBN 0 471 27649 9 Pbk

Photo typeset in India by The Macmillan Co. of India Ltd., Bangalore–1
and printed in Great Britain by The Pitman Press, Bath, Avon

For Anita and Stella

an antidote to my Witch messages

Contents

viii

Editor's Preface

This, the second, volume in the series *Methods in Psychotherapy* presents a form of treatment very different from that described by Michael Fordham in his *Jungian Psychotherapy: a study in analytical psychology.* Indeed, the very term 'treatment' is probably less appropriate in the context of Transactional Analysis than in that of the more conventional psychotherapies. The psychoanalyst is traditionally a medically qualified person, and even the psychotherapist whose skills have been acquired through other channels is invested with quasi-medical authority. The 'therapy' afforded by Transactional Analysis (TA) is not so much interventional action directed at 'cure' as an ongoing process through which the 'client' is afforded an opportunity of attaining insight into a personal problem.

To reach this goal a client has to learn the language and understand the concepts of TA. I have no wish to pre-empt Mavis Klein's lively and persuasive exposition; I would only suggest that there is perhaps less disparity between her interests and Dr Fordham's than might appear on the surface. In introducing Dr Fordham's book and the series as a whole I referred to a 'broad spectrum of orientation'. Much of Jung's teaching is concerned with the more recondite (but nevertheless real) aspects of human experience; TA is very much a matter of the here and now. That being so the two systems may be located at opposite ends of the spectrum, but it is a spectrum deriving from a single light source—the teaching of Freud. Eric Berne, the creator of TA, was himself a trained Freudian analyst, and while academics like to play with the idea of 'the unconscious without Freud', what Berne proposed was essentially 'Freud without the unconscious'.

Whether such a concept is feasible is something the reader must judge for himself. One should not be put off by the ultra-colloquial language in which much of the literature of TA is couched, nor should one assume from the title of Berne's best-known book *Games People Play* that TA is mainly concerned with how to 'win' in social encounters. TA has progressed, both in theory and in practice, since Eric Berne laid its foundations, and Mavis Klein has herself, I feel, contributed significantly to its development.

B. SEMEONOFF

Preface

The basic interest of Transactional Analysis is the study of ego states. Ego states are not roles, but real, separate parts of each of us which together make up our sense of 'self'.

Since Eric Berne first developed Transactional Analysis in the early 1960s, TA has reached the stage where it is now a language in which it is possible to speak and make sense of all the experiences of our conscious lives, both inside our own heads and hearts and in our interactions with others. It is of course true that we can speak and make sense of all our conscious experiences in English — and many other languages as well — and there is no specious grandiosity in TA which seeks to invalidate other languages in order to prove its own worth. What it does claim as uniquely its own, however, is its enormous precision and concision, which make possible a tangible and easy communicability of those truths which are clearly felt but only partially or fuzzily expressed by our novelists, poets and psychoanalysts. An analogy which often springs to my mind in comparing TA to ordinary language as a vehicle for expressing psychological wisdom is that of set theory to ordinary algebra. For all the 'rightness' and beauty of algebra there are many problems where the application of set theory provides through its graphical immediacy an incomparably quicker and aesthetically more pleasing solution. Such, I believe, is the advantage of TA over ordinary language in referring to and understanding psychological truths, and I hope this book will validate that claim.

My expectation is that most of my readers will already have some acquaintance with TA which they will be seeking to further in reading this book, and I am confident that there is enough originality in theory and exposition in what I have written to provide interest for already fluent speakers of the language. However, I make no presumption of any previous knowledge of TA in my exposition and therefore hope very much that it will also succeed in persuading non-professionals of the validity and potency of TA in understanding and coping with personal issues in everyday life. But for those seeking personal psychotherapy this book cannot be a substitute for the living experience of a therapeutic group, any more than an A-level course in French can provide the same fluency in that language as can be acquired by living in France for a year or so. A combination of good grammar and practice and a wide vocabulary provides the greatest fluency and expressiveness, of course.

I believe that as well as being a new language with which to express old truths, TA can also lay some claim to being an original theory. Certainly its direct descent from Psychoanalysis is obvious throughout and, less explicitly but also very closely it is related both to Adler's individual psychology and Skinner's operant conditioning. But in the binding of these diverse elements Berne produced not a mixture but a new compound. Even the core concept of *ego states* alone — so clearly derivatives of the Superego, Ego, and Id — presents, I believe, a radically new framework within which to experience ourselves. For the separateness of the ego states furnishes us with permission to experience ourselves as *necessarily inconsistent*, which — a simple thing in itself — I have seen provide immense relief from suffering for many anguished people.

Eric Berne wrote six books on TA, beginning with *Transactional Analysis in Psychotherapy*, first published in 1961, and culminating in *What do you say after you say hello?* published posthumously in 1970. He also edited (and largely wrote) the *Transactional Analysis Bulletin*, beginning in January 1962 and published quarterly thereafter until his death in July 1970. For those of my readers who revel in the evolution of ideas and the appreciation of genius I recommend these writings in TA above all others. Paperback editions of all Berne's books are now widely available and a bound collection of all the Bulletins is obtainable from *Transactional Pubs*, 1772 Vallejo Street, San Francisco, California, 94123, U.S.A.

Since January 1971, the official organ of the International Transactional analysis Association has been the quarterly *Transactional Analysis Journal*,[1] in whose pages TA theory and application have continued to evolve. Many important concepts now familiarly used by TA therapists and teachers were only incipient in *What do you say after you say hello?*,[2] but fortunately there have been many brilliant followers of Berne in whose minds these ideas have germinated and been brought to life. Books on TA have also proliferated. *I'm OK-You're OK*[3] by Thomas Harris, first published in 1967 and *Born to Win*[4] by Muriel James and Dorothy Jongeward, first published in 1971, have familiarized millions of people all over the world with TA's basic concepts, whilst Claude Steiner's *Scripts People Live* (1974)[5] is fast becoming an essential reference book for people involved in the rare possibility which TA makes available to us for rewriting our own destinies. TA books expressing specialist viewpoints have also been published, most notable amongst these being Jacqui Schiff's *Cathexis Reader*,[6] in which she reports on her astonishing success in the transactional analytic treatment of schizophrenics. Several excellent books have also been written with a view to introducing TA to children.

Currently TA is taught at undergraduate and post-graduate levels in over a thousand colleges and universities in the United States as well as to children in primary and secondary schools there.[7] In America it is also widely taught and known and used in business and industry as a highly potent psychological theory and method of understanding human communication.

In this country TA is only now becoming more than a fringe theory and method, occasionally taught and applied in its appropriate settings, but rarely more than superficially. Why it has taken such a time arriving here is open to speculation, but my own view is that anything that has happened on the other side of the Atlantic since 1776 is still suspect as a bit too new-fangled for us to accept readily or take seriously. However, largely through the indomitable efforts of Michael Reddy, England's first and Europe's second member of the ITAA to attain its highest membership status of Teaching Member, the (British) Institute of Transactional Analysis was constituted in November 1975. Its second conference, held in London in May 1976, was attended by nearly two hundred people. Among those present at the 1977 and 1978 conferences were a considerable number of representatives of prestigious British organizations and businesses who, in their working lives, are now using many TA concepts and methods.

Through my own work as a transactional analyst I am aware of a continually increasing interest in TA in the community at large. I tend no longer to be the party to take the initiative in setting up courses I run for people in business and in the helping professions, and more and more prospective patients who contact me are looking specifically for a TA therapist rather than a good 'general' psychotherapist, traditionally having a broadly based psychoanalytic orientation combined with some eclectic pragmatism.

All this augurs well — I believe and hope — for this present book. Two separate wants provided the impetus for its writing. Most importantly, I saw a need for a comprehensive and up-to-date account of TA theory, much of which has never been published outside the official TA Journal. Many excellent introductory books on TA are now in print, but all concentrate essentially on whetting the appetites of readers with easy-to-digest accounts of TA's basic concepts, ready-mixed in the minds of their authors. But I believe there are also many people who are looking for a bit more intellectual meat in their diet — people who wish to feed their heads as well as their hearts and digest TA into their thinking as well as their feeling selves. It is to such people that this book is primarily addressed.

My second impulse in writing this book had to do with personal and national pride. I got sick of answering 'No' to people who asked, 'Are there any *English* books on TA?' and I felt I would like to be the author of the first. So here it is. Vocabulary, spelling, idiom, and examples are proudly British, although I hope, too, there will be Americans amongst my readers who will find it worthy of the effort of translation. It represents the distillation of my experiences of reading all the theory that has ever been written in TA (mercifully still a finite task), of practising as a TA therapist for three years, and of listening to admired colleagues, particularly at the first two European TA conferences held at Villars, Switzerland, in July 1975 and at Enschede, Holland, in July 1976.

All perception is selective, being related to emotional and cognitive vested interests in the perceiver. To the extent that it is logically possible, I feel it behoves me to inform my readers objectively of my subjective biases which have inevitably been involved in the writing of this book. As a theoretical psychologist

I believe in qualitative accuracy and do not believe in quantitative precision in understanding human nature. A straight ruler measuring to tenths of an inch is a better instrument than a bent one measuring to hundredths. As a psychotherapist I believe in the primacy of words as the stuff out of which our sense of 'self' is fashioned and the primacy of laughter in the achievement of curative insight. And as a consumer of other people's theories, I am drawn to the clearest, the most concise, and the most general.

To a very large extent, these are values which inhere in TA itself and which I share with all my TA colleagues. It is on the therapeutic issues of laughter and words that I am most likely to be at odds with other TA practitioners, since it is these that bias me towards practising a strictly verbal form of therapy compared with others who feel the necessity to supplement TA with other modalities incorporating sensual as well as cognitive curative techniques. For me, cathartic as non-verbal expressions of self may be, dynamically they are at best self-knowingly treading the water of life whilst waiting for a lifeboat to appear on the horizon, at worst creating the delusion that treading water is itself a style of swimming.

From a meta-psychological point of view I recognize that what I have just propounded is itself determined by my own needs to rationalize and reinforce an existential position I chose to adopt when very young as the most useful adaptation to my idiosyncratic environment. But by this admission I have just now jammed myself between two facing mirrors and am staring impotently at infinity. The only viable next move must be to smash one of the mirrors, pretend the other one is not there, stick my neck out and let the reader get on with reading. The first draft of this book was so 'objective' as to be suffocating in its conceptual density. In this version, without further apology, I also incorporate my beliefs, convictions, speculations, interpretations and hunches. To all those parts in you which are also parts in me I commend this book.

The core of the text is a straightforward, up-to-date presentation of TA theory and application — that is, the way I make sense of TA for myself.[8] Unless otherwise stated, all concepts are attributable to Eric Berne and are taken to be valid. Authors other than Berne are acknowledged alongside statements of their ideas, and these may also be taken as familiarly accepted in the TA community unless otherwise stated.

Most of Berne's ideas did not achieve their final form in his mind at first writing, and various definitions of even some of his most basic concepts can be found scattered throughout his works. For this reason I have avoided citing specific references to his books or articles unless for a special purpose. Other authors — perhaps more constrained by Berne than Berne was by Berne! — by and large seem to have achieved publication of their ideas in final form first, so they are referred to specifically in the text.

In accordance with accepted nomenclature the names of particular *ego states* are capitalized throughout the text. In addition I have chosen always to capitalize the *roles* of Karpman's *drama triangle*, the *positions* in Kahler and Caper's *miniscript*, and the terms *Witch* and *Ogre*, since they have in common with the *ego states* that they are names of specific existential states of being. 'TA' is regularly used as the customary abbreviation for 'Transactional Analysis'. Technical terms, including common English words which are used more specifically and precisely in TA than in ordinary usage, are italicized throughout.

Each chapter concludes with a summary of the main ideas contained in it, author's notes, and references to sources.

Notes and References

1. The *Transactional Analysis Journal* may be obtained by subscription from the International Transactional Analysis Association, 1772 Vallejo Street, San Francisco, California 94123, USA. Back issues can also be purchased.
2. E. Berne, *What do you say after you say hello?*, Bantam, 1973.
3. T. Harris, *I'm OK– You're OK*, Harper & Row, 1967.
4. M. James and D. Jongeward, *Born to Win*, Addison-Wesley, 1976.
5. C. Steiner, *Scripts People Live*, Bantam, 1974.
6. J. Schiff, *Cathexis Reader* Harper & Row, 1975.
7. M. James and contributors, *Techniques in Transactional Analysis*, Addison-Wesley, 1977, p. 28.
8. I am grateful to Bill Holloway, immediate past president of the International Transactional Analysis Association, for this definition of 'theory', which he gave at the TA conference in Holland in July 1976.

INTRODUCTION

Eric Berne and the ITAA

The life of Eric Berne[1]

Eric Bernstein was born on 10 May 1910 in Montreal, Canada, the elder child of David and Sarah Bernstein. His father was a general practitioner, his mother a professional writer and editor. His sister, Grace, was born in 1915. In 1919 his father died, at the age of thirty-eight, of tuberculosis.

In 1935 Eric Bernstein graduated in medicine from McGill University and commenced his internship at Englewood Hospital, New Jersey, USA. From 1936–38 he served his psychiatric residency at Yale University School of Medicine. At this time he became an American citizen and shortened his name to Eric Berne.

In 1940 he established himself in private practice in Norwalk, Connecticut and married his first wife, by whom he had two children. Between 1941–43 he was Clinical Assistant in Psychiatry at Mount Zion Hospital in New York and during this time began training at the New York Psychoanalytic Institute, an analysand of Paul Federn.

He joined the US Army Medical Corps as a psychiatrist in 1943 and in this capacity first began practising group therapy. On his release from the army in 1946 he was divorced from his wife and resumed his psychoanalytic training in San Francisco. His first book, *The Mind in Action*, was published in 1947.

In 1949 he met and married his second wife, by whom he had two more children. At the time of his second marriage he became the analysand of Erik Erikson and from about 1950 submitted himself to the demanding, self-regimented discipline of psychiatric practice and writing which characterized the rest of his life. Shortly before his death, he was divorced from his second wife and married his third.

The conception in Eric Berne's mind of the embryo that finally became Transactional Analysis probably dates from the first in a series of five articles on 'Intuition'.[2] In the fifth of these, published in 1957, the realities of the Adult and Child *ego states* were clearly differentiated in the now legendary anecdote about the New York lawyer who, in response to Berne's question, 'How are you?' answered, 'Are you talking to the lawyer or the little boy, Doc?'.

1

But the most important impetus for the development of TA was probably the repeated rejection in 1956 of Berne's application for certification as a psychoanalyst. He was deemed 'not ready' and out of his despair he determined to 'show them' with a completely new approach to psychotherapy. His emotional and intellectual relationship to establishment psychoanalysis is clearly in evidence in these brilliant articles and it is fascinating to witness the changes in him, over the years, from an attitude of compliance to rebellion to a self-confident insistence on reciprocal respect.

The essential disagreement between Berne and establishment psychoanalysis concerned practice, not theory. He was, and remained all his life, committed to traditional psychoanalytic theory, but his frustration with the slowness of psychoanalysis as therapy to effect measurable change in his patients made him baulk at the overtly passive role demanded of the analyst. He questioned the assumptions behind the 'rules' of psychoanalysis as therapy and decided that in one respect they were false. Where psychoanalysis insisted that Unconscious conflicts must be resolved before manifest personality changes could effectively and permanently be achieved, Berne claimed that patients could be made better *first* — and quickly — and have their underlying conflicts resolved *later*. Thus, out of a practical concern to *cure people quickly*, TA came into being and developed as a theoretical elaboration of psychoanalytic Ego psychology and a systematized approach to Ego therapy.

Between 1958 and 1968 Berne wrote and published five books. Tragically, for those who knew him and recognized his genius, he died of a heart attack in 1970 at the age of sixty, leaving the manuscripts of *Sex in Human Loving* and the crowning fulfilment of his life's work, *What do you say after you say hello?* to be published posthumously.

Such are the factual bare bones of Eric Berne's life and work. But what kind of a man was he? Since I never met him I am not in a position to describe his personality at first hand, although I have heard him described and understood psychologically by several of his friends and colleagues. Externally, he was socially shy and had difficulty in relinquishing his intellectual control of situations. Internally, he seemed to long most of all for profound and lasting intimate relationships, which he never quite achieved. But if he was never quite capable of laying thought aside entirely in favour of feeling, he certainly seems to have inspired uncontaminated love in others, and his death was deeply mourned by very many people. A particularly loving appreciation of the man has been expressed by his close friend and colleague, Claude Steiner, as an introduction to his book, *Scripts People Live*.[3]

At a strictly analytical level, my own understanding of Berne is based on the fact of his father's death when he was nine years old. Of all the traumas that we may suffer in childhood, the death of a parent is surely the greatest, and Berne himself insisted that no parent should be allowed to die before his youngest child is eighteen.[4] Empirically, the effect of such a trauma is that of leaving the individual, for the rest of his life, with a disproportionate amount of psychic energy bound in the personality structure of that stage of his development. For

Berne that stage was latency, that matter-of-fact stage sandwiched between turbulent infancy and turbulent adolescence. The three-to-six-year-old resolution of the Oedipal conflict had been achieved and, with it, the capacity for gender identification and future intimacy with the opposite sex. But not quite. The function of adolescence is, to a large extent, to reiterate and finalize the achievements of the earlier Oedipal period and for Berne, with his father no longer present, this function was incomplete.

His three marriages probably reflect most directly the nearly but not quite achieved completion of his emotional maturation. But there is also, I believe, significantly corroborating evidence in the theory of TA itself, as Berne originally expounded it, which implicitly but consistently values the intellectual functioning of the Adult *ego state* above the other *ego states*, whilst paying ardent lip-service to the free emotional expression of the Child and tending to undervalue the generalizing, believing Parent, whose clear-cut differentiation in the personality is the most important conclusion of adolescence.

However, in making such an analysis which, like all psychoanalysis, clarifies by magnification of minutiae, I am at risk of making mountains out of molehills. The only limiting effect of this imbalance in Eric Berne on the actuality of his work seems to me to be that he observed Parent/Adult and Adult/Child contaminations only in the structure of personality and failed to see the obvious possibility of Parent–Child contaminations. (For an elaboration of this issue see Chapter 5.) But is also true that, by a different name, the Parent/Child contamination is the central theme of psychoanalysis, Berne's rebellion against which produced Transactional Analysis. Perhaps the many thousands of people whose lives have been made more joyous through TA would be the sadder had Berne's father lived.

History of the ITAA

In the mid-1950s Eric Berne was the supervisor of group therapy at Mount Zion Hospital in San Francisco. At this time, transactional analysis was still embryonic in his mind and his psychotherapeutic practice, but several psychologists employed at Mount Zion expressed an interest in the clear novelty of his approach and asked if he would conduct some after-hours seminars for them. He agreed, and six people attended the first meeting on 18 February 1958. By the fourth meeting the group had grown to thirteen, and six months later to forty. By the middle of 1959 the seminars were becoming unwieldy. Not only were more and more people crowding into the small space of Eric Berne's office, but there was also a conflict of interest developing between newcomers to the meetings who had little or no knowledge of the subject and those who had been attending the meetings for a long time and had acquired sophistication in the subject. Reluctantly — and this reluctance reflects the continuing spirit of TA from then to the present day — it was decided that some form of organization was necessary. As Eric Berne himself put it, 'The title of the organization was carefully chosen to avoid pretentious words like "Institute" and "Society" ',[5] and the 'San Francisco Social Psychiatry Seminars' (SFSPS) was decided on. At the same time, the first formal introductory course in transactional analysis was organized. It was called '101' (modelled on similar nomenclature used by American colleges) and ran for ten weekly sessions, starting on 29 September 1959.

This expansion and formalization of membership in turn necessitated financial organization. A charter was granted by the State of California, and the SFSPS became a 'non-profit educational corporation' in May 1960. With the publication of Eric Berne's first (and superb) book on TA, *Transactional Analysis in Psychotherapy* in 1961, and as time passed and word spread, more and more people living out of San Francisco wanted to be associated with the SFSPS. Accumulated funds were used to keep in regular touch with interested people through the *Transactional Analysis Bulletin*, whose first issue, published in January 1962, consisted of three pages. The TAB was published quarterly thereafter until October 1970. In January 1971 it was replaced by the *Transactional Analysis Journal*, which has continued to be published quarterly since then. The first Summer Conference on TA was held in 1963 and is still held annually.

The first membership list of the SFSPS, published in the TAB in April 1962, numbered eleven. From then until 1964 knowledge and practice of Transactional Analysis continued to spread and slowly to infiltrate establishment psychiatric practice in America. But with the publication of *Games People Play* in 1964 Berne and his brainchild achieved overnight fame, and membership of the association grew hugely. This took Berne (and his publishers, Grove Press) totally by surprise. The first print was 3000 copies, in expectation of a modest success amongst practising psychiatrists, but little more. Within a year it was a world bestseller. Ironically enough (in my view and the view of most TA practitioners today) *Games People Play* is of comparatively minor lasting value in the corpus of Berne's work and especially so compared with his earlier *Transactional Analysis in Psychotherapy*. Perhaps it was the neat and beguiling packaging of the title, or that some impossible-to-predict right moment occured in 1964 in the popular imagination, but whatever vagaries of human response may account for it, *Games People Play* established TA as a major contribution to twentieth-century psychology. In October 1964 the International Transactional Analysis Association was formed with a membership of 279. The San Francisco Social Psychiatry Seminars continued as a branch of the ITAA until Berne's death in 1970.

The Present ITAA and Its Affiliates

There are now about 8000 members of the ITAA, the vast majority living in the United States, but about 1200 spread over more than 30 other countries. At the time of writing there are 85 members in Great Britain.[6]

The headquarters of the ITAA is still in San Francisco,[7] from where are published the quarterly official *Transactional Analysis Journal* and *Script*, a newsletter issued ten times a year. The *TAJ* and *Script* are posted to all paid-up members of the ITAA, but both may be purchased independently of membership, on application to the ITAA.

Since 1971 an Eric Berne Memorial Scientific Award has been made annually in recognition of outstanding contributions to TA theory.

The By-Laws of the ITAA make it governable by a Board of Trustees, which consists of twenty-four elected members plus the President, two Vice-Presidents, Secretary, Treasurer, and immediate Past President. No member of the Board may hold office for more than three successive years. Current committees include By-Laws, International Relations, Public and Professional Information, Scholarship Loan Fund, Training Standards, Ethics, Prisons, Licensure, Long Range Policy Planning, Publications, Social Action, Educational Applications, Grievance, Finance, and Education and Research.

In 1974 the handful of people in this country then actively interested in TA got together and began publication of the *British Transactional Analysis Bulletin*, which has been published quarterly since then. In November 1975 the (British) *Institute of Transactional Analysis* was formed with a Founder Membership list of 40 people. As yet it is the first and only formally constituted national TA organization outside the United States. The ITA holds a conference annually in May.

In the summer of 1975, under the inspirational and organizational guidance of Bob and Mary Goulding, two well-known American TA teachers and clinicians, the ITAA organized a conference (additional to its regular San Francisco one) at the magnificent Club Med. in the Swiss mountain resort of Villars. The combination of a French chef, the scenic beauty, and tax deductibility, drew 135 people, 75 of them Americans. During the course of this conference, Michael Reddy collected the 60 Europeans present into a Tower of Babel huddle (Peter Sellers would have adored it!) and the *European Association for Transactional Analysis* was born. EATA has since then been wholly responsible for the organization of annual summer conferences in Europe (1976 Holland, 1977 Austria, 1978 Denmark 1979 France, 1980 Britain) as well as for Joint European Workshops in winter in London. Each member country of EATA may elect two people to represent it on the Council. EATA publishes its own Newsletter several times a year.[9] Year by year since 1975 the European conferences have become more and more European, and in 1978, the Americans were as swamped by us as we were previously by them. At the 1978 conference in Helsinor, Denmark, were 297 Europeans, 35 Americans, 3 Australians, 1 Canadian, and 1 Israeli. More than 600 people from 19 different countries attended the 1979 conference in Aix-en-Provence.

ITAA Training and Licensing Regulations

There are two broad categories of membership of the ITAA, Regular Membership and Advanced Membership. Only Advanced Members are licensed to call themselves 'transactional analysts' and they are voting members. Regular

Members of three or more years standing and Regular Members in training for Advanced Membership may opt to become voting members. Regular Members constitute about 90 per cent of the membership of the ITAA.

Regular Membership is obtainable by attendance at a twelve-hour '101' introductory course run by a certified Provisional Teaching Member or a Teaching Member of the ITAA. Certification of satisfactory attendance at the course and the first annual membership fee are then submitted to the ITAA, which then sends the candidate certification of Regular Membership. A Regular Member receives the *Transactional Analysis Journal* (four times a year), the *Script* newsletter (ten times a year), and is listed in the *ITAA Membership Directory*. Regular Membership is a prerequisite for pursuance of Advanced Membership. '101' courses are run several times a year in Britain and are regularly advertised in the *Transactional Analysis Bulletin*.

Advanced Members are either Clinical Members or Special Fields Members. Clinical Members are licensed to practice transactional analytic psychotherapy, Special Fields Members are licensed to engage in educational and consulting applications of TA (in accordance with their nominated 'special field'). Training for Clinical Membership is restricted to people who already have some qualification in one of the 'helping' professions (although exceptions are made in some cases at the discretion of individual supervisors).

Training for Advanced Membership takes a minimum of about two years, and the core of the training is practice under supervision. Trainees are also required regularly to attend advanced seminars and to make several presentations at them, and to complete successfully both a written and an oral examination. Especially in the case of trainees for Clinical Membership, considerable emphasis is placed on trainees acquiring a high degree of awareness and resolution of their own psychological problems before becoming licensed to practise as transactional analysts. Consequently, most TA supervisors require of their trainees that they spend at least some months as members of ongoing therapy groups.

Shortly after becoming a Clinical Member or a Special Field Member, an Advanced Member may choose to apply for Provisional Teaching Membership. Application is made through attendance at a PTM (Provisional Teaching Member) Contract Workshop, at which certified Teaching Members of the ITAA determine candidates' suitability to be further trained to become Clinical Teaching Members or Special Fields Teaching Members as the case may be. Once accepted as a PTM, training to TM (Teaching Member) status takes a minimum of three years. Both PTMs and TMs are authorized, in addition to their clinical or special fields work, to conduct '101s' and to train and supervise Regular Members working towards Advanced Membership. However, until they are fully-qualified TMs, PTMs must do their training and teaching under the supervision of a TM.

As of now, all Advanced Members have gained their credentials directly through and by the ITAA in San Francisco. However, there is currently concerted debate and negotiation between EATA and the ITAA, out of which it is hoped that EATA will emerge with some degree of autonomy with respect to training standards and the examining and licensing of European candidates. As Europeans are factually accepting more and more responsibility for the conduct of their TA affairs, it seems only fair to most of us that the ITAA should gradually reward our 'growing up' with some loosening of their parental reins.

In Europe, at the time of writing, there are three TMs and a couple of dozen PTMs. At the moment the demand for TA teachers far exceeds the supply. The prospect for TA in Europe looks great.

Summary

Eric Berne (1910–1970) was a Canadian-born psychiatrist who, for many years until his death, lived and practised psychotherapy in San Francisco. Committed as he always was to the theory of traditional psychoanalysis, he developed Transactional Analysis out of his dissatisfaction with the slowness of psychoanalysis as therapy to achieve observable cures in his patients. The most crucially determining event in Eric Berne's life was probably the death of his father when he was only nine. Consequent on this trauma his emotional maturation was incomplete and he was unable to form the lasting intimate relationships he so longed for. However, this very limitation in him is probably directly related to his creation of Transactional Analysis.

In the 1950s and 1960s Eric Berne conducted weekly seminars under the title of 'San Francisco Social Psychiatry Seminars'. With the publication of *Games People Play* in 1964, TA and Eric Berne gained world fame almost overnight, and shortly afterwards the *International Transactional Analysis Association* was formed.

There are now about 8000 members of the ITAA, including about 1200 outside the United States. The ITAA publishes the *Transactional Analysis Journal* four times a year and the *Script* newsletter ten times a year. It also makes an annual Eric Berne Memorial Scientific Award for outstanding contributions to TA theory. The ITAA has many special interest committees, all of which function under the auspices of its Board of Trustees.

The quarterly *British Transactional Analysis Bulletin* began publication in 1974 and the (British) *Institute of Transactional Analysis* was constituted in 1975, and now holds annual conferences. The *European Association for Transactional Analysis* was formed in 1975 and since then there have been annual European TA conferences.

There are two categories of ITAA membership, Regular and Advanced. Advanced Members may be Clinical or Special Fields Members. The highest status of membership is Teaching Member. Regular Membership is attainable after a twelve hour '101' course, Advanced Membership takes about two years training, and Teaching Membership a minimum of three further years of training. At present all standards and examinations are set by the ITAA in San Francisco, but negotiations are taking place between EATA and the ITAA with a view to EATA gaining some autonomy from its parent body.

Notes and References

1. The biographical data of this chapter are derived from the first issue of the *Transactional Analysis Journal* (January, 1971), which was also a memorial to the life and work of Eric Berne.
2. 1949: 'The Nature of Intuition', *Psychiatric Quart.* **23,** 203–226.
   1952: 'Concerning the Nature of Diagnosis', *Int. Rec. Med.* **165,** 283–292.
   1953: 'Concerning the Nature of Communication', *Psychiatric Quart.* **27,** 185–198.
   1955: 'Primal Images and Primal Judgement', *Psychiatric Quart.* **29,** 634–658.
   1957: 'The Ego Image', *Psychiatric Quart.* **31,** 611–627.
   An edited and bound edition of these articles is now available. It is published under the title *Intuition and Ego States: the Origins of Transactional Analysis*, by Eric Berne (Ed. Paul McCormick), Transactional Publications, 1772 Vallejo Street, San Francisco, California 94123, USA, 1977. Price $2.95 (plus 75 cents p.&p.)
3. C. Steiner, *Scripts People Live*. Grove Press, 1974.
4. E. Berne, *What do you say after you say hello?* Bantam, 1973, p. 197.
5. E. Berne, Editorial in the *Transactional Analysis Bulletin*, **2,** no. 5, January 1963.
6. *International Transactional Analysis Association Membership Directory, 1978–1979.*
7. At 1772 Vallejo Street, San Francisco, California 94123, USA.
8. Enquiries concerning membership of the ITA and subscription to the *BTAB* should be addressed to: The Secretary, ITA, Cabrae House, Calderbridge, West Cumbria.
9. Information concerning membership of EATA may be obtained (in Britain) from: Juliette Pollitzer, Flat 5, 64 Rutland Gate, London, SW7.
   The present Chairman of the Council of EATA is: Raymond Hostie, Minderbroederstraat 11, 3000 Leuven, Belgium.

PART I

Theory

CHAPTER 1

The Structures and Functions of Personality

All of us in all of our waking lives are in one or another of three possible *ego states*. These are not *roles*, but different real parts of our being. Nor are they synonyms or near-synonyms for the psychoanalytic Superego, Ego, and Id, which are concepts that refer to forces in the Unconscious. *Ego states*, by contrast with these concepts, are phenomenological realities — that is observable states of being — and are all contained within the (psychoanalytic) Ego. They are all conscious or pre-conscious — that is either actually in awareness or accessible to awareness. Existentially we switch from one of these states of being to another throughout our lives, hour by hour, minute by minute, second by second. They are called Parent, Adult, and Child and are represented[1]

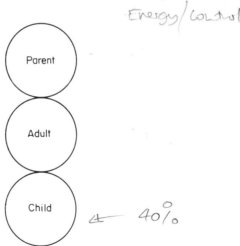

The Structures of Personality

The Child ego state contains our feelings. At birth we have only our Child. When in our Child we cry when we are miserable, laugh when happy. We are all the things a baby is — demanding, self-centred, loving, spontaneous, honest, uninhibited, and lovable. But in any human society the Free Child we are born as to some extent has to be bridled in the interests of our socialization. And so, having learnt that we are more likely to get an icecream if we ask for one politely rather than screaming for it, that we cannot always get what we want, and that others in general have power over us to gratify or thwart our wishes, our Child *ego state*, after early infancy, is differentiated into Free and Adapted parts. People differ from each other in the degrees to which the Free Child is inhibited by the Adapted Child in accordance with differences between parents and societies in the ways in which they 'rear' their children.

The Adult ego state is our storehouse of facts and skills gained from the objective environment. It is without feeling. It begins its formation in our early months of life with our first awareness of the separateness of our own bodies from the rest of the universe. It has become a clearly differentiated *ego state* by some time between one and three years of age.

The Parent ego state contains our taught concepts of life, the values and generalizations explicitly given us by our parents and other influential people in our lives. When we are in our Parent we are usually behaving like one of our parents did or in accordance with precepts they taught us when young, although our Parent is also capable of change and growth throughout our lives. We may reject old values and acquire new ones as a consequence of new experiences and meetings with admired people. But our Parent *ego state* is essentially formed between the ages of about three and six, although it finds its precursor in some imitative behaviours in the Child between one and three years of age. A little polishing up is usually achieved in adolescence, but thereafter our Parent is an automatic and therefore a comfortable place to be. We don't have to think before being kind to people in distress, since our parents were kind to us. Nor do we have to think about looking both ways before crossing the road, since our parents taught us to long ago. These early *messages* are as if recorded on tape and stored but always ready to play whenever the situation is appropriate.

The structure of the whole personality may be summarized thus:

Ego State	Contents
Parent	explicitly taught concepts in general, including beliefs, values, morality; generalizations made by the individual himself out of his (Child) experiences.
Adult	facts and other objective data such as skills.
Child	innately given feelings, and feelings learnt in the process of adaptation to parents' and others' demands.

Diagnosis of ego states

The table which follows may be helpful in the practical task of identifying *ego states*.

Characteristics of the *ego states*

	Parent	Adult	Child
Words	good/bad, should/shouldn't, must/mustn't, always/never, right/wrong	how, what, why, when practical, possible, interesting	wow, want, can't, won't, wish, hope, please, thank you, I wonder if . . . . . ., I have a feeling that . . . . . ., That's phoney!
Voice	concerned, comforting, critical	even, calm	free, loud, energetic, whining, excited, pleading
Gestures or expression	open arms, points finger frowns, smiles	thoughtful, alert, open	uninhibited, loose, spontaneous, naive, cute, sad, happy, assertive, whimsical, knowing
Attitude	judgemental, understanding, caring, giving, authoritarian, moralistic	erect, evaluative of facts	curious, compliant, defiant, ashamed, volatile, creative, fun-loving, manipulative, hypothesizing

In every-day life most people can readily and quickly acquire the facility for recognizing their own and others' *ego states* with a minimum margin of error. However, strictly speaking, the complete diagnosis of an *ego state* requires four separate viewpoints to be recognized and validated. To quote Berne:

> 1. The diagnosis made by the observer is behavioural. For example, a behavioural diagnosis can be made if someone inappropriately bursts into tears, so that the observer is irresistibly reminded of the behaviour of a child at a certain age, or if the agent exhibits coyness, sulkiness or playfulness which is reminiscent of a special phase of childhood.
> 2. Those participating in *transactions* with the agent make the diagnosis on social grounds. If he behaves in such a way as to make them feel fatherly or motherly, he is presumably offering childlike stimuli, and his behaviour at that moment can be diagnosed as a manifestation of his Child. . . .
> 3. The subjective diagnosis comes from self-observation. The individual himself realizes that he is acting the way his father did, or that he is objectively interested in what is going on before him, or that he is reacting the way he did as a child.
> 4. The historical diagnosis is made from factual information about the individual's past. He may remember the exact moments when his father behaved in a similar way; or he learned how to accomplish this particular task; or exactly where he was when he had a similar reaction in early childhood.
> The more of these standards that can be met, the sounder the diagnosis. . . .[2]

Thus the structures of our personalities, which we have now outlined, refer to the various existential states of being available to us in our waking lives. Let us now turn to the functions of these *ego states* in our lives.

The Functions of Personality

Executive ego State

Whereas the structures of the *ego states* refer to various kinds of ideational content, the functions of the *ego states* refer to various kinds of energy which may be expressed. Broadly speaking, the Parent believes, the Adult thinks, and the Child feels. At any moment, the *ego state* containing the most active energy is said to be in the *executive*, even though the person may be phenomenally in another *ego state*. For example, a man in his Child enjoying drinking at a party may keep his Adult in the *executive* in order, realistically, to remain capable of driving home. Or a mother rationally arguing in her Adult the merits of pre-marital chastity to her teenage daughter probably has her Parent in the *executive*. (A father in the same situation probably has his Child in the *executive*!) And someone concentrating in his Adult to build a house of cards actually has his Child in the *executive*. When the phenomenal and *executive ego states* are not one and the same the feeling in the individual is of another 'self' hovering in the background, informing the more present 'self' of the *meaning* of what is going on.

Summarily, the autonomous functions of the three *ego states* are as follows:

Ego state functions

Ego State	Functions
Parent	believes, protects, controls, directs, nurtures
Adult	thinks, computes, analyses
Child	feels, wants, demands, plays, adapts, fights

Rissman's trilog

Now apart from the appropriateness of sometimes being in one *ego state* whilst keeping another in the *executive*, there are also occasions that call for the conscious collaboration of two or more *ego states* in equal or near-equal measure. Some simple situations are most appropriately experienced in a single, autonomously functioning *ego state*, for example, writing out cheques (in Adult), riding a roller coaster (in Child), or 'kissing it better' (in Parent). But in many situations in life one *ego state* is not enough, and at the time of his death Berne was beginning to be aware of this and to consider the relationships of the *ego states* to each other *within* the healthily functioning personality. However, he did not get as far as any clear articulation of the problem or its solution, and it was not until 1973 that this vital piece missing from Berne's jigsaw of human nature was discovered by Arthur Rissman and named by him the *trilog*.[3] The *trilog* shows how the three different pairs of *ego states* collaborate within the personality. Parent and Adult collaborate to form *judgements*, Adult and Child find and choose between *alternatives*, and Parent and Child form *compromises*.

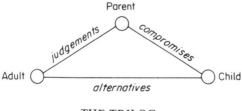

THE TRILOG

For me, this is the single most useful construct developed in TA since Berne's death. It is a brilliant conception and, like all great ideas — in TA and elsewhere — combines profundity of meaning with instantly comprehensible simplicity of form. Let us consider some examples.

Parent–Adult collaboration: A judge in court combines the wisdom in his Parent with the knowledge of the law in his Adult before making a *judgement* and passing sentence. Should any reader doubt the necessary influence of a judge's Parent, consider the variability of sentences passed for similar crimes by different judges. The awareness of this is expressed as appropriate confidence or trepidation by barristers on behalf of their clients once they know which judge is sitting on their case. 'Harsh' judgements usually imply an imbalance on the side of the critical Parent, 'lenient' judgements a bias either towards Adult or towards indulgent Parent, and 'cold' judgements suggest a leaning towards Adult with less than average compassionate Parent.

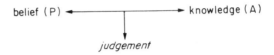

Adult–Child collaboration: A man whose Child yearns for a five-bedroom house on the edge of Hyde Park realizes (Adult) it is beyond his means, so considers and chooses between such *alternatives* as a five-bedroom house in Wembley or a two-bedroom flat near Hyde Park. A bias towards Adult in setting up *alternatives* will tend to make the list 'cautious', a bias towards Child will deem the options 'unrealistic' or make their achievability doubtful.

Parent–Child collaboration: A young woman whose Child would like to exhibit her body as a nightclub stripper, *compromises* with her controlling Parent by becoming an artist's model. Here the collaboration is between the two feeling *ego states*, with no input from the Adult, so in terms of actual *possibilities* the individual may choose any point on the continuum from all Parent to all Child. But, of course, in terms of the psychological reality of the individual, choosing the appropriate degrees of Parent and Child is crucial in determining his experienced sense of well-being. Too much Child in the *compromise* and the Parent will probably inflict guilt, too much Parent and the Child will be bitter on account of the frustration.

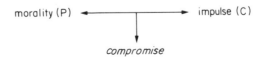

Parent–Adult–Child collaboration: The most complex and significant of life's decisions — such as marriage, divorce, to have or not to have children — probably all require the harmony of all three *ego states* for a happy outcome to be achieved. This may account for the emphasis in traditional education — from the ancient Greeks to latter-day British public schools — on the importance of games, since these provide a singular opportunity for training the effective collaboration of all three *ego states*. Consider a boy playing football. His Parent is obeying the rules, his Adult skills are being exercised and developed, and his Child is having a marvellous time.'

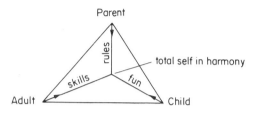

A BOY PLAYING FOOTBALL

Now, having described the essential structures and functions of the *ego states* within the individual personality, we are ready to proceed to an analysis of the ways in which separate people interact with each other. But in case any residual doubt remains in the mind of the reader, it is worth emphasizing that no *ego state* is 'better' or 'worse' than another. People beginning to become familiarly aware of their own and others' *ego states* often misconstrue TA as positively valuing the Adult and/or Child and giving negative value to the Parent. This is not the case. As I hope this chapter has shown, we need to have all three readily available in order to function adequately in everyday life. *Appropriateness* to the situation is the one and only criterion in evaluating each of the *ego states* as they manifest themselves.

Summary

All of us in all of our waking lives are in one or another of three possible *ego states*. These are not *roles*, but different, real parts of our being. They are called Parent, Adult, and Child. Structurally, the Parent *ego state* contains our taught concepts of life, the Adult *ego state* contains knowledge and skills, and the Child *ego state* contains our felt concepts of life.

Functionally, the Parent believes, the Adult thinks, and the Child feels. At any moment, the *ego state* containing the most active energy is said to be in the *executive*. This is not necessarily the *ego state* which is most observable. Rissman's *trilog* shows how the three different pairs of *ego states* collaborate within the personality. Parent and Adult collaborate to form *judgements*, Adult and Child find and choose between *alternatives*, and Parent and Child form *compromises*. The most important decisions in life usually require the collaboration of all three *ego states* for the outcome to be a happy one. All *ego states* have equal value in the personality. The healthy personality chooses, at any moment, to be in the *ego state* most appropriate to the given situation.

Notes and References

1. The first person to use the concept of *ego states* was not Eric Berne, but Paul Federn, whose ideas Berne quotes often. In 1957, in 'Ego states in psychotherapy' (*The American Journal of Psychotherapy*, **11**, 293–309) Berne remarked, 'What Federn (1952) calls "a mental duologue between two parts of the ego, the adult and the infantile", becomes clearer when the boundaries between the two ego states become well defined and both are in an active state.' (P. Federn. *Ego Psychology and the Psychoses*. New York: Basic Books, 1952.) So we see that the core concept in the theory that gained Berne world fame did not originate in Berne's mind. But none of the greatest and most revolutionary ideas in history have sprung parthogenetically from one mind. It is the one who, at the right time in the right way, takes the seed of an idea and nourishes it to maturity, whom the world acclaims as 'genius'.
2. E. Berne, *The Structure and Dynamics of Groups and Organizations*. Grove Press, pp. 133–134.
3. A. Rissman, 'Trilog', *Transactional Analysis Journal*, **5** no. 2, April 1975. A detailed account of the 'trilog' is also available on cassette tape; *TA For Creative Living*, no. 18, Boyce Productions, Corte Madera, California, 1973.

CHAPTER 2

Transactions, Strokes, and Time Structuring

Transactions

When two people meet *transactions* occur between them (even if no words are spoken). The Parent, Adult, and Child contained within one skin meet a Parent, Adult, and Child contained in another skin: From this diagrammatic repre-

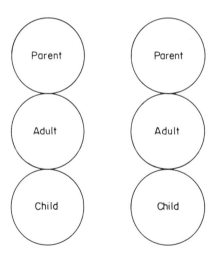

sentation of the two personalities it is clear that, since either person may choose to be in any of his three *ego states* and to address any of the three *ego states* of the other, there are nine possibilities for any single *transaction*.

For example:

Wife to husband who arrives home with a streaming cold:

(a) 'You poor thing. Get into bed and I'll make you a nice hot toddy.' (Parent to Child) Or,

(b) 'That's a bad cold you've got. There's some aspirin and some vitamin C tablets in the bathroom cabinet if you want them.' 'Adult to Adult) Or,

(c) 'Wow, you've got a corker! Keep away from me. I don't want it'! (Child to Child) Or,

(d) 'I hope you're not going to go on about this cold. Remember you promised to take me out tonight.' (Child to Parent)

What happens next depends on how the husband chooses to respond.

Complementary transactions

If, for example, he responds to (a) with:

'Thank you darling. That's just what I feel like' (Child to Parent) or to (d) with

'I'm sorry, I'll have to break my promise then.' (Parent to Child), the transactions will have been *complementary*. The *ego state* addressed responded to the *ego state* which addressed it and communication, though not necessarily happy, is clear and straightforward and, as long as it continues *complementarily*, will not result in misunderstandings.

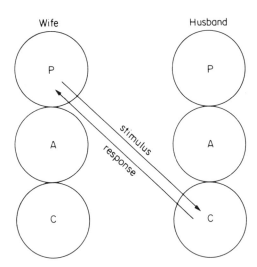

A COMPLEMENTARY TRANSACTION

Crossed transactions

Consider, however, the possibility that the husband responds to (b), his wife's stimulus, 'That's a bad cold you've got. There's some aspirin and some vitamin C tablets in the bathroom cabinet if you want them', with 'For goodness sake, woman! Don't you realize that once you've got a cold there's nothing you can do about it?' (Parent to Child). The result is a *crossed transaction* of the commonest kind, where an Adult to Adult stimulus gets a critical Parent to Child response and communication breaks down. A good case could be made, I believe, for describing the vast majority of fights between individuals and nations as being at least precipitated by just such *crossed transactions.*

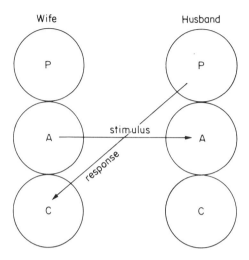

A CROSSED TRANSACTION

Although the most common *crossed transactions* are self-evidently defined as such by the actual intersection of the stimulus and response lines of communication, the category of *crossed transactions* also includes non-*complementary* but parallel stimulus and response lines and some *angular* relationships between stimulus and response.

Examples: If the husband had responded to his wife's Adult to Adult stimulus of 'There's some aspirin and some vitamin C tablets in the bathroom cabinet' with 'We must get a kid-proof lock on that bathroom cabinet', we would have

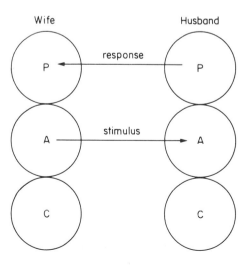

Or if he had responded, 'If you come with me', to his wife's 'Get into bed and I'll make you a nice hot today', we would have

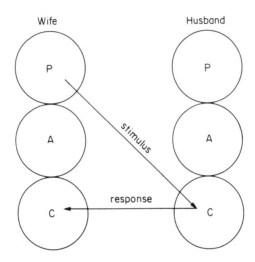

These two examples, as well as the previous one, are kinds of *crossed transactions*.

Ulterior transactions

As well as *complementary* and *crossed* there is a third kind of *transaction* between people. These are called *ulterior transactions* and are the stuff of which much of our working and social lives are made. They occur when communication nominally takes place between two *ego states* but when, covertly, at least one other *ego state* is involved. At the hidden level, at least one Child *ego state* is usually involved. The covert stimulus and the covert response always contain the more important communication. The covert lines of communication are always drawn as dotted lines in *transactional* diagrams. *Ulterior transactions* are subdivided into *angular* and *duplex* types. An *angular ulterior transaction* is typically a conning *transaction*. Example:

Salesman: (Stimulus$_1$, overt) It's a beautiful fit, sir, but perhaps you'd prefer one not so youthful looking.
(Stimulus$_2$, covert) Buy this if you want to look young.
Customer: (Response, overt) I'll have it.

Only stimulus$_1$ is spoken, but the more powerful stimulus is the covert, Adult to Child one. In such an *angular ulterior transaction* the salesman aims to hook the customer's Child into the *executive* whilst the salesman stays in his cool Adult.

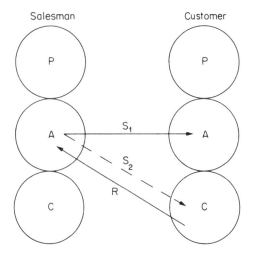

In *duplex ulterior transactions* the Child *ego states* of both parties are usually involved. Example:

Man: (S₁) Would you like to come and see my etchings?
   (S₂) Let's have it off at my place!
Woman: (R₁) Oh yes. I've always been very interested in etchings.
   (R₂) Yeah, let's!

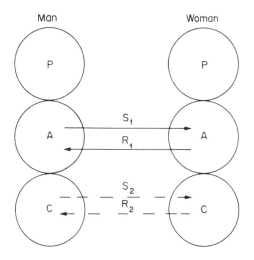

A DUPLEX ULTERIOR TRANSACTIONS

Ulterior transactions may occur for many different reasons, but they all have in common that they provide a face-saving way out for either or both parties. In the example of the man and the woman above, the woman may have replied, 'Thanks, but I'm not interested in etchings' (Adult to Adult), but meant, covertly, 'No, I don't fancy you' (Child to Child), in which case, though her meaning was clear, the situation was resolved with less loss of face for the man and less gracelessness for her than if the Child to Child *transaction* had been openly expressed. Furthermore, the man was, from the start, protected against the woman repudiating his Child to Child transaction openly. Had she replied, overtly, 'Buzz off buster!' (Child to Child), he could hotly deny that he had meant anything more than what was contained in his overt Adult to Adult *transaction*. Similarly, if the customer in the previous example had replied to the salesman with, 'I'll thank you to mind your manners!' (Parent to Child), the salesman could 'legitimately' reply, 'I beg your pardon sir. Did I say something wrong?' (Child to Parent).

Thus many commonplace *ulterior transactions* have generally conceded positive social value in providing important protection for the parties to the *transaction* while they explore the potential for their future *transactions* with each other. However, it is important to distinguish these from the definitively maladaptive *ulterior transactions* involved in *games*, which are considered later in this chapter and also in Chapter 6. In *games*, the protagonists are far less likely to be aware of the *ulterior transactions* they are involved in and yet be much more compulsively driven to use them than when they use them consciously in a socially adaptive way. Straightforward manipulation of others is generally far less harmful than unconscious manipulation of self, as we shall see.

Strokes in General

> The ability of the human psyche to maintain coherent
> *ego states* seems to depend upon a changing flow of
> sensory stimuli.[1]

There is a great deal of evidence that, deprived of sufficient stimulation through human touch, the human infant will degenerate organically (as well as psychically) in much the same way as if deprived of food. For Berne, this finding — for which he repeatedly acknowledges his indebtedness to the findings of R. Spitz[2] — led him to postulate the need to be *stroked* as the primary psychological motivator of all our behaviour from the cradle to the grave.

Physical intimacy, epitomized in a loving mother's healthy handling of her baby, most completely satisfies this need. And once the period of close intimacy with his mother is over the individual, for the rest of his life, perpetually strives to recapture the perfect, *unconditional stroking* he once received. But in the grown-up world this is often, for many and various reasons, hard to come by. So

> Under most conditions he will compromise. He learns to do with more
> subtle, even symbolic forms of handling, until the merest nod of
> recognition may serve the purpose to some extent, although his

original craving for physical contact may remain unabated. As the complexities increase, each person becomes more and more individual in his quest, and it is these differences which lend variety to social intercourse.[3]

In TA a *stroke* is any act implying recognition of another's presence — from the primary physical *stroke* to its most symbolic derivative, from the intensely valuable 'I love you' to the very slightly valued nod of recognition from a passing acquaintance. Although the primary quest for the original *strokes* to the sensual Child remains, derivatively *strokes* may be given from and received by any ego state. A child who is thanked by his mother for looking after his little brother so well while she was out receives a *stroke* to his Parent from his mother's Parent. A child given a present for being top of her class in maths is given a Parent to Adult *stroke*. A man telling his girlfriend that she is the most beautiful woman in the world is giving her a Child to Child *stroke*.

As well as being intrinsically gratifying to the recipient, *strokes* also serve to reinforce the behaviour they are given for. Thus the boy who is praised by his mother for looking after his little brother will tend to look after his brother even better the next time he is given the opportunity; the child who came top in maths will work even harder to maintain her position; and the girl praised for her beauty will feel, and hence be, more beautiful in future.

Our continual need — and consequent quest — for *strokes*, as for food, provides the basic structure for the whole of our lives. And since *strokes* can only be obtained by engaging in social contact, *transactions* with others are a vital not an optional requirement for our well-being. Giving oneself *strokes* is, by definition, only possible through drawing on our internal *stroke bank*, our account in which represents an accumulation of *strokes* previously received from others. This remains true notwithstanding any authenticated accounts of people living as total hermits. For such people it need hardly be said that *strokes* from others must have been paid into their accounts at some time or they would not have survived more than a few hours of life.

The Six Ways of Structuring Time

Throughout our lives there are six different ways we may choose from to *structure time* when we are with other people — that is for our various *ego states* to *transact* with the various *ego states* of others and thus receive *strokes*—each way having its attendant advantages and disadvantages.

Withdrawal is a limiting case of *time-structuring* in which there is no interaction with another person. It has the advantage that it contains no risk of rejection, the disadvantage that no *strokes* are received (except by the depletion of the individual's internal source accumulated from the past in his *stroke bank*).

Rituals are highly stylized *transactions* between people, which are completely predictable. They range from the informal greeting ritual of two acquaintances when they meet to highly formalized ceremonies such as weddings and funerals. Next to *withdrawal*, engaging in *rituals* is the *safest* way of *structuring time*. That is, there is very little risk of being rejected and some *strokes* are guaranteed. However, such *strokes* are usually just *sustenance strokes* of minimal value since there is a basic lack of differentiation in the giving and receiving. A typical *four-stroke* greeting *ritual* would be

1A: Hello.
1B: Hello.
2A: Terrible weather, isn't it?
2B: Yes. I hope the farmers are pleased.
3A: Yes. See you soon.
3B: Yes. Take care.
4A: Bye.
4B: Bye.

Pastimes, like *rituals*, have a certain predictable, repetitive quality about the nature of the *transactions* involved, but are more open-ended than *rituals*. They are usually socially programmed and consist of talking about acceptable subjects in acceptable ways, but different *pastimes* are appropriate to different groups of people whereas, within a given culture, *rituals* are much more nearly universal. *Pastiming* offers the stimulus of some unpredictability combined with some certainty of receiving some comparatively superficial *strokes* as well as providing a platform for 'psyching out' people as potential for more profound giving and receiving of *strokes*. However, there is some risk of being rejected in *pastiming* as well as of boredom with the comparative superficiality of the *transactions*. *Pastimes* include watching the telly, playing Scrabble, Monopoly, cards, discussing the news, football results, clothes, cars, going to the pub, to the pictures, for a walk, etc.

Activities (work) are *transactions* which are stimulated by a situation external to the relationship between the participants. They are typically Adult to Adult *transactions* and oriented to the reality of the task. *Activities* can provide many highly valued *strokes*, both through the interpersonal approval each person may give the other in sharing the task and from the internal *strokes* the individual may give himself for the task well done. (This is not actually in contradiction of my earlier contention that we cannot give ourselves *strokes*. When we give ourselves 'internal' *strokes* we are actually remembering and reiterating *strokes* given us by our parents for similar behaviour in the past.) However, there is no guarantee of *strokes* from the other person or of success in the task. Thus there is a definite risk of the situation forcing the individual to face his own deficiencies.

Games are sets of *ulterior transactions*, repetitive in nature, with a well-defined and specific psychological *payoff* for each of the players. They also involve each of the players in being party to a secret unspoken position built on deception, self-deception, half-truth, distortion of facts, or any combination of these.

Games are basically destructive of TA's most highly prized qualities of psychological health, viz. *spontaneity, authenticity*, and *autonomy*, binding energy in self- and other-destroying compulsive *transactions*. The profound meaning of *games* in our lives will become clear when we discuss *structural pathology* in Chapter 7. For the present, in the general context of *strokes*, it is sufficient to know that *games* provide many more *strokes* than *rituals* or *pastimes* and, for most people, more *strokes* than they find themselves able to obtain from *activities*. From the point of view of recognizing that a *game* is being played, be alert for the feeling of 'Here we go again' and listen for 'Yes, but. . . .' and 'If it weren't for. . . .', by far the commonest lines used in a very wide variety of *games*.

Intimacy is the second limiting case of ways of *structuring time* (*withdrawal*, as noted on p. 25, being the first). When bilateral, it is a candid *game-free* Child to Child relationship with mutual giving and receiving of *strokes* without exploitation or reservations. The *stroke* yield is the absolute maximum both in number and profundity, but the demands of total honesty and total vulnerability are more than the majority of us can bear most of the time. Sadly, for some people the risk involved in intimacy is so terrifying that *game-playing* is the closest they ever get to another person.

Four Kinds of Strokes

We have now delineated the six ways available to us for fulfilling our fundamental and life-long need to receive *strokes*. For each of these ways there are four different kinds of *strokes*. They are *unconditional positive, conditional positive, conditional negative*, and *unconditional negative* which, in descending order of gratification, provide to our self-esteem and therefore to our sense of well-being with the world. *Strokes* are so vital to us that any *stroke*—that is, any act of recognition — is better than none. We would rather receive a *negative stroke* — an angry word, a put-down, a hostile glance — than be ignored and receive no *stroke* at all. Every parent and teacher is familiar with the child who, being unable to get any *positive strokes* for being 'good' at least makes sure of some *negative strokes* for being 'bad'.

A healthy parent's loving attitude towards his or her child provides the prototype of all *unconditional positive strokes*, which effectively say, 'I love you because you are you, irrespective of anything you do to please or displease me'. These are the original *strokes* for which we yearn for the rest of our lives and typically obtain as grown-ups in loving sexual intimacy.

But the *transactions* from which we can derive these most highly prized *strokes* are too rare in our lives to suffice for all our *stroke* needs, so we also need and seek the more readily available *conditional strokes* offered us in our everyday encounters. These may be *positive* or *negative* and their prototypes are also found in childhood mother–child *transactions* such as 'You can watch television if you're good and tidy up your toys' (*positive*), or 'Do that once more and I'll wallop you!' (*negative*). The feeling conveyed in *unconditional negative strokes* is 'You are unworthy of love irrespective of anything you might do to please me'.

The consequences of a child receiving such *messages* from a parent are inevitably tragic for the rest of his life.

The development of our idiosyncratic *stroke* needs is the subject matter of Chapter 6, but it is of prime importance to recognize that, regardless of individual differences in *what* we learn to get *strokes* for, *negative (conditional* or *unconditional) strokes* are as powerful as *positive (conditional* or *unconditional) strokes* in reinforcing the behaviours they are given for. Thus, 'Mummy is cross with you when you don't eat up all your dinner' will as surely create a grown-up man who does *not* eat up all his dinner as 'What a good boy, eating up all your dinner' will create a grown-up man who licks his platter clean.

Some elucidation of this 'anti-commonsense' view is needed. What punishment (*negative stroking*) does accomplish is to suppress the undesired behaviour momentarily *while the punishment is being inflicted*, so, from a harrassed parent's point of view, 'a good wallop' does achieve the immediate aim. But the behaviour will reassert itself with increased vigour (having been *negatively stroked*) as soon as the punishment is lifted. This long-term personality effect (directly contrary to the short-term effect) is largely unrealized by most people — although good animal trainers have always known it.

The inefficacy of punishment in eliminating undesired behaviour has been indisputably demonstrated in the experimental results of B. F. Skinner,[4] the far-reaching conclusions from which I find dishearteningly little appreciated in the relevant professions. True, the treatment of adult and child offenders is increasingly oriented to 'rehabilitation' rather than an eye-for-an-eye philosophy, but this is almost always rationalized morally in terms of 'humaneness' and 'cost to the community'. Until the pragmatic truth — *that punishment simply does not work* — is realized, the morally inhumane will continue to do battle with the morally humane on an equal footing. For example, to those who still advocate corporal punishment in schools, supporting inhumane morality with phoney pragmatism, a question rarely asked is, 'How can it be that if hitting children works the same children receive the same punishment time and time again for the same offences?'. In fact — again irrefutably demonstrated by Skinner — the only way undesired behaviour can be truly extinguished is by consistently ignoring it (that is by *giving it no strokes of any kind*) in which case, slowly but surely, the frequency of its manifestation will decrease to zero. Thus Skinner's theory and experimental results are completely congruent with TA *stroke* theory.

Stroke Currencies and Target Strokes

Which kinds of *strokes* were the typical *currency* of our childhoods will largely determine the *stroke currency* we will typically *transact* with for the rest of our lives. And our particular characteristics and behaviours which were *stroked* (in their various ways) in childhood will determine our *target strokes* for the rest of our lives.

Families vary in their favoured *stroke currencies*, which may be seen as explicitly acknowledged Parent values. Some popular *stroke currencies* are food, money, power, intelligence, physical attractiveness, prestige, and status. Our *stroke currencies* define the ways we measure the worth of ourselves and others with our Parent.

Our *target strokes* are more idiosyncratic and are felt in the Child. We each have *positive* and *negative target strokes*, respectively the nicest and the nastiest things we can remember our parents saying about us when we were children, and which remain, throughout our lives, the *strokes* which give us the greatest pleasure and the greatest pain. The *target strokes* for a particular individual are often hard to discern without direct questioning, although a clue to them is what kind of *strokes* the person tends to give to others. Thus, 'What a sweet woman' is likely to be said by a woman whose own *target stroke* is 'sweetness'; 'What a good-looking man' by a man whose *target stroke* is his own good looks. There is nothing more conducive to good feeling between people than knowingly giving the other person his *positive target stroke* — and scrupulously avoiding his *negative* one!

Stroke Balance

As well as deciding in childhood *what* we will be stroked for for the rest of our lives, we also decide relatively *how much positive* and *negative stroking* we are entitled to as our lifelong due. And failure to maintain our chosen *stroke balance* in our *stroke banks* will create intense discomfort in us until such time as the appropriate balance is restored. This idea of a necessary *stroke balance* is probably a near-universal myth — but nonetheless a myth — which finds its expression in a wide variety of superstitious attitudes from 'Laugh before breakfast, cry before supper' to the convinced 'I lost so much money on the horses last week, I'm bound to win this week'. Unexpected job promotion is a quite common source of a discomforting excess of *positive strokes*, an extreme response to which may be a nervous breakdown. A more moderate example of promotion-induced *stroke imbalance* occurred to a man in one of my therapeutic groups. His first response to his surprise promotion was, 'For some reason I'm not as happy about it as I would have thought I'd be'. But by the next time the group met, a week later, he was obviously euphoric about his success. It was not until quite late in that session that he mentioned, quite 'incidentally' that he had had a bad week quarrelling with his wife about aspects of his behaviour of which she disapproved. Though he was unaware of the fact, it was absolutely clear to everyone else in the group that only after receiving a comparable number of *negative strokes* was he able to enjoy his 'undeserved' excess of *positive* ones.

The exposure and destruction of the *stroke balance* myth is one of the chief tasks of psychotherapy.

Summary

When two people meet *transactions* occur between them. The Parent, Adult, and

Child contained within one skin meet a Parent, Adult, and Child contained in another skin. For these six *ego states* there are nine simple possibilities for any single *transaction*. In *complementary transactions* the *ego state* addressed responds to the *ego state* which addressed it, so the lines of communication are parallel. In *crossed transactions* the ego state addressed does not respond to the *ego state* which addressed it. In *ulterior transactions* communication nominally occurs between two *ego states* — often Adult and Adult — but, at the hidden level, other *ego states* — usually Child — are also communicating. The *transactions* occurring at the covert level are the more powerful. In *angular ulterior transactions* the Child of one party is usually involved. In *duplex ulterior transactions* the Childs of both parties are usually involved. *Ulterior transactions* have socially adaptive value as well as maladaptive value (when they are used in *games*).

For human infants, physical stimulation through touching is as vital to survival as food. In later life, though the longing for physical touch remains, human beings can survive on symbolic derivatives of touching. In TA a *stroke* is any act of recognition from the primary physical *stroke* to its most symbolic derivative.

From the cradle to the grave we *structure our time* in order to get *strokes*. There are six different ways in which we may *structure time* with others, that is, *transact*, for *strokes*. *Withdrawal* is the limiting case in which no *strokes* are given or received, but there is no risk of rejection. The five other ways of *structuring time*, in increasing order of *stroke* satisfaction *and* risk of rejection are *rituals, pastimes, activities, games,* and *intimacy*.

For each of the ways of *structuring time*, there are four different kinds of *strokes: unconditional positive, conditional positive, conditional negative,* and *unconditional negative*, which, in descending order of gratification, provide to our sense of self-esteem.

Our *stroke currencies* define the ways we value ourselves and others in accordance with Parent values we were given in our childhood families. Similarly, our *target strokes* are those *strokes* (*positive* and *negative*) which were given to our Child by our parents and which provided us then, and continue to provide us throughout our lives, with our greatest pleasure and our greatest pain to our self-esteem.

Throughout our lives we aim to maintain a particular *balance* between *positive* and *negative strokes* in our *stroke banks*, based on a childhood estimate of the proportionate balance to which we are entitled. Psychotherapy exposes and attempts to destroy this myth.

Notes and References

1. E. Berne, *Transactional Analysis in Psychotherapy*, Grove Press, 1961, p. 83.
2. Especially, R. Spitz, 'Hospitalization in genesis of psychiatric conditions in early childhood', *Psychoanalytic Study of the Child*, 1, 53–74, 1945.
3. *Transactional Analysis in Psychotherapy, op. cit.*, p. 84.
4. See B. F. Skinner, *Science and Human Behaviour*, Macmillan, New York, 1960.

CHAPTER 3

Child Development I. Functional Development of the Ego States[1]

Implicit in TA, as in traditional psychoanalytic theory, is the assumption that we are each born with a fixed amount of biologically derived psychic energy. This energy is quantitatively conserved in the totality of a given personality.

In healthy child development the congenitally given reservoir of energy gradually becomes differentiated into the various *ego states* in accordance with biologically and culturally programmed developmental stages. But each stage in development from birth to maturity manifests an unstable equilibrium in the distribution of energy between the various *ego states*, and the task of parenthood is essentially that of reinforcing specific *ego states* at each particular stage. For this special kind of parental reinforcement I have coined the phrase 'stroking up'. I intend it to convey the usual meaning of 'bringing up' combined with the concept of *stroking*. *Stroking up* the relevant *ego states* at each stage of development effects the child's healthy transition from that stage to the next.

The categories of ages and stages I have chosen are based on the traditional psychoanalytic model of child development. For individual children, of course, the ages are not precise, although the stages themselves and their order are assumed universal. My justification for choosing this model is that both theoretically and through my living experience with my own and others' children it best fits the observable facts. Over and over again in the development of my own children (who are now, at the time of writing, eighteen and fifteen) I have witnessed — without essential prejudice, I believe — how right Freud was.

It is appropriate also to acknowledge here that there are some inconsistencies between my delineation of the stages of child development and those of Pam Levin[2] and Jacqui Schiff,[3] two TA authors who have also written on this subject. Most of these inconsistencies are, I believe, comparatively trivial in that we have each chosen to delineate the same emergent phases with slightly different focuses. However, I am committed to the psychoanalytic view that the structures and functions of personality are essentially complete by about six years of age, which is not the view of Pam Levin. I am prepared to concede that the Parent *ego state* may not be *externalized* until late in latency, but I am unconvinced by her account of the turbulence of six to twelve years, which she associates with the *formation* of Parent. On the contrary — assuming that the previous development stages have been healthily completed — the vast majority of parents will, I believe, testify to the validity of the psychoanalytic description of latency as singularly the calmest (most Adult-oriented) stage in the whole of development from birth to maturity.

For the inspiration of diagramming the developmental stages in a histogram-type form I am indebted to Jack Dusay, who invented the *egogram* and for which he won the Eric Berne Memorial Scientific Award for 1973.[4] It should be noted that in my diagramming, as in Dusay's *egograms*, there is no attempt at precise quantification of differences between energy levels of different *ego states*. The best validity in the use of *egograms* is obtainable from a spontaneous, intuitive drawing.

Stage I Birth–one year

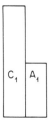

In the beginning we are all Natural Child, designated C_1. The Natural Child is biologically given and is universally demanding, self-centred, loving, spontaneous, honest, uninhibited, and lovable — all the characteristics of a new-born baby. In early infancy C_1 demands and healthy parents instinctively *stroke* these demands.

By the second half of the first year of life some part of the Natural Child becomes differentiated into another *ego state* through the infant's dawning awareness of the separateness of itself from the rest of the universe. This new *ego state* is called the Adult-in-the-Child or the Little Professor and is designated A_1. It is manifest in the crawling, exploring, and 'getting into things' so typical of the infant from the age of about six months.

Although it is the precursor of the Adult *ego state*, the Little Professor is still part of the Child *ego state* and is therefore as much a feeling as a thinking state. More than anything else it grants the child the capacity for 'psyching things out'. On its own, A_1 is probably recognized as simple cunning, but developed hand-in-hand with the purely objective Adult, it is potentially the most rewarding and valuable *ego state* throughout life, granting intuition, hypotheses, insight, and the basis of all forms of creativity. (It does Edward de Bono's 'lateral thinking', whilst the Adult does 'vertical thinking'.)

Healthy development of the infant through Stage I depends on parents' willingness to let go of their Parental omnipotence of the very early months and emphatically *stroke* the emerging Little Professor from about six months onwards. Jean Liedloff[5] cites empirical evidence which underlines the importance of sufficient A_1 stroking at this stage: 'Drs. Doman and Delacato in their Philadelphia clinic . . . . . found that people who had not been allowed to creep about on all fours at the appropriate time in babyhood, who had been hampered by playpens or some other cause from fulfilling their requirement to crawl and creep, failed to develop fully their verbal abilities.'

Stage II One–three years

At about one-year-old the infant is beginning to become 'self-willed' and, in the interests of socialization, parents impose constraints, usually beginning with 'Don't'. In this way energy is differentiated into a third aspect of the Child, the Adapted Child, which is designated P_1, and which is usually contrasted with the Free Child, which consists of the Natural Child, C_1, plus the Little Professor, A_1. (Although some authors argue that the Free Child consists only of C_1, since both A_1 and P_1 represent adaptations to realities the child discovers, it makes most sense for me, personally, to see the capacites of the Little Professor (A_1) as innately given, and therefore part of the Free Child.)

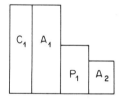

Learning to say 'please' and 'thank you', not spitting or screaming for what he wants, and generally learning to delay gratification are important components of the Adapted Child, P_1, which are developed in this stage by parental *stroking up* of these behaviours. In general, P_1 may be thought of as the imitative precursor of the Parent *ego state*, which is not fully developed until about six years of age. At two years of age a little girl may imitatively 'share' some chocolate with her doll but then 'eat it for Dolly', whereas at six years of age she will be capable of truly sharing some chocolate with a friend.

Parents need to be particularly aware at this stage — as again in early adolescence — that *negative strokes* are as powerfully reinforcing as *positive* ones. Thus 'a good hiding', for example, in response to a child's purposefully tipping a plateful of food on to the floor will, in the long run, be less effective in teaching him social control than 'What a good, well-mannered boy you've been' in response to his having behaved with appropriate constraint.[6]

Between the ages of one and three there is a secondary *stroking* emphasis on the emerging Adult *ego state*, A_2. This is manifest largely in practical skills — building a tower of blocks, blowing one's nose, pouring water from one container to another — but above all else on the acquisition of language.

The child's healthy development through Stage II depends on parents' awareness of the difference between constraints necessary for socialization and those which maladaptively bind an excess of energy into P_1 (the Adapted Child) to the detriment of the other *ego states*.

Stage III Three–six years

From about three years on, until the personality is functionally complete at about six years of age, the *stroking* emphasis continues to be directed to A_2 the Adult and also to the newly emerging Parent *ego state*, P_2, manifested in sharing and caring behaviours. Parent *ego state stroking* of the child is concerned with the explicit teaching by parents of their own idiosyncratic code of morality and values as well as of those values endemic in the larger community of which the family is a member. The Adult, A_2, continues to be *stroked* for an expanding repertoire of language and other skills such as toileting self, doing up shoe laces, and adroitly handling a knife and fork.

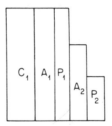

Healthy development of the child through Stage III depends essentially on the same-sexed parent's willingness to forgo his/her jealousy of the attachment of the child to the opposite-sexed parent.

Stage IV Six-years-old

Energy is harmoniously distributed amongst all the *ego states* and all of them are now available to the child for their appropriate uses.

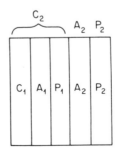

Stage V Six–twelve years

But the harmony of the six-year-old is disrupted through the demands of culture, and the six- to twelve-year-old personality responds to these demands by heavily energizing the Adult at the expense of the Parent and Child. Much of the child's healthy development through this stage is handed over to teachers who *stroke up* the culturally demanded skills of literacy, numeracy and social skills. Subsidiarily, parents *stroke up* their child's Adult in their own individualistic ways (with their Parent in the *executive*), taking the child on outings, arranging swimming and music lessons, etc.

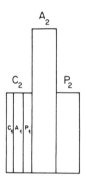

The dominating matter-of-factness of this stage of development provides for parents a bonus calm after the intensity of the earlier years and before the storm of puberty. Now is the time in which children are less vulnerable than previously, or than they will be subsequently, to traumatic events that may befall them. So this is the time to teach them the facts of sex and generally to grant them knowledge of emotionally charged aspects of reality, which they are able to assimilate with their Adult appropriately in the *executive*. So much is their Adult in the *executive* at this stage that they can be excrutiatingly boring at times, such as when they pin you down while they tell you every single *fact* of what happened in the film they have just seen!. This is also the time — if needs be — when the separation or divorce of parents is likely to produce the least damaging long-term effects on the child.

Stage VI Thirteen–sixteen years

At puberty the child is suddenly overwhelmed by a biologically determined surge of sexual/aggressive energy into C_1, and manifestly demands its fulfilment as if in infancy again. But, unlike Stage III of which this stage is so reminiscent, there is now no escape for the child from the established realities of A_2 and P_2. Much as he might wish, he cannot escape into the naïvety of infancy and he is desperate for help. Instinctively, parents *stroke up* P_1 With 'Don'ts' and appeal to A_1 with spending money in order to redress the balance *within* C_2, while teachers do their utmost to keep on *stroking up* A_2. But P_2 remains essentially swamped.

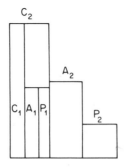

This is a holding-on stage, and healthy development through it depends on parents' self-confidence, through their A_1 awareness, in keeping their own A_2 in the *executive* while *stroking* from their P_1 to their child's P_1 and A_1.

Whereas in the earlier critical stage between one and three the Adapted Child expressed essential compliance, it is equally necessary for healthy maturation that, at this stage, the Adapted Child express the other side of its coin, namely rebellion.

The way this necessity makes most sense to me is in terms of the emergence out of the Child of the autonomous Parent which needs, most importantly, a sense of *responsibility* for the nurturance of the next generation. But no qualities exist without their opposites, and the opposite of responsibility in this context is *blame*. My fourteen-year-old daughter *must* tell me (from her P_1) that I am 'ruining her life' when I tell her to be in by eleven o'clock at night, (though her Little Professor has enough sense actually to be home by then). Out of the natural expression of blame for the generation before us emerges the capacity for the only healthy and natural kind of *guilt* — for what we do to the generation after us.

When this healthy model of blame by children and guilt by parents is distorted, I believe we have the basis for most of the problems that bring people to psychotherapists. When parents consistently blame their children schizophrenia may be the outcome for the children. When children feel guilty towards their parents we get the commoner neuroses, the cure for which has been, since psychoanalysis was invented, the catharsis of blame towards parents at a later date, in therapy. And notwithstanding the increasing psychological enlightenment of recent generations of parents, the inhibition of thirteen- to sixteen-year-old *blame* is still — in my experience — one of the commoner causes of psychological difficulties later in life.

Stage VII Late adolescence

By this stage A_2 has normally received some potent *stroking* through educational attainment and energy is now more harmoniously distributed between C_2 and A_2 than it has been since the age of six, but P_2 still needs its share of energy for the early harmony of Stage IV to be restored.

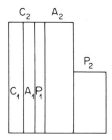

The child knows now that he still needs his parents to help him achieve this final stage in his maturation. But usually, for a complex of reasons including sexual rivalry with his same-sexed parent and the taboo against sexual intimacy with his opposite-sexed parent, he needs to play *games* around getting this need fulfilled. Often he will use his A_2 — now capable of deduction and sophistry — to defend the unrealistic demands of his C_1. He may launch a two-pronged attack on his parents' A_2 and P_2 with his now self-confident A_2, but covertly he is begging for P_2-P_2 *strokes* from them, which will enable him to leave home safely and function as an *autonomous* adult.

The child's healthy development through this stage depends on his parents' awareness of the *game* he is playing and their self-confidence in gently insisting that in some matters of values and morality reason is irrelevant — that is, that the Parent as well as the Adult has the right to *autonomy* within the personality.

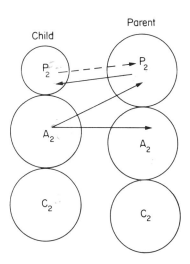

What has just been said should not be misconstrued as advocating rigid *impermeability* as a healthy state for the Parent. Mature and healthy personalities make changing *judgements* in accordance with Adult reality testing as well as given Parent values, and the Parent itself is capable of structural change. But this mature *collaboration of ego states* (see Chapter 2) is only possible *consequent* on clearly delineated contents and boundaries for each of the *ego states* in the first place. The wise parent appreciates this and sends his adolescent out to face the world properly armed with a set of Parent values which will stand him in good stead until such time, as an adult established in the larger world, he may safely and assuredly reassess his Parent in the light of changing realities in his life.

Stage VIII Maturity

The harmonious distribution of energy into all *ego states* — previously only manifest transiently in the charming six-year-old — is restored and maturity is achieved.

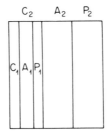

Summary

Implicit in TA is the assumption that we are each born with a fixed amount of psychic energy, which is conserved in the totality of the personality. In development from birth to maturity the congenitally given reservoir of energy gradually becomes differentiated into the various *ego states*. At each stage of development parents *stroke up* emerging *ego states* in order to effect the child's healthy transition from that stage to the next.

At birth, the personality is wholly the Natural Child, C_1. In the second half of the first year the Little Professor, A_1, emerges. From one to three years the emphasis is on the emerging Adapted Child, P_1, and the Adult, A_2. Three to six years emphasizes the emerging Parent, P_2, and by six years of age the personality is complete.

From six to twelve years the Adult, A_2, is dominant, but at puberty the Child, C_2, particularly the Natural Child, C_1, and the rebellious aspect of the Adapted Child, P_1, again overwhelms the personality until about sixteen years of age. Late adolescence restores energy to the Adult, A_2, and maturity is achieved when the Parent, P_2, is re-energized and all the *ego states* are in harmony again, as they were transiently at the age of six.

Notes and References

1. This chapter is based on an article called 'Stroking Up Our Children' which I wrote and which was published in the *Transactional Analysis Journal*, **7**, no. 4, October 1977.
2. P. Levin, *Becoming the Way We Are*, Trans. Pubs., 1974.
3. J. Schiff, *Cathexis Reader*, Harper and Row, 1975.
4. J. Dusay, 'Egograms and the "Constancy Hypothesis"', *Transactional Analysis Journal*, **2**, no. 3, July 1972. Although Jack Dusay and I both use the histogram form to represent the distribution of energy between *ego states*, his *egogram* consists of 'Nurturing Parent', 'Critical Parent', 'Adult', 'Free Child', and 'Adapted Child'. I do not believe that 'Nurturing Parent' and 'Critical Parent' are distinct functional entities; he does not believe that the Little Professor is a distinct functional entity. The idea of delineating developmental stages in *egogram* form is mine.
5. J. Liedloff, *The Continuum Concept*. Futura Publications, 1975, p. 134.
6. As a parent, I am only too well aware of how much easier said than done it is to be in such control of oneself. However, parents in my groups who — in the first instance experimentally — have taken the trouble self-conciously to avoid giving their children *negative strokes*, have reported 'incredible' and 'immediate' favourable changes in their children's behaviour.

CHAPTER 4

Child Development II. Structural Development of the Ego States

In Chapter 3 we saw how, in the course of normal human development, energy becomes gradually differentiated into our various *ego states* in accordance with an inbuilt biological programme supported by the cultural structure of society.

But we differ from each other as individuals primarily in the *contents* of our *ego states*, which are determined by the idiosyncratic programming of parents and other influential people in our early years of life. This programming comes to us in the form of *messages*, which consist both of words and actions, out of which we make *decisions* about ourselves, others, and the nature of the world. We remain committed to these *decisions* for the rest of our lives unless, through the radical opening up of the personality, we re-examine the *messages* we received and *redecide* their meanings with the expanded data of our grown-up Adults combined with new insights in our Little Professors.

The overall understanding of how our structural programming takes place is called *script theory*, which is that aspect of TA which has been elaborated and developed most rapidly in the last few years. Both during Berne's lifetime and since his death, Claude Steiner has been primarily responsible for the development of *script theory*, which is crucial in the diagnosis and treatment of individual pathology when therapy seeks to go beyond the surface understanding and control of social interaction. *Script analysis* makes available material which causally relates the present to the past and opens up the possibility for radical changes in the individual's perceptions of himself, others, and the world. Claude Steiner won the first Eric Berne Memorial Scientific Award in 1971 for his article 'Script and Counterscript'.[1] His most recent book is *Scripts People Live*.[2]

The *script matrix* below diagrams the way the structure of our personalities is filled-in in childhood. The arrows in the *script matrix* represent the paths of communication between parents and child. Each *ego state* in the child receives *messages* from the corresponding *ego states* of Mother and Father, and the child amalgamates and interprets these *messages*, thus forming his own unique ego.[3]

Generally speaking, the earlier in life *messages* are received the more immutable will be the *decisions* made around them. However, it is also true (see Chapter 3) that at different ages between birth and maturity the personality is

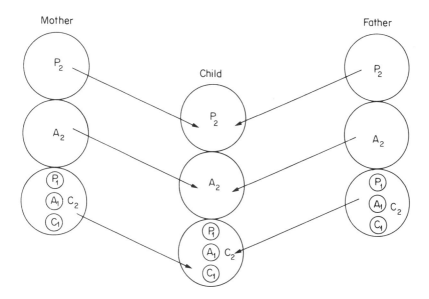

more open to the receipt of *messages* of one kind than another. Thus table manners have the best chance of being incorporated into the personality between one and three years of age when P_1 is at the peak of its development, honesty when P_2 is developing between three and six, and arithmetical tables between six and twelve when the personality is dominated by the development of A_2.

Most parents and teachers educate children with an instinctive awareness of these optimal times for the incorporation of different material into the various *ego states*. However, many over-zealous parents fall prey to the delusion that, if they try hard enough, their nine-month-old baby can be potty-trained or their two-year-old taught to share. A nine-month-old baby does not have P_1 yet available to *obey commands* to defecate on a potty, nor does a two-year-old have P_2 available to *share* with. (In the light of the emergence of P_2 at around three years of age, I believe a good case can be made for spacing children in a family by between three and six years. By this means, no child will be subject to a premature demand to care for and share with a younger sibling, whilst at the same time — for all but the youngest in the family, who will have to make do with a pet — the instruction to share and care will begin to be imposed at the optimum time for the incorporation of these values into the personality.)

Let us now consider the ways in which the various elements of the *script matrix* are developed.

Counterscript and the Acquisition of Skills (Parent and Adult)

All normal parents want the best for their children and pass on to them precepts like 'Be honest', 'Succeed in life', 'Be loving and kind to others'. These are the *taught* concepts of life, called *counterinjunctions*, which travel along the P_2-P_2 paths, mostly between the ages of three and six years. They are explicitly given, usually in words, and consist of socially acceptable values and controls, including *stroke currencies*, which we defined in Chapter 2. The collection of instructions we have in our P_2s, together with our *decisions* derived from them, is called our *counterscript*. By virtue of the child's psycho-sexual attachment to the parent of the opposite sex between the ages of three and six, when P_2 is at the peak of its development, there is a tendency for the child to receive P_2 *messages* with greater impact from the parent of the opposite sex than from the parent of the same sex.

A_2-A_2 transmits *how-to messages*. They are usually received by the child through observing Mother and Father in action. Thus the child learns how to mend a fuse, peel onions without crying, dress attractively, do long division a quick way, play the piano, and swim. A_2 *messages* begin to be received from about one year of age onwards throughout life, with a peak between about six and twelve years. Sexual identification (after the age of about six) usually grants somewhat greater impact to the *messages* received from A_2 of the child's same-sexed parent.

Thus if Mother swims well and is religious and Father plays the piano well and is ambitious, a son is more *likely* to play the piano well (A_2) like Father and be religious (P_2) like Mother, the daughter more *likely* to swim well (A_2) like Mother and be ambitious (P_2) like Father.

Script Permissions (Natural Child and Little Professor)

C_2-C_2 transmits — often covertly and therefore more powerfully than P_2-P_2 and A_2-A_2, since actions speak louder than words — the parents' feelings about life. C_1 is biologically given and is called the Natural Child. As indicated in Chapter 1, it is universally the same in content — demanding, self-centred, loving, spontaneous, honest and lovable — all the things a new-born baby is. Thus no *messages* need to be given from parents' C_1 in order for their child's C_1 to be activated, although the child's observation of Mother and Father in their C_1s will serve as a *stroke* — that is, reinforcement — to his own C_1 and grant him various *permissions*. In other words, through the examples of Mother and Father some freedoms are more likely than others to be manifest in the child's C_1. In practice, this usually amounts to a well-developed capacity to *enjoy* particular things. Thus if the growing child is witness to Mother or Father enjoying cooking, shopping, reading, walking, golf, arranging flowers, etc., the child is more likely than not also to enjoy these things. The peak time for the reception of these *permissions* is probably between birth and three years of age. As well as all the socially acceptable *permissions*, such as the examples I have just given, there may also, of course, be *permissions* given to feel and do 'bad' things. Some cases of lawlessness, for example, are clearly manifestations of behaviour that was *stroked* in childhood. An example of such a *permission* was evident to me in a member of one of my therapeutic groups whose father used to bring him presents when he was a child which had 'fallen off the back of a lorry'. For the son, this was received as *permission* 'to be dishonest in small ways' — which is quite different from *antiscript* stealing so common amongst adolescents. (The nature of *antiscript* is elaborated later on in this and the next chapter.)

A_1 is the Little Professor and A_1-A_1 *messages* are concerned with 'psyching out' people and situations and generally in being creative. By the time an infant keeps banging his spoon on his high-chair tray while his mother is talking to a friend — until she stops and gives *him* some *strokes* — he has clearly received some A_1 *messages*. So too will his later talents for drawing, writing poetry, sculpting etc., be largely a result of early *strokes* to these A_1 behaviours. As with C_1-C_1 *messages*, A_1-A_1 *messages* probably serve to *stroke* and therefore to reinforce biologically inherent capacities of the child rather than actually to teach him things of which he would otherwise be incapable. Beginning with the emergence of A_1 at about six months of age, peak learning through A_1 continues until about three years of age.

The innately given capacity of the Little Professor to 'psych things out' also gives it the responsibility for making the *decisions* (*script*) arising out of the reconciliation and assimilation of *messages* given to C_1 and P_1 as well as to itself.

Script Inhibitions (Adapted Child)

In the interests of socialization and of self-preservation the Free Child needs to have some of its expression inhibited as well as encouraged. Constraints usually begin to be necessary at about one year of age as the child becomes mobile, and P_1, the Adapted Child, then emerges and continues its development until about three years of age.

Now the problem with the Adapted Child is that, by definition, it must constantly do battle with the Free Child. 'Don't pick your nose in public', 'Don't scream, ask politely', 'Don't poke things in power points' are *injunctions* which undoubtedly need to be obeyed in order for the child to function happily amongst other people and, indeed, to survive. Between one and three years of age, when obedience to such *injunctions* becomes practically necessary — at least in our culture — the child's Adult is not sufficiently developed to appreciate the good sense of not poking things into power points nor has his Parent (which will later support the Adapted Child with generalizations about considering others' feelings) begun its emergence. So at this early stage parents need to pour a great deal of energy into *stroking up* P_1 until the slightest cue activates an immediate and unquestioned obedience to the appropriate *injunction*. When a child has learnt always to say 'please' and 'thank you', never to put coins in his mouth, and to get no closer than five feet away from the stove before stopping in his tracks (and possibly saying to himself 'Don't touch') the relevant P_1 *messages* have become like *electrodes*, buttons in his head which precipitate an immediate response in his behaviour even if Mother or Father are not present. From then on any disobedience to these *injunctions* will precipitate him into *giving himself negative strokes*—just as we explained in Chapter 2, we analogously give ourselves *positive strokes* for behaviours manifesting our *permissions*.

So far so good. But parents have hang-ups and these too are transmitted along the P_1-P_1 paths and also quickly achieve the immutable power of *electrodes*. Very often these *messages*, which are usually covert and non-verbal, conflict with overt, verbally given P_2 *messages*. But because P_1 *messages* pre-date P_2 *messages* and because actions speak louder than words, the Adapted Child, P_1, will always have equal if not greater power over the individual's life than any Parent, P_2, values, no matter how explicitly the Parent values are given and *stroked*. The invitations sent to children urging them to misery and other forms of self-destruction are called Witch *messages* when they come from Mother and Ogre *messages* when they come from Father.

For example, consider the father who instructs his children (P_2-P_2) in the value of sobriety, but comes home drunk every other night (P_1-P_1 invitation to alcoholism); or the mother who tells her children (P_2-P_2) that marriage is the surest way to happiness, but has frequent unhappy rows with her husband (P_1-P_1 invitation to be unhappily married). The give-away in a grown-up overtly complaining of his fate but covertly being deeply gratified by the *stroke* to the Witch or Ogre in his Child is often a barely camouflaged verbal statement of intent, such as 'Oh boy, (smiling) am I paying for my night on the town' or 'I don't know why I married him. My mother always told me not to fall for a no-hoper like my father'.

Because P_1 contains all the *messages* inviting us to bad and sad endings, Claude Steiner calls this *ego state* the Pig Parent (rather than the Adapted Child). I think this fails to do justice to the positively adaptive elements — especially simple good manners and life-preserving inhibitions — which need to be manifest in the personality long before the Adult and Parent are between them capable of making relevant *judgements*.

Although in very many cases the P_2-P_2 *messages* directly contradict the P_1-P_1 *messages* that are given, it can also happen that the P_2 and P_1 *messages* are in harmony. Thus a parent may make an explicit P_2 statement that 'Life is one long misery' and give a completely congruent *message* from P_1 by actually *being* a misery most of the time. In such a case, though the child need never experience any conflict between *injunctions* and *counterinjunctions* he is even less likely than otherwise to escape the Witch or Ogre's curse.

Rackets (Adapted Child)

One very important kind of *injunction* children receive concerns what kind of bad feelings they should feel. The bad feeling(s) selected by the parents for their children become their children's *racket(s)*. Unlike a genuine — and therefore spontaneous — emotional response, a *racket* is an habitual, stereotyped emotional response. In every family, certain feelings are more likely to be noticed — that is, *stroked* — than others. Every child learns very early in life which feelings *his* parents will respond to, and thereafter, these feelings will be part of the repertoire of his Adapted Child, to be used in *games* and other exploitative *transactions* (see Chapter 6). There is a necessary verbal component in the successful transmission of *injunctions* leading to *rackets* through the *naming* of the bad feeling concerned, for which realization I am indebted to Fanita English,[4] whose theory of *rackets* and *games* is discussed in detail in Chapter 6.

Rackets are universal because, inevitably, in the process of growing up things go wrong in our families. Parents quarrel, fathers lose jobs, mothers get ill, the household is disrupted by the presence of a widowed grandparent. Though some of us as children are witnesses to more unhappiness than others, none of us completely escapes things going wrong in our families when we are young. The way we find to adapt best to such situations provides us with our chosen *racket feeling*, which we may pursue for the rest of our lives. Anger, guilt, fear, frustration, embarrassment, helplessness are all very common *racket feelings*.

Whichever *racket* is our own favourite became so by being *stroked* — albeit often *negatively* — in childhood. Take, for example, the case of a child who witnesses his parents quarrelling. The first time he experiences this situation he is frightened, but nobody seems to notice it. His fear is not *stroked*. So next time his parents quarrel, he seeks to get *strokes* by being angry with them, shouting at them to stop. This response, too, is ignored. The next time he acts sad and cries, and this time he is noticed. He might be given the *positive stroke* of a hug and a consoling, 'Don't be sad. Everybody quarrels sometimes'. Or he might be shouted at, 'Stop that snivelling! I've got enough to contend with without you being sad as well!' Either way, his sadness has been *stroked* and his bad feeling and the word 'sad' (which his mother or father used in responding to his behaviour) both become inextricably linked in his mind as the best (i.e. *stroke-getting*) response whenever things go wrong in future.

Whenever, for whatever reasons, we are not getting enough *strokes*, we tend to seek out situations which lend themselves to our feeling our *racket*. Sometimes we can achieve our *racket* without *transacting* with others, simply by remembering things that have happened that made us feel angry, guilty, frightened, etc. But more often than not we seek out other people to play *games* with, the *payoffs* of which will include *racket feelings* for ourself and for the people playing *games* with us. In adult life we tend to insist on the 'naturalness' of our own *racket* and are surprised if we enquire and find that other people do not feel the same bad feeling as ourselves as a usual response to things going wrong.

This was brought home to me very vividly when one evening in December I walked into my living room to conduct a group therapy session and, as I entered the room, I heard one group member saying to another, 'Thank you for your Christmas card. I'm sorry I haven't sent you one yet. I know I must seem very *ungrateful*'. I took this up and asked the rest of the group how each of them would feel on meeting someone who had sent them an unreciprocated Christmas card. The responses were 'triumphant', 'embarrassed', 'angry', 'guilty', and 'worried'. As each person named his or her own *racket* the rest of the group looked on in amazed *disbelief*. I have very successfully used this method — of asking for people's responses to a commonplace discomfitting situation — ever since, to define and elucidate the nature of *rackets*.

The *final payoff* to a *game* is more than just a *racket feeling*. It incorporates also a thought element (originally construed by the Little Professor), an interpretative statement about life-in-general, whose reinforcement is also repeatedly sought throughout the individual's life. These *existential positions* may be highly idiosyncratic, and in Chapter 8 this will be demonstrated, with examples of complete *script matrices*. However, a couple of popular *racket* and *existential position* combinations are a resentment *racket* accompanied by the thought 'I always get the rough end of the wedge' and a misunderstood *racket* accompanied by 'No matter what I do for people they never appreciate me'. Such are the ultimate *script decisions* made by our Little Professors, based on the totality of all the *messages* received into the Adapted Child and the Little Professor himself as well as the (*permissions* received by the) Natural Child.

Antiscript (Adapted Child)

In general, our *scripts* determine our ultimate destinies and our *counterscripts* determine the styles of our lives and provide temporary protection (often dominant in our personalities until middle-age) from the more destructive and tragic elements in our *scripts*. There is also a third aspect of our planned destinies called *antiscript*. This is a highly unstable *rebellious* aspect of the Adapted Child, which gives the illusion to the individual using it of refuting his *script* while, in fact, he is obeying his *script* by a devious route. Thus a teenage girl may run away from home, swearing never to be caught in the trap of marriage as she saw her mother so unhappily was, only to end up in a very short time choosing marriage to an unsuitable man as the 'best' option consequent on her pregnancy. As well as providing the delusion of escaping from *script*, *antiscript* is commonly observed in adolescence as a self-conscious rebellion against *counterscript*, and is observable in the many 'anti-social' acts of adolescents, including transient stealing, vandalism, trespassing, and drug-taking. Between the ages of approximately thirteen and sixteen *antiscript* is expressive of a natural and necessary stage in maturation, but it is also observable as a pathological fixation in some adults who may stay in it for many years at an enormous cost of psychic energy. (The nature of *antiscript* is further elaborated in Chapter 7 in the discussion of the *miniscript*, in which it is very well exemplified.)

Episcript (Little Professor)

The fourth and final aspect of our *life-plans* is the *episcript* or *hot potato*, as it was named by its discoverer, Fanita English.[5] It is a manifestation of a parent's compulsion to get rid of the spell of his or her own Witch or Ogre by passing it on to someone else. In life, the parent makes this attempt by very heavily imposing some particular *injunction* on his child, and the Little Professor of the child picks this up as one particular rule he is duty bound to obey in order to relieve his parent of some of her or his onerous life burden. To some extent the device works as, for example, when an alcoholic father is never so sober as when his teenage son becomes a drug addict, only to return to his old drinking patterns if his son is rehabilitated, that is, chucks the *hot potato* back to whence it came. Even if the son continues on his path to self-destruction, however, the curse is only partially lifted for the father, who is unlikely to find any long-lasting relief from his own symptoms by the imposition on his son. The son, of course, is likely to pass it on to his children and on through the generations, although nature provides a gradual cooling of the potato over the generations through the introduction of spell-free marriage partners into the generation game. Sometimes the *hot potato* can be disguised by *antiscript*, as was the case of one man I knew whose father — objectively a very successful scientist — had a *final script payoff* of 'I am worthless and my life has been a failure' which he justified by the fact that he had not won the Nobel Prize! When I knew his son, at the age of forty, he (the son) had been unemployed and living from hand to mouth for the past ten years, despite having an engineering degree (gained in *counterscript* in his early twenties). Miserable though he manifestly was, he *hotly* asserted the superiority of his way of life over a conventional one incorporating professional achievement and ambition.

Summarily, we may now express all the material of this chapter so far, graphically, the enlarged Child indicating the dominance of this *ego state* in the whole structure.

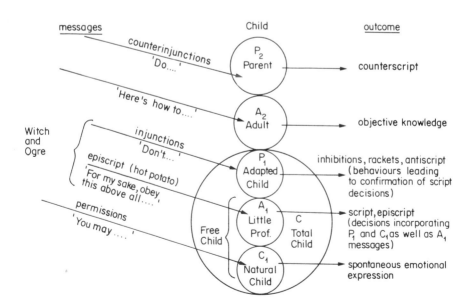

The Need for Script

In the light of all the unhappiness in our lives for which our *scripts* are so often responsible, we may well ask why we write them in the first place and why we stick to them in the long run.

In the first place *all* our behaviour is ultimately *stroke-seeking*, and obedience to *injunctions* and *counterinjunctions* is the most obvious way we can obtain *strokes* (overt or covert, positive or negative) from Mother and Father. Therefore, such obedience, in our childhoods and for as long as we go on living with our parents, is vital to our self-preservation. And by the time we leave our parents our obedience to *injunctions* and *counterinjunctions* is so firmly entrenched through childhood *stroking* as to make such behaviours automatic in the world at large, regardless of the fact that they may be maladaptive in *transactions* with people outside our families. However, such is the cleverness of our Little Professors that they nearly always manage — with uncanny regularity and precision — to make sure that the people with whom we form our most intimate relationships psychologically match—especially in terms of Adapted Child characteristics — members of our original families, so that our childhood behaviours will continue to get their predictable responses and we need not learn anything new.

But even more critically determining of our lives, in terms of our short- and long-term destinies as well as our moment-by-moment *transactions*, are our *script decisions*, which seem less related to our primary need for *strokes*. Certainly some of our ultimate existential *decisions* and related *payoffs* meet with Mother's and Father's approval, but they need not. *Script decisions* we make may actually displease Mother's or Father's Witch or Ogre, such as when a child *decides* in response to 'Don't ever be happy with what you've got' that 'When I grow up I will always be happy with what I've got' — and is. Such a *decision* must, of course, be distinguished from a *decision* that 'Nobody can ever be happy with what they've got', camouflaged by continuous 'trying hard to be happy with what I've got' — and failing.' (See the Try Hard *miniscript*, Chapter 7.) *Decisions* made by the Little Professor in direct opposition to a particular *injunction* may be likened to 'reaction formation' in psychoanalytic terminology, in which a characteristic opposed to a parent's deepest wishes for the child becomes a deeply entrenched part of the Child's character, (i.e. incorporated into both his *script* and *counterscript*). However, both psychoanalysis and *script theory* recognize that no characteristic exists without the possibility of its opposite, so the original *injunction* remains in the child's mental constructs even if it never finds manifest expression.

However, regardless of whether or not our childhood *decisions* are ultimately pleasing to Mother or Father, these original *existential decisions* remain core issues in our lives and we seek to reaffirm them over and over again. Why, when we have proved their validity once, are we not satisfied and why do we not go on to something else?

This is explainable in terms of another need, equally innate and as vital as our need for *strokes*, namely the need *to organize our experience*. Out of the chaos which it is inferred is our perception of the world at birth we continually strive to make cohesive sense of every element in our experience in order to provide for ourselves the sense of well-being and security that is only found in *predictability*.

The world has two chief aspects, the physical and the psychological, both of which we need to make sense of. Usually, making sense of the physical world proceeds smoothly and with minimal frustration. The grown-ups around us have it all worked out and, recognizing our need to share their security in the knowability of things, they readily and willingly, in response to our uncertainty and curiosity, *impose on us* their own self-consistent concepts concerning physical cause and effect. Thus we acquire security derived not only from the repeated patterns that our Child experiences in, for example, balls always falling down when we throw them up, but also from the repeatedly reaffirmed 'reason' for this experience which we are given, namely that 'Gravity makes everything fall down'. And should any of us as children be sceptical enough to test Mother's or Father's answers for congruence with other people's answers, we find that Grandma and Grandpa, aunts and uncles, neighbours, and any other grown-up we ask all say the same thing — 'Gravity makes everything fall down'. And thus, by the age of no more than about four or five, we have acquired a near enough complete knowledge of physics experientially — in our Child, that is — which we supplement with compatible data fed into our Adult by all the colluding grown-ups in the world, for as long as and to the extent that our curiosity prompts us to ask.

I say 'colluding grown-ups' because, of course, metaphysically, 'our' physics is only one self-consistent picture of 'reality' that the human brain may have invented (and there is strong inferential evidence that the Hopi Indians, for example, have invented a quite different 'reality' from ours). This was brought home to me pointedly when one of my daughters at the age of four asked me, 'Why are all the big aeroplanes at the airport and all the little ones in the sky?'. In answering, 'The ones in the sky only *seem* little . . . .' I was aware, with some poignancy, of closing her mind once and for all, in order to give her the comfortable cognitive certainty she needed in order to get by in the (ordinary) world.

In an entirely analogous way we also need to make sense of our psychological worlds and therefore seek and find answers from our early instructors, who are the members of our immediate family circle. And it is my belief that the tragedy for each of us — in being human — lies in our Little Professor's mistaken but overwhelming conviction that our own family's idiosyncratic ontology is as universally agreed upon as the 'laws' governing our understanding of the physical world.

This is the determinism which we all find so unpleasant to acknowledge. The threat to the illusion of *autonomy* posed by this knowledge is more than most people can bear, so they defend against it with crude denial, discounting it as unjustifiable 'pessimism'. Yet, paradoxically, it is only those who are brave enough to face this essential 'pessimism' who may, in fact, achieve some degree of real 'optimism' through achieved control over their *scripts*. Freud knew all this, of course, and so do many writers. The novels of Iris Murdoch and Fay Weldon and T. S. Eliot's 'The Cocktail Party' immediately come to mind as exhibiting these writers' deep understanding of the overwhelming power of *script decisions*. And, of course,

> 'Men at some time are masters of their fates;
> The fault, dear Brutus, is not in our stars,'
> But in ourselves, that we are underlings'.

TA can make this understanding explicit for the individual through *script analysis*. In the chapters on diagnosis and therapy we will see how such analysis provides the possibility through *awareness* of gaining at least some freedom from the compulsion of *script* and, in its place, achieving new *spontaneity* and *autonomy*.

Protocol and Palimpsest

The child's decisions derived from his earliest experiences are called his *protocol*. Later experiences in childhood will basically reaffirm the original *protocol* but may modify it somewhat through an increased sophistication of the Little Professor and additional Adult data. This later version of the *script* is called the *palimpsest*.

The *protocol* is laid down in the first six years of life, the *palimpsest* between approximately six and twelve. Some final polishing up of the *palimpsest* takes place in adolescence, when the resurfacing of the turbulent Child allows the possibility of some last-minute changes in the *script* before the child begins to enact the drama he has written for himself. Adolescence is the time when, as we saw in Chapter 5, the personality is again — as it was before, in infancy — in a state of disequilibrium and is wide open to influences. Although in the normal course of events (parents having retained *their* personalities of ten to fifteen years previously), the adolescent will usually simply receive the old *messages* anew and reaffirm old *decisions* around them, this does not have to be the case. Aware parents, regretting some of the *messages* they transmitted years ago, *do* get a second chance to reinform their children at this later stage. My own experience as a parent has confirmed the validity of this possibility, which I have personally found an enormously rewarding, albeit exhausting, task.

The *protocol* itself is made so early in life that it is inevitably a mixture of verbal and pre-verbal thought-feeling. And the verbally articulated aspects are often very far removed from the sophisticated interpolations that all grown-ups make use of. Every parent is daily a witness to the literal-mindedness of children under the age of about six which so charms grown-ups. One such example which delighted me at the time was when one of my daughters, aged six, was playing 'Reading the News' and she announced: 'Here are the headlines. Today a lion escaped from the zoo, so now the zoo-keeper will have to get another one'. Such naïvety also alerts us to the vulnerability of the young child to every word that is spoken to him, since his *script protocol*, which colours all the rest of his life, is made out of such a literal-minded and limited interpretative capacity. And because the *protocol* is inevitably made up of such a tangle of non-articulated feeling plus the peculiar distortions of literal-mindedness with respect to words, it is very difficult to get at in later life. Rediscovering it and making new sense of the *messages* from which it was formed is the task of psychoanalysis. TA *script analysis* and therapy deals with the later version of the *script* as it is manifest in the *palimpsest*.

Occasionally, however, as a TA therapist, I hear some of the literal-minded conclusions of the *protocol*. A vivid example concerned the four-year-old son of a woman who was a member of one of my groups. He asked his mother one evening as she was getting ready to come to a therapy session, 'Why are you going out?'. The mother, whose *contract* in the group was to improve her unhappy marriage, replied, 'I'm going to get some help so I can live with Daddy'. The next morning the little boy got up early and, by the time his parents were awake, had pulled all the books off the bookshelf, smashed ornaments, turned chairs upside down, and generally wreaked havoc in the sitting room, and he continued to behave in an inexplicably rageful way for several days. 'During the course of several subsequent therapy sessions with the boy's mother, I sought to make sense of this violent incident in the context of the whole family situation. By chance, we hit on the contiguity of the child's violent outburst with his mother saying, 'so I can live with Daddy'. It was clear that the mother's tone of voice, inflexion, and emphasis had led her son to presume that unless she went out and got help *she would die*. He had understood the word 'live' in the only way he was capable of. Had she not been able to trace this construction in her son's mind and help him *redecide* its meaning, we can infer that he would have incorporated into his *protocol* a lifelong rage together with a *decision* (bearing in mind his Oedipal attachment to his mother and jealousy of his father at this time in his life) such as 'Whenever I love a woman she will need help to stop my love killing her'.

Once the *script protocol* has been written the child immediately begins to live it, in so far as he will *selectively perceive and remember* from then on those items of experience which will serve to reinforce it. Let us hypothesize that the little boy I have just spoken of did incorporate into his *protocol* 'Whenever I love a woman she will need help to stop my love killing her'. Let us say that when this little boy is ten his parents decide they 'can no longer live with each other' and they get divorced and Father leaves the family home. By this stage — at the age of ten — the little boy is clearly putting together insights in his Little Professor in a much more sophisticated way than he was at five, and he is also aware now in his Adult that it is not his love for his mother which has caused his parents' divorce. But his Child, of course, experiences enormous loss in the event of his parents' divorce and he will need to make sense of the event in a subjective as well as an objective way. He will use his already established *protocol* (probably unconsciously) as a backdrop and will probably form an Adult/Child *con-tamination* (see Chapter 8 for an elucidation of the meaning of *contaminations*)

52

which will serve to make sense both of the Adult reality of the situation and of his Child's feeling of loss, in a single mental construct. For this particular boy we might guess that he would arrive at a *decision* rather like 'I will save women I love from destruction by sacrificing my own needs'. At the same time — recalling the traumatic event which led to his *protocol decision* — he may feel a deep *rage* towards his father. This new *decision* — a modified version of the original one — will be incorporated into his *palimpsest* together with *rage* as his *racket*.

As a sixteen-year-old, we may speculate that he will fall in love with a girl whom he dreams of Rescuing (see Chapter 6 for the meaning of Rescuing) from a boyfriend who abuses her in some way, and as a twenty-one-year-old gives up his studies to marry a girl who is pregnant by another man.

And in an Old Age Home, at eighty, he will sit rocking and *raging* at the loss of his *wife* and at being neglected by his *daughters* for whom he has *sacrificed* so much.

Summary

We differ from each other as individuals primarily in the contents of our *ego states*, which are determined by programming by parents and others in the early years of our lives. Each *ego state* receives *messages* from the corresponding *ego states* of Mother and Father. The child obeys these *messages* and also makes existential *decisions* around them, *decisions* which will have validity for him for the rest of his life. Parent *messages* are *counterinjunctions* and *decisions* made around these are called the *counterscript*. Adult *messages* are 'how to' *messages*, communicating skills. Child *messages* and *decisions* made around these are called *script*.

The *script messages* consist of *permissions* and inhibitions (*injunctions*) of the Free Child. The child also chooses from his parents' Child *messages* which bad feelings to have and these feelings become his *rackets*. The child also learns to camouflage his compliance to his parents' *messages* by rebellious behaviour called *antiscript*, which leads to *script payoffs* by a devious route. The *episcript* is a 'hot potato' contained in the *script*, which is often passed down from parents to children in order to relieve the parents of some of their own *script* burden.

We obey our parents' *injunctions* and *counterinjunctions* in childhood in order to get the *strokes* from them which are so vital to our survival. By the time we are grown up, our obedience to them is so entrenched through childhood *stroking* that we go on obeying them even when we are no longer living with our parents. However, we nearly always manage to make our intimate relationships in adult life match the relationships in our early families, so that we tend to go on giving and receiving *strokes* throughout our lives in the ways that were taught us when we were children.

As well as for getting *strokes* we also need *scripts* because we have another innate *need, to organize our experience. Scripts* organize our psychological experience just as the laws of physics organize our experience of the material world. The earliest form of our *script* is made before the age of six and is called the *protocol*. Later childhood experiences basically reaffirm the *decisions* of the *protocol* but may modify it somewhat in the light of increased sophistication in our Little Professors and increased Adult data. The later version of our *scripts* is called the *palimpsest*. Some final modification of the *script* may be made in adolescence, when the personality is again — as it was before in infancy — in a state of disequilibrium and is wide open to influences.

Notes and References

1. C. Steiner, 'Script and Counterscript', *Transactional Analysis Bulletin*, **5**, no. 18, April 1966.
2. C. Steiner, *Scripts People Live*, Grove Press, 1974.
3. In the early 1970s, when *script* theory was still being developed by Claude Steiner and others, consideration was given to delineating the *script matrix* in other forms. It was suggested, for example, that parents may transmit *messages* from their Parent to their child's Child. Eventually, however, it was generally agreed that such alternative representations added complexity without adding meaning, so the present *ego state*-to-corresponding-*ego state* form became standard.
4. F. English, 'Rackets and Real Feelings' (Part I), *Transactional Analysis Journal*, **3**, no. 4, October 1971 and (Part 2), *Transactional Analysis Journal*, **2**, no. 1, January 1972. For this work, Fanita English was awarded the 1978 Eric Berne Memorial Scientific Award.
5. F. English, 'Episcript and the "Hot Potato" Game', *Transactional Analysis Bulletin*, **8**, no. 32, October 1969.

PART II

Diagnosis

CHAPTER 5

Functional Pathology[1]

Functional pathology is to do with energy flow between *ego states*. It is concerned with the profound adaptations we make in order to *avoid awareness* of painful aspects of our *scripts*, and is manifest in the relationship between our *ego states* within our individual personalities.

Individual Differences in Healthy Functioning

Let us first remind ourselves of the healthy personality in action, as described in Chapter 1. In the healthy personality energy flows freely between the *ego states*, which are used separately or collaboratively according to the needs of the situation in which the individual finds himself. The Parent *believes*, the Adult *thinks*, and the Child *feels*. Parent and Adult collaborate to make *judgements*, Adult and Child choose from amongst *alternatives*, and Parent and Child form *compromises*. The most important decisions we make in life usually require the harmony of all three *ego states* for the outcome to be a happy one and the total 'self' to be content.

Now even the most healthily functioning personalities differ from each other in the comparative strengths (that is amounts of energy) of the various *ego states*. The completely balanced personality may be an ideal, but one rarely if ever achieved in real people. As well as preferentially *stroking* behaviours reflecting *messages* they give their children, parents also tend to value each particular *ego state* somewhat more or less than the others and thus *stroke* their children into some degree of bias in choosing which *ego state* to function from on any particular occasion.

In his article on the 'trilog'[2] Arthur Rissman realized the existence of such individual differences, and he proposed that in each personality one *ego state* will be the *power point*, and another *ego state* the *low point*. The third *ego state*, of middling energy, will be the *flow point*. The energy flow (and collaborating potential) for the pair of *ego states* opposite the *power point* may be *blocked*, opposite the *low point* will be free, and opposite the *flow point* may be *damaged*. These variations of energy distribution and associated variability of collaborating potential between different pairs of *ego states* can be clarified in a diagram. Thus, for example, a person who functions best in his Adult (*power point*)

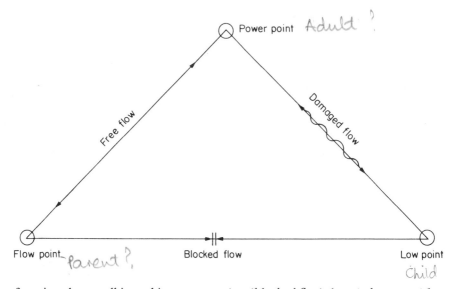

functions least well in making *compromises* (*blocked flow*); best *judgements* (*free flow*) imply least Child (*low point*); best Parent (*power point*) implies least awareness of *alternatives* (*blocked flow*). These normal differences between people may be used co-operatively or destructively in everyday working situations. Three different people whose respective *power points* are Parent, Adult, and Child, may, with good-will and awareness of their differences, make a marvellously functioning team by collaborating in an analogous way to the three *ego states* within one personality. Without awareness and positive appreciation of their differences, each will constantly insist that the others 'miss the point entirely' and will 'get nowhere' in their *transactions* with each other.

There is one other way in which healthily functioning personalities differ from each other, and that is in the degree of *permeability* of *ego state boundaries*. A greater than average *impermeability* of *ego state boundaries* is manifest as slow responsiveness of the individual to changing situations. It takes him a long time to shift *ego states*. Too great a *permeability*, however, is also maladaptive in making the individual restlessly shift *ego states* too often, so that he will tend to apply his various *ego states* irrelevantly in a given situation. A middling degree of *permeability* of *ego state boundaries* is the most adaptive in life in general. My hunch is that the degree of *permeability* of *ego state boundaries* in an individual is determined both by genetic factors and learning through childhood *stroking*.

Functional pathology begins when *ego states* (within one personality) are 'getting nowhere' with each other. Since the *ego states* are functionally different from each other, the possibility of disagreement between them is always present. Functional pathology may be defined as *unresolved disagreement between ego states*.

Impasses: First-degree pathology

In general, *impasses* are manifest as equally energized *ego states* which disagree with each other and cannot be reconciled. Failing to achieve a healthy resolution, the individual hurls himself backwards and forwards between the *ego states*, desperately trying to sweep first one and then the other under the carpet of consciousness. Usually he only succeeds in substituting an acute state of anxiety for the previous feeling of two equally matched parts of himself bashing themselves impotently against each other. *Parent–Adult impasses* are manifest as *indecisiveness*, for example, a parent who cannot find a satisfactory state school for his children (Adult), but is inhibited in sending them to a fee-paying school because of his socialist principles against privilege (Parent). *Adult–Child impasses* are manifest as *struggle*, for example, a woman longing to flee with her three children from her brutal husband (Child) but who can find no way to do so and at the same time materially to support herself and her children (Adult). *Parent–Child impasses* are manifest as *conflict*, for example, an unhappily married man in love with another woman (Child) who cannot reconcile his love with his sense of responsibility towards his children (Parent).

Inasmuch as such *impasses* are inevitably part of everyday life, in many cases they are 'pathological' only in a technical sense. For most of us on most issues they produce a temporary dis-ease, which is dealt with by relevant dialogue between *ego states* until healthily resolved into appropriate *judgements, alternatives*, or *compromises*. But when an *impasse* over some issue dominates an individual's awareness over an extended period of time and is accompanied by chronic anxiety, then pathological functioning is clearly present. The difference between health and pathology is mostly a matter of degree.

Contaminations: Second-degree pathology

Rather than continuing to feel the discomfort of the *impasse*, many people settle for a *contamination* between *ego states*, which resolves the issue by finding expression for the impulses of both *ego states* in a single percept or attitude. But such resolutions are actually *pseudo-resolutions*, because the individual pays a high price for them. They bind an excessive amount of psychic energy (in the *contamination*) and also severely restrict response options to relevant situations presenting themselves in life.

Parent/Adult contaminations

Example: A man doing battle with a Parent *message* which says 'The Irish are idiots' and the Adult reality of his very intelligent Irish neighbour may settle for, 'My Irish neighbour is very intelligent, but of course he's the exception that proves the rule'. This is *prejudice*. It is worth mentioning that 'The Irish are idiots' is not, in itself, a prejudicial statement. It may simply be a given Parent generalization. However, there are some Parent values — such as 'The Irish are idiots' — that are intolerable to the Free Child compassion, Adult reason, and Parent humanitarianism of most civilized people everywhere. Many TA

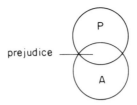

practitioners refer to such values as 'prejudiced Parent', although, technically, this is a misnomer. Such values only become *prejudices* when they are 'justified' by *contamination* with Adult data. This is an important distinction to make when we are attempting to challenge and overthrow bigotry. Otherwise we are likely to fail in our best intentions through allowing ourselves to fall into the trap of our own *prejudice*.

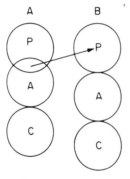

A: "You're prejudiced"

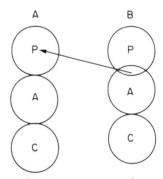

B: "No I'm not! You are!"

If we ever wish to influence another person into modifying the structure of his Parent we will inevitably be more *effective* in doing so if we recognize our own and others' Parents as having autonomy within our respective personalities and realize that we will sometimes have to agree to disagree. The only debates which have any real hope of effecting changes in people's opinions are those which take place amongst the *uncontaminated* Parents and Adults of the debaters.

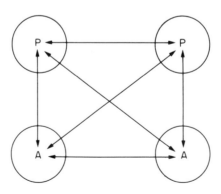

A HEALTHY DEBATE

Very many so-called 'objective discussions' between colleagues in working situations are in fact of an 'I *think*. . . .', 'Well, *I* think. . . .' type of *transaction*.

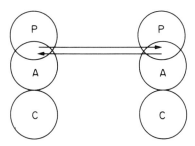

The giveaway, of course, is the highly-charged emotional tone of the *transactions*. It is as if — in this secular age of ours — it is somehow shameful to 'believe' anything.'

Adult/Child contaminations

Example: A girl in love (Child) with a man who in reality (Adult) is barely aware of her existence, may delude herself with, 'He must be in love with me or he couldn't possibly have avoided me at the party last night the way he did'. This is *delusion*, the equivalent of psychoanalytic 'rationalization'.

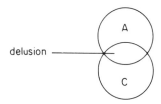

Parent/Child contaminations

For some reason he did not account for, Berne only considered cases of the Adult being contaminated by either the Parent or the Child, although at one point in *Transactional Analysis in Psychotherapy* he actually came very close to differentiating a Parent/Child *contamination*.[3] The fact that the usual vertical representation of Adult over Child and Parent over Adult has to be varied in order to represent a Parent/Child *contamination* does not seem to be a sufficient cause for Berne's oversight. It seems likely that Berne's own *power point* was very much his Adult, and Parent/Child his *blocked flow*, and that it is this fact that accounts for his blind spot which prevented him seeing Parent/Child *contaminations*.

Theoretically, the 'trilog' calls for the possibility of a Parent/Child *contamination* and, irrespective of theory, my own clinical experience repeatedly convinces me that this is the case. Example: A man whose Parent says, 'Sex is a sin' but whose Child is very lusty, may achieve happy sexual congress so long as he simultaneously suffers guilt and remorse. This is *confusion*.

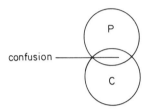

Subjective versus objective views of contaminations

In clinical practice one becomes aware of incongruity between the *felt experience* of a person in a *contamination* and the usual *perception of an observer*. It is important in group therapy to make this incongruity explicit in order to maintain clear, *complementary transactions* between a person in a *contamination* and the rest of the group. The subjective and objective perceptions are linked in tabular form.

Contamination	Felt experience	Observed manifestation
Parent/Adult	threatened	prejudice
Adult/Child	desperate	delusion
Parent/Child	confused	inflexibility

(The alert reader may have noticed that, in the examples I gave previous to this table, I labelled the Parent/Adult and Adult/Child *contaminations* in terms of their 'observed manifestations' ('prejudice' and 'delusion' also being Berne's nomenclature for them), but the Parent/Child *contamination* in terms of the 'felt experience'. I did this because, in perceiving *prejudice* and *delusion* the objective Adult is usually in the *executive* whereas in the case of *confusion*, since there are no objective data at all in the *contamination* itself, the 'felt experience' is usually in the *executive* in perceiving it.)

Richard Erskine[4] argues that all *script decisions* are themselves made in an Adult/Child *contamination* and are continually reinforced throughout life by Parent/Adult *contaminations* and further Adult–Child *contaminations* based on selective perception of reality. So within the framework of his *script* the individual personality looks like this:

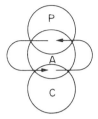

This is congruent with my own view, expressed in Chapter 4, that our *script decisions* are based on an inbuilt need to experience reality as predictable. So when pure Adult reality conflicts with the comfortable certainty of early *decisions* (which were made within the very limited reality we perceived in our childhood family lives), we prefer to distort the larger reality available in our grown-up lives in order to reinforce our childhood *decisions*, rather than face the prospect of disproving the validity of our *scripts*.

Exclusions: Third-degree pathology

There is an even more radical resolution for the problem of an *impasse* between *ego states* than *contamination* and that is *exclusion*. By relegating the attitudes or percepts of one or two *ego states* to unconsciousness, *impasses* are *denied by complete evasion*. The choice of *exclusion* is only available to those individuals who can maintain sufficiently *impermeable boundaries* between *ego states* that they can, in practice, dissociate their sense of 'self' from one or more of their *ego states*. Clearly, this leads to a greatly impoverished personality and life. There are six different possible forms of *exclusion*, three *exclusions* of one *ego state* and three *exclusions* of two *ego states*. The effective *exclusion* of two *ego states* from most of an individual's daily life is clearly the most impoverishing defence of all against awareness of *impasses*.

The uncaring person

An *excluded* Parent leaves a person without the necessary generalized precepts to behave responsibly or in a caring way towards himself or others.

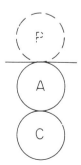

64

The joyless person

An *excluded* Child makes a person lack joy, sorrow, spontaneity, and insight.

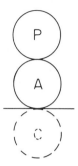

The turbulent person

An *excluded* Adult results in a chronic condition of emotional turbulence, in extreme cases manic-depressive psychosis.

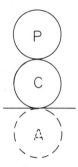

The cold person

The cold person can be observed in the stereotype of the utterly boring scientist who insists on using his Adult exclusively to deal with all of life in order to avoid facing his unresolved Parent–Child *conflicts*.

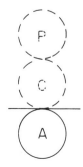

The harsh or smothering person

Such a person is found in the stereotype of the preacher — all Parent — who, metaphorically, refuses to take his dog-collar off — even in bed — rather than bring Adult reality to terms with his Child fantasies. The smothering version is personified in the archetypal Jewish mother of Portnoy fame.

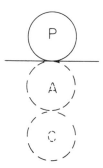

The infantile person

The infantile person is found in the stereotype of the woman who impulsively lives the whole of her life according to the whim of the moment (Child), rather than testing her (usually harsh) Parent against (Adult) reality and extracting some useful generalizations from the dialogue.

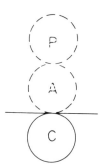

Diagnosis and Cure

For me, diagnosis is made by a combination of Little Professor and Adult. I usually feel *exclusions*, hear *impasses*, and perceive *contaminations* by a combination of hearing and feeling — all in terms of the definitions and categories of this chapter. Thus, there are *key words* (or near-synonyms of them) which I am constantly alert for in listening to anyone talking about himself and his problems. 'Believe' is Parent, 'think' is Adult, 'feel' is Child; 'indecision' is Parent–Adult *impasse*, 'struggle' is Adult–Child *impasse*, 'conflict' is Parent–

Child *impasse*. When I perceive *prejudice* (Parent/~~Child~~ Adult *contamination*) I infer a feeling of being *threatened*; when I perceive *delusion* (Adult/Child *contamination*) I infer *despair*; and when I perceive *inflexibility* (Parent/Child *contamination*) I infer *confusion*.

The process of cure consists of returning *exclusions* and *contaminations* to the original *impasses* from which they were derived, and enabling the individual to resolve these *impasses* healthily into *judgements, alternatives*, and *compromises*.

First, excluded *ego states* are energized by insistence and *permission* (through example) of the therapist and the group. (This is often a lengthy process and may take several months.) Second, *contaminated ego states* are wrenched apart by charging the *contamination* with the energy of the non-colluding *ego state*. For example, the therapist and group may bombard the person in a Parent/Child *contamination* with Adult energy until he, too, cathects Adult and wedges it between his own Parent and Child. A woman in one of my groups had a Marxist-type Parent/Adult *contamination* which seriously marred all her social *transactions*. In the course of therapy she fell in love (Child) and her newly energized Child enabled her effectively to separate her beliefs from factual reality. Adult/Child *contaminations* are so typical of adolescence largely because, at this stage of development, the Parent is mostly rescinded. Thus the adolescent girl in love with the man who doesn't notice her 'resolves' her despair with an Adult/Child contamination of 'He must be in love with me or he wouldn't ignore me the way he does'. Were her Parent fully energized she would be more likely to introduce a Parent shrug and 'There are plenty more fish in the sea' and find her love reciprocated elsewhere. Third, the *impasse* is revealed and the discomfort of it felt. The felt discomforts are *indecision* between Parent and Adult, *struggle* between Adult and Child, and *conflict* between Parent and Child. Fourth, the *impasse* is resolved into an effective *judgement*, choice of *alternatives*, or *compromise*. The key experiences and steps (from *contamination* to cure) are tabulated below.

| | Pathology | | Cure | |
Contamination	Felt experience	Observed manifestation	Through	To
Parent/Adult	threatened	prejudice	indecision	judgement
Adult/Child	despair	delusion	struggle	alternatives
Parent/Child	confusion	inflexibility	conflict	compromise

Just in case the reader at this stage is still in any doubt, let me reiterate that the difference between health and pathology is a matter of degree. Functionally, it is a matter of how much of the individual's psychic energy is available for *free* functioning and how pervasive in his life are the issues around which he binds energy in *impasses, contaminations*, or *exclusions*.

Paradoxically, the 'noisier' a pathological issue in a person's head, the closer he is to health. People whose lives are seriously constrained by *exclusions* rarely feel any dis-ease — there is too much repression. If they seek psychotherapy it is almost certainly in response to threats by husbands or wives to leave them if they do not!

Conversely, a person in the middle of a major *impasse* is overwhelmed by felt distress and acutely aware that he is not well. But his very *indecisiveness, struggle,* or *conflict* show how close he is to health. When somebody in therapy has achieved huge progress from *exclusion* towards health and is now experiencing the acuteness of an *impasse* for the first time, he will almost certainly accuse the therapist of making his unhappiness 'worse'. This is the meaning of the commonplace, 'You've got to get worse before you can get better.' But 'getting worse' means 'getting more alive'. In later chapters we will see how TA therapy sets about bringing people to life.

Summary

Functional pathology is to do with energy flow between *ego states*. It derives from adaptations we make in order to avoid awareness of painful aspects of our *scripts*. All personalities have some bias away from perfect balance of energy distribution amongst the *ego states*. The *ego state* having the greatest strength is the *power point* of the personality, the second strongest is the *flow point*, the weakest *ego state* is the *low point*. The energy flow between the pair of *ego states* opposite the *power point* may be *blocked*, opposite the *flow point damaged*, and opposite the *low point free*.

Individuals also differ from each other in the degree of *permeability* of their *ego state boundaries*. Too little *permeability* makes for slowness of response to changing situations, too great *permeability* to inappropriate restlessness. A moderate degree of *permeability* is the most adaptive to life in general.

Impasses between *ego states* are first-degree pathology, felt as *indecisiveness, conflict,* or *struggle,* which are usually accompanied by anxiety.

Contaminations between *ego states* are second-degree pathology felt as *threat, confusion,* or *despair,* and respectively observed by others as *prejudice, inflexibility,* or *delusion.*

Exclusions between *ego states* are third-degree pathology and are usually unaccompanied by feelings. When the Parent is *excluded* the person seems to others to be 'uncaring', when the Adult is *excluded* he seems 'turbulent', and when the Child is *excluded* he seems 'joyless'. When Parent and Child are both *excluded* the person seems 'cold'; when Adult and Child are *excluded* the person seems 'harsh' or 'smothering'; when Parent and Adult are *excluded* the person seems infantile.

Paradoxically, the closer the individual is to health, the more felt distress he experiences in his functional dis-ease.

68

Notes and References

1. This chapter is based on an article I wrote recently called 'Thoughts and feelings: A functional description of health, pathology, diagnosis, and cure', which has been accepted for publication by the *Transactional Analysis Journal.*
2. A. Rissman, 'Trilog', *Transactional Analysis Journal,* **5,** no. 2, April 1975.
3. E. Berne, *Transactional Analysis in Psychotherapy,* Grove Press, 1961, p. 55.
4. I first heard Richard Erskine express this view in a paper he presented at the second ITAA European Conference in Enschede, Holland, in July 1976. An abstract of his theory is also published in the *Transactional Analysis Journal,* **6,** no. 3, July 1976.

CHAPTER 6

Structural Pathology I.
Various Viewpoints

Whereas functional pathology is concerned with the adaptations we make in order to avoid awareness of painful aspects of our *scripts*, structural pathology is concerned with ways in which we seek to reaffirm our *script decisions*. Functional pathology is manifest in the relationships between our *ego states* within our individual personalities, whereas structural pathology is manifest in the *content of our transactions* with others.

Structural pathology is to do with *script* content. The more inhibiting of the Free Child are the *injunctions* and the more tragic the *script decisions* and the *episcript* the greater the felt distress in the life of the individual.

We have already seen that *script* content has a twofold derivation, that is a *stroke-yielding* response to *injunctions* and *counterinjunctions* and the gratification of a biologically inbuilt need for certainty of outcome in our interactions with the material and psychological worlds. The laws of physics provide the material certainty, our *script decisions* provide the psychological, existential certainty. Chapter 4 was concerned with the dynamics of acquiring our existential certainty, this chapter is concerned with the dynamics of maintaining it.

Games

Playing *games* with other people is the chief means by which we each repeatedly re-experience our *racket feelings* and reaffirm our *script decisions*. Games are set series of *ulterior transactions*, with a well-defined psychological *payoff* for each of the parties to the *game*. The *payoff* is the culmination of and the most essential feature of a *game*, since the aim of the *game* is to achieve the *payoff*, which consists of a reaffirmation of a *script decision* accompanied by a *rackety* feeling. There are short-term *payoffs*, long-term *payoffs*, and ultimate *payoffs* which are analogous to the ends of scenes, acts, and whole plays in the lives of individuals. Long-term and ultimate *payoffs* are written into the *script* of an individual and tend to be achieved in a once-and-for-all manner, whereas short-term *payoffs* are achieved repetitively in *games*.

In *Games People Play* Berne divided the *payoffs* (or 'advantages') of *games* into five coexisting levels. He saw all *games* as having the 'general advantage' that they serve the purpose of 'stabilizing (homeostatic) functions', and he analysed this 'general advantage' into five components:[1]

(1) The 'internal psychological advantage', which directly affects the 'psychic economy' of the libido.

(2) The 'external psychological advantage', which is the avoidance — by playing the *game* — of a feared situation.

(3) The 'internal social advantage', which is the *time structuring* that is provided by the stereotyped dialogue involved in playing the *game*. This particular 'advantage' may be summarized into the *name* of the *game*, although the name will usually only refer to the 'internal social advantage' for one of the players. Other players in the same *game* will have different 'internal social advantages', which could also provide names for the *game* — from their points of view.

(4) The 'external social advantage', which is the *time structuring* that is provided by talking *about* the *game* with others.

(5) The 'existential advantage', which provides the 'confirmation of a position', i.e. what today is called the 'reinforcement of a *script decision*'.

Interestingly, Berne correctly prophesied the increased relative importance in TA theory of the 'existential advantage', when he added to the classification of 'advantages' above,

> The most likely candidate for a systematic, scientific classification is probably the one based on the existential position, but since knowledge of this factor is not yet sufficiently advanced, such a classification will have to be postponed. Failing that, the most practical classification at present is probably a sociological one.

A sample analysis of a *game* will elucidate the nature of the different levels of *payoffs* ('advantages') Berne discerned.

Let's You & Him Fight — a three-handed game

The action
1. Miss A, at a party, makes a pass at Mr B in the presence of Mrs B
2. Mr B responds positively
3. Mrs B attacks Mr B
4. Mr B attacks Mrs B
5. Miss A leaves the party with Mr C

Payoffs

Miss A
Internal psychological: sexual excitement
External psychological: avoidance of intimacy

Internal social: Let's You & Him Fight
External social: Married Men are All the Same
Existential: Men are suckers

Mr B
Internal psychological: sexual excitement
External psychological: avoidance of intimacy
Internal social: If it Weren't for Her (Mrs B)
External social: I am desirable
Existential: I am blameless

Mrs B
Internal psychological: justification for rage
External psychological: avoids confronting own deficiencies
Internal social: Now I've Got You, You Son-of-a-Bitch!
External social: You have to watch them (men) all the time
Existential: Sex is revolting

Thus it can be seen that by a specious projection of responsibility onto others, *games* give temporary relief from feeling *not-OK*. But this relief is inevitably contaminated by awareness — however vague — of the spurious and inauthentic nature of the relief. People we choose and are chosen by to play *games* with have elements in their *scripts* complementary to our own. The seeking and finding of suitable partners with whom to play our own favourite *games* undoubtedly forms the basis of many friendships and marriages and may also provide us with an understanding — albeit cynical — of the nature of falling in love.

Games teach us nothing. *Games* may be stopped by: (1) Not taking the bait. (It takes two to tango.) (2) Finding out *why* you and the other person are playing, and discovering alternative, *authentic* ways of giving each other the *positive strokes* you both most want.

In *Games People Play* Berne differentiated a large number of different *games* and fascinatingly spelt out the typical moves of the players leading to their separate *payoffs*. Such titles as 'Blemish', 'Let's You & Him Fight', 'Rapo', and 'I'm Only Trying to Help You' succinctly abstract pertinent 'internal social advantages' that we are all familiar with in our daily lives. For several years after the publication of *Games People Play* a favourite *pastime* (see Chapter 2) amongst TA practitioners was 'discovering' and naming new *games* and drawing up ever longer and more comprehensive lists of them. However, the naming of *games*, though fun, is no longer considered useful in therapy, since Berne's original 'advantages' are now subsumed under the single *script payoff* ('existential advantage') for each of the players. Nevertheless, some 'internal social advantages', such as '"why don't you. . . . ?" "Yes, but. . . ."', 'Kick Me', 'Now I've Got You, You Son-of-a-Bitch', and 'If it Weren't For You/Her/Him/Them/It', are so pervasive in everyday life that they are commonly interpolated, as a colloquial shorthand, in conversations between TA therapists and patients.

Karpman's Drama Triangle

In recent years, most TA therapists have favoured a more general approach to *games* than Berne did and many, including myself, find it sufficient to define all *games* simply in terms of the *roles* of Stephen Karpman's *drama triangle*.[2]

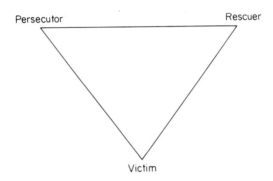

Persecutor, Rescuer, and Victim are the possible *roles* each of us may play in any *game*, and these three *roles* essentially define all the characters in all our best-loved fairy-tales and myths. Thus, asking a person what was his best-loved fairy-tale or other childhood story and the character he most identified with in it is often a very economical way of eliciting a wealth of *script* material.

Typically, we start from one position and *switch* (few or many times) during the course of a *game*, until ending up in the *role* which is congruent with the existential position the *game* is serving to confirm for us. It is important to distinguish the *roles* of the *drama triangle* from *ego states*. Persecutor, Rescuer, and Victim are all *roles* which exist in the Adapted Child *ego state*, although Rescuer and Persecutor masquerade as Parent and Victim masquerades as Natural Child.

'Why Don't You? Yes, But' — probably the most commonly played *game* of all — elucidates well the dynamics of the Karpman Triangle. Typically, A (Victim) asks B (Rescuer) for advice. B offers several suggestions, each of which is rejected by A with a 'Yes, but'. Eventually, B realizes A is not going to accept any of his suggestions and B becomes angry and accusing (Persecutor) towards A (still Victim). A then *switches* to Persecutor and accuses B of not being a real friend after all and slams the phone down on B (Victim). At this point A may well reaffirm a *script decision* such as 'Everybody wants to dominate me' and B that 'I'm never appreciated'. (The *roles* of the *drama triangle* do not deny the existence of real persecution, rescuing, and victimization in the world. However, depth-analysis of many apparently *game-free* situations reveals unambiguous — although unconscious — *script* determinants at work. Thus, for example, it is likely to be more than 'chance' that determines a woman be widowed three times, that a boss often has to sack incompetent employees, or that a father repeatedly needs to bail his grown-up children out of financial difficulties.)

Trading Stamps and Racketeering

Sometimes, instead of simply providing a straightforward reaffirmation of a *script decision*, together with a *racket* feeling and a familiar behavioural response, the *racket payoff* is separated from the other *game* elements and silently saved up in a collection of *trading stamps*, to be used, when the collection is large enough, for a larger *script* prize. Thus a woman collecting resentment *stamps* may play *games* with her husband every night for a week until she has collected enough to back his new car into a lamp-post and do £50 worth of damage (guilt-free), but she may need to play similar *games* with him for several years before amassing a large enough collection to cash in for a 'free' accusation of adultery and a divorce writ.

The analogy between commercial and psychological *trading stamps* is perfect. Each person, according to his upbringing, tends to handle both kinds in the same way, whether it be to save and savour them and cash them in for a big prize (divorce or suicide, perhaps); to get lots of small prizes (niggling complaints to others, for example); to gloat over them ('Do you remember. . . . ?'); or to forget them for years, only to discover them with glee one day at the back of the cupboard. Like the commercial variety, psychological *trading stamps* usually represent a counterfeit gain (paid for in the higher prices of the 'shops' which give them). Talking straight (like shopping without benefit of stamps) is much less wasteful of psychic energy, and the true savings thus achieved can 'buy' more rewarding and intimate relationships with others. That 70 per cent of the adult population of this country is known to collect the tangible stamps that are stuck in books is probably a direct reflection of that proportion of the population that collects psychological stamps. But the recent news that Tesco, who serve a large part of the population, have decided to trade with Green Shield Stamps no longer may perhaps be a symptom of a healthy trend towards *authenticity* in British society as a whole. And the currently increasing popularity of many forms of humanistic psychotherapy espousing personal *authenticity* as their goal also provides corroborating evidence for this hypothesis.

Therefore sometimes, instead of playing out a fully-fledged *game* we content ourselves with simple *pastiming*, through which we may acquire — in the presence of a willing partner — some more *stamps* for our collection, but without benefit of the profound existential reinforcement that only a fully played-out *game* would provide. This procedure was first described by Fanita English, and she called it *racketeering*.[3] Some commonplace *racketeering pastimes* might succinctly be named When *I* Was a Girl, They're All the Same (Men Only or Women Only varieties), and Ain't It Awful (inflation, the inefficiency of public services, the weather, etc.). Fanita English distinguishes *racketeering* from *game-playing* by virtue of the fact that, so long as both parties are willing, the *racketeering* may continue *complementarily* for an indefinite period without any *ulterior transactions, crossed transactions*, or *role switches*. Bearing in mind that all *racketeering* and *game-playing* actually takes place between Adapted Child *ego states*, *racketeering* may be Parent–Parent-type, for example, 'The trouble

74

with kids these days is that they have it too easy'. 'Yes, when you think how grateful we used to be for 6d for blacking the stove'. . . . Or Child–Parent-type, for example, 'Tom was late home from the office again last night. I think he's having an affair with his secretary. I'm so depressed, I just don't know what to do'. 'Oh you poor thing. Come on over. I'll make us a nice cup of tea and we'll have a chat'. . . . Or Parent–Child-type, for example, 'How many times do I have to tell you to clear up your room? I'm not your servant, you know!'. 'No, you're not, but you treat me as if I was your slave!'. . . . Or Child–Child-type, for example, I'm sick to death of being bossed around in this dump. I've a good mind to pack it all in and be a milkman'. 'Yeah, you spend the best years of your life slaving your guts out. What for?!'. . . .

Fanita English's Theory of Rackets and Games

But if one of the *racketeers* tires of *racketeering* before the other and withdraws from or *crosses* the last *transaction*, the other player will be frustrated in his quest for *stamps* and will *switch* to a *game-position* and an even more satisfying *payoff*. For Fanita English, '*a game is a racket that has failed*'. Although, in theory, people may *racketeer* for an indefinite period with a willing partner, in practice each person will eventually *switch* from *racketeering* into his *game-position*. The comparative lengths of times spent in *racketeering* and *game-playing* will vary amongst individuals and according to the situation. There are only two kinds of *payoffs* available for both *rackets* and *games*, that is, '*Kicked*' and '*Now I've Got You You Son-of-a-Bitch*' (originally named by Berne). People who *racketeer* from NIGYYSOB (helpful Rescuer or bossy Persecutor) *position* have a *kicked* (helpless or rebellious Victim) *game payoff* and people who *racketeer* from a *kicked position* have a NIGYYSOB *game payoff*.

Example:

Mrs Black: I could kill you! Look at the time! I specially asked you to come home early to look after the kids so I could get out to my evening class.

Mr Black: I'm terribly sorry dear. The boss wanted to see me just as I was leaving and I couldn't get away.

Mrs Black: Well, it's about time you had the guts to come straight out and say your family comes first sometimes. You're so mealy-mouthed to everyone!

Mr Black: I can't afford to speak my mind. There are plenty of people just waiting to take my job.

Mrs Black (withdrawing from *racketeering*): Well, the kids are asleep. I'm off now.

Mr Black: Thanks very much I must say! What about my dinner? What kind of a wife are you? (*Switches* to *game-position* and gets resentment/NIGYYSOB *payoff*.)

Mrs Black: (Bursts into tears): You wanted me to have an interest of my own. Just because I can't do *everything* like some people, you don't love me! (*Switches* to *game position* and gets guilt/kicked *payoff*.)

For Fanita English, corresponding to the two positions for *racketeering* and for *game-playing* there are also only two broad categories of people: Type I, those who *racketeer* from a (pseudo) Natural Child and *switch* into a (pseudo) Parent *payoff* and Type II, those who *racketeer* from a (pseudo) Parent and *switch* into a (pseudo) Natural Child *payoff*. Based on her clinical experience, Fanita English claims that Type II people, though they less often seek therapy, have usually been more tragically *stroke-deprived* in childhood. They are the people who were forced into a Rescuing *position* vis-à-vis the 'helpless Child' of Mother or Father and were only *stroked* at all when in this spurious (and doomed to fail) Parent *role*. Type I people, in childhood, did at least have their Childs *stroked*, even if only for unhappy feelings. Their existential *game payoff* is generally a triumphant one, whereas Type II people generally feel existentially worthless and have learnt neither to ask for nor to expect any *strokes* from others for their own Child wants.[4]

Pam Levin's Two Types of People

A slightly different way of differentiating people into the same two broad categories is in terms of Pam Levin's two basic *injunctions*, 'Don't grow up' (Type I) and 'Don't be a child' (Type II).[5] To some extent we all receive both of these *injunctions*, although each of us will tend to receive one in significantly greater measure than the other. For example — all other things being equal — oldest children will tend to be of the 'Don't be a child' type and youngest children of the 'Don't grow up' type. Only children very often seem to get a heavy dose of both, that is, they lack the *permission* for Natural Child to Natural Child *transactions* through having no siblings to practise on ('Don't be a child') and at the same time are bound in a Child to Parent symbiosis, since they are continually the sole focus for their parents' nurturing behaviour ('Don't grow up'). Thus being a parent, in general terms, seems to me to be a feat of tightrope walking, with the overall aim of giving the child *permissions* to be a child *and* to grow up, the emphasis on each *permission* being maintained in a fine balance for each step towards maturation that the child takes. No wonder we are none of us hang-up-free!

However, there are marked differences between people in the degrees of heaviness with which 'Don't be a child' and 'Don't grow up' are imposed on them. These differences may be represented graphically, as below, the wavy line along the horizontal axis representing the precarious tightrope walking of all parents, and the numerical divisions representing increasing heaviness of the *injunctions*. Thus health and pathology may be seen to exist on a quantifiable continuum.

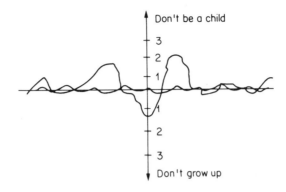

My clinical experience is increasingly leading me to believe that we tend to choose our *friends* from amongst people on the same side of the horizontal line as ourselves (for contented *racketeering*) and our *lovers* from the opposite side (for *game-playing* and *script payoffs*). And our Little Professor, with his uncanny precision for hitting the nail exactly on the head, almost always manages to find us a lover or spouse whose *degree* of pathology exactly matches our own (but on the opposite side of the horizontal)!

To the extent that this picture of intimate human relationships is valid, the sad but certain truth is that the most *intense* attraction (love?) exists between people whose capacity for destructive *game-playing* with each other is the greatest. And the least pathological liaisons—companionship between people on the same side of the horizontal—must inevitably be comparatively emotionally dull! Probably, 'ideal marriages' exist between people who each have no more than one degree of pathology and are also on opposite sides to each other.

Kahler's and Capers' Miniscript

One other major description of the process whereby we reaffirm our *scripts* remains to be discussed. That is the *miniscript* developed by Taibi Kahler and Hedges Capers, which deserves a chapter to itself.

Summary

We re-experience our *racket* feelings and reaffirm our *script decisions* over and over again throughout our lives.

Playing *games* with other people is the chief means by which we reaffirm and reinforce our *scripts*. *Games* give us 'external' and 'internal' psychological *payoffs*, 'external' and 'internal' social *payoffs*, and existential *payoffs*. In playing *games* we *switch* around amongst the three possible *roles* of Karpman's *drama triangle*: Persecutor, Rescuer, and Victim.

Sometimes we *racketeer* instead of playing out a *game* to its final *payoff*. When we *racketeer* we collect *trading stamps* (of bad feelings) and save them up for cashing in for a greater or lesser prize (*payoff*) later on. Fanita English argues that people *switch* into their *game* position when they are frustrated in their attempts to *racketeer*. For her, there are only two positions for both *racketeering* and *game-playing*: 'Kicked' and 'Now I've Got You, You Son-of-a-Bitch'.

Pam Levin's two broad personality types, based on 'Don't be a child' and 'Don't grow up', represent a variation of Fanita English's theory. It is hypothesized that we tend to choose our *friends* from people of the same type as ourselves, in order to *racketeer*, and our *lovers* from people of the opposite type to ourselves, in order to play *games* and get our *script payoffs*.

Notes and References

1. E. Berne, *Games People Play*. Andre Deutsch, 1966, pp. 56–58.
2. S. Karpman, 'Fairy-tales and script drama analysis', *Transactional Analysis Bulletin*, **7**, no. 26, April 1968. Stephen Karpman received the Eric Berne Memorial Scientific Award in 1972 for his *drama triangle*.
3. F. English, 'Rackets and real feelings' (Part I), *Transactional Analysis Journal*, **1**, no. 4, October 1971 and (Part II) *Transactional Analysis Journal*, **2**, no. 1, January 1972.
4. A detailed account of Fanita English's theory of *rackets* and *games* is obtainable on cassette tape, *TA For Creative Living, no. 32*, Boyce Productions, Corte Madera, California, 1973.
5. P. Levin, *Becoming the Way We Are*. Transactional Publications, 1974.

CHAPTER 7

Structural Pathology II.
The Miniscript

Definition

The *miniscript*[1] is defined as a sequence of behaviours, occurring in seconds or minutes, which reinforces early *decisions*. Like a *game*, it is a stereotyped process leading to a *payoff*. But whereas the number of steps in a *game* may vary, the *miniscript* process is tightly defined as consisting of three or four steps always. Each step achieves a defined existential position, which is both idiosyncratic to the individual in its particularity and universal in its general meaning. The four general positions of the *miniscript* are the Driver (*counterscript* position), a Stopper (*racket* response to a *script injunction*), Vengeful Child (*antiscript* position), and a Final Miniscript Payoff (reaffirmation of a *script decision*).

The four parts correspond to the positions of the *OK Corral*, developed by Franklin Ernst,[2] which delineates four possible existential positions we may be in: 'I'm OK-You're OK' (I + U +); 'I'm not OK-You're OK' (I − U +); 'I'm OK-You're not OK' (I + U −); and 'I'm not OK-You're not OK' (I − U −). These positions are used variously by TA therapists to define both phenomenal attitudes of the moment and fundamental *life positions*. I am happy to use the *OK Corral* in the former way, but with respect to *life positions* I believe I + U − is only a defensive-aggressive camouflaging aspect of I − U + and not really separable from it. As used in the *miniscript* the four positions are useful correlates of the transitory *roles* being played out.

OK and Not-OK Miniscripts

According to Kahler and Capers, the Little Professor in each of us has positive and negative charges fed into it by positive and negative *messages* in the Parent (received from Mother's and Father's Parent *ego states*). Each of us has a *not OK miniscript* and an *OK miniscript*.

In the *not OK miniscript* the Drivers are *messages* which *seem* to bring the individual out of a Stopper (obedience to a *script injunction*) but actually only drive him deeper into it. The Vengeful Child is a spiteful 'I'll show you!'

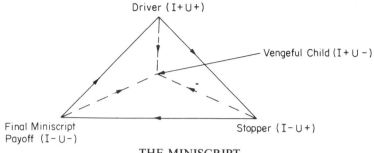

THE MINISCRIPT

(*antiscript* position), which also provides the individual with the delusion of avoiding the *script payoff*, but inevitably leads him to it, albeit by a devious route. The whole process may be diagrammed in a triangle, as above. The Vengeful Child may or may not be used in the total process and is therefore linked to all the positions by dashed lines. Individuals have their own typical progression round the *miniscript*, some, for example, proceeding from Driver to Stopper to Vengeful Child to Final Miniscript Payoff, some from Driver to Stopper and straight on to Final Payoff, and others from Driver to Vengeful Child to Stopper to Final Payoff.

Each person's Final Miniscript Payoff will be an idiosyncratic *script decision*, but there are five and only five Drivers. These are Be Perfect, Be Strong, Please Me, Try Hard, and Hurry Up. Although we nearly all use all of the Drivers at some time, each of us usually has his or her own favourite one or two which most efficiently serve the *payoffs* they are (unconsciously) designed to achieve. Deprived of the use of our favourite Driver for any reason we automatically shift into our next favourite and so on down the line. Taibi Kahler argues that depriving people of the use of all the Drivers (in therapeutic intervention, for example) will prevent them ever achieving the *not OK* Final Payoff. For most TA practitioners this is an optimistic but unrealistic view. Although awareness of Drivers and their purposes does enable people to gain a much more increased degree of control over their *scripts* than previously, the empirical evidence is strong that people will, one way or another, achieve their *script payoffs* anyhow, until and unless they deal with their *script decisions* head-on and gain new *permissions* for their Childs. I did, in fact, once meet a man who gave no evidence at all in his *script matrix* of the use of any Drivers. This man had been brought up on a farm in an isolated part of Yugoslavia where time and life were reckoned very slowly in terms of the seasons and crops and the life events of the farm animals. The usual 'driven' behaviour we are familiar with in our urban and less than isolated country lives was entirely absent, and yet this man experienced in his life a usual number of *not OK decisions* to which he returned no less often than most people do.

Parallel to the *not OK miniscript*, Kahler and Capers describe an *OK miniscript* consisting of an Allower (instead of a Driver), a Goer (instead of a Stopper), an Affirming Free Child (instead of a Vengeful Child), and a Wower (instead of a

Final Payoff). They see the sequence of change from the *not OK* to the *OK miniscript* as one in which the individual chooses to spend less time in I − U −, moving up to I − U +, to I + U −, and finally to spending a major amount of time in I + U +.

Critique of the Miniscript Concept

For me, the *miniscript* is the most useful and brilliant theoretical development in TA since Berne's death. Some people object to the *miniscript* as an alternative to *games* in describing the process involved in achieving *script payoffs* on the grounds that it does not incorporate *transactions* with other people. I find this objection spurious. In playing *games*, anyway, the *transactions* involved are much more like a psychological form of mutual masturbation than a congress of spontaneously giving and receiving autonomous individuals. Eric Berne himself predicted that the analysis of *games* would evolve towards a greater focus on existential *payoffs* (as opposed to immediate *transactional payoffs*) and the *miniscript* does just this.

However, there are two minor matters over which I take issue with Kahler and Capers, one technical, the other empirical. First, I do not accept the concept of *OK* and *not OK* aspects of the Parent *ego state*. The Parent simply contains all the individual's beliefs, values, and generalizations about life, which by definition, are neither *OK* nor *Not OK*, (although individuals of course differ in the contents of their Parents and may not like what they see in others' Parents). Furthermore, the incorporation of the Parent *ego state* into the concept makes the system, as described by Kahler and Capers, extremely (and, I think, unnecessarily) complex and unwieldy. So for me the whole of the *miniscript* exists, by definition, in the Adapted Child.

Secondly, the whole sequence of behaviours in the *miniscript* need not take place in so short a time as seconds or minutes — although it usually does. A

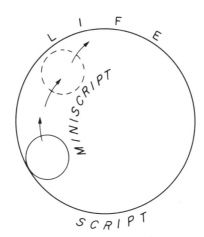

woman in one of my therapy groups regularly exhibited an approximately six-week cycle in the Please Me *miniscript*, proceeding from being 'a good and conscientious housewife' (Driver) to a Stopper position of feeling 'exhausted through being used' (by her husband and son), to a Vengeful Child position of lying in bed all day and refusing to do anything at all, to a Final Payoff of resentful 'People always try to push me around, but in the end I win'. In relation to the *script*, the *miniscript* may be seen as a small temporal cycle of varying length, constantly repeating itself within the total span of the individual's lifetime.

When I first encountered the *miniscript* it seemed to me to be very abstract and abstruse and to lack the pithy precision and usability of other ways of viewing structural pathology (see Chapter 6). However, the more experience I gained as a clinician the more often did the *miniscript* intrude itself into the foreground of my consciousness as the obvious frame of reference for describing what was going on. And as I have continued to look and listen and generalize from my experience I have found that each of the *miniscripts* implies, with a high degree of reliability, a whole cluster of traits and some profound meanings. So elaborated have these implications become in my mind that I now see all Adapted Child behaviours as manifestations of elements contained in one or other of the five *miniscripts*. Item by item I have collected qualitatively *simple everyday feelings, thoughts, attitudes, and behaviours* and categorized them in the fifteen spaces of the five *miniscripts*. One fact or bit of behaviour or statement may now be enough for me to infer the whole essential nature of a person's *script*. The rest of this chapter represents the fruits of my experience in the use of the *miniscript*. I hope I succeed in infecting the reader with some of my enthusiasm.

The Personality Types of the Five Miniscripts

Be Perfect is a close relative of the psychoanalytic 'obsessive-compulsive' syndrome. It is often associated with a religious background, and it is generally a safe hypothesis that anyone with a Roman Catholic or Jewish background has Be Perfect as his or her favourite or second favourite *miniscript*. Be Perfect is exemplified in the scholastic *pastime* of arguing how many angels can dance on the point of a needle or the rabbinical one of whether or not it is lawful to eat an egg that was laid by a hen on the Sabbath. In Roman Catholics (and others) Be Perfect is often focused on sexual behaviour and finds its expression in Driver behaviour which abstains from all sex unless it is associated with 'perfect love' or else, in the Vengeful Child position, loves some people and has sex with others, but never finds sex and love with one and the same person. 'Guilt' is a favourite Stopper (*racket*) and a feeling of 'worthlessness' a favourite Final Miniscript Payoff. The third-degree manifestation of Be Perfect is psychotic depression. At the deepest levels of the personality Be Perfect is superstitious behaviour used to ward off calamity, and ultimately reflects a fear of death. This deepest level usually comes close to articulation in the mind of a child who always (or never) steps on the lines of the pavement. Anything carried out 'religiously' is a sure sign of Be Perfect. To an outsider Be Perfect may induce a feeling of sympathy for its pathos. When the user projects it outwards on to others he is nit-picking in argument and critically blemishing of others' actions. Be Perfect needs to learn that attitudes and values can be relative as well as absolute.

Be Strong is caricatured in the stiff-upper-lipped English gentleman. It is often a response to a heavy 'Don't be a child' and a rejection by Mother or Father of the child's attempts to get close to them. The child longs for closeness but has to make do without, so makes a 'virtue' (Be Strong) out of what he sees as a lifelong 'necessity' to be solely dependent on himself for *strokes* to his Child. He is often a committed Rescuer, through which he makes doomed-to-fail attempts to get close to others and through which he commonly achieves an 'unappreciated' *racket*. The truth, of course, is that *nobody's* attempts to get close are successful all the time, but Be Strong uses every rejection to 'prove' the 'absolute' impossibility of *ever* getting close. Thus the antithesis to Be Strong involves the individual in the realization that to be accepted (some of the time) involves being rejected (some of the time) as well. From the outside, especially in its Vengeful Child position of 'invulnerability to others', which is often manifest as 'boredom', Be Strong often appears superiorly stand-offish.

Please Me is typically a response to 'Don't grow up'/'Don't leave me' and particularly to 'Don't feel what you feel, but what I tell you to' and is often found in only children or youngest children or any other child specially singled out by a parent as the apple of the parent's eye. The child grows up perceiving all emotional *transactions* on the Parent–Child controller–controlled dimension. Please Me cuts both ways. It says, 'I will please you (Child to Parent) but, when it's my turn, you have to please me (Parent to Child)'. In our culture where, anyway until recently, most women were bound to finding their chief life gratification in their motherhood role, 'Don't leave me' is an *injunction* more commonly given by mothers than fathers. The dominant manifest feature of Please Me is the individual's unwillingness (which he feels as inability) to make any clear-cut or committed statement of his autonomous feelings. If a defining characteristic of all the *miniscripts* is inauthenticity, then Please Me is inauthenticity squared. Please Me tends to live life from a Victim position. In the Driver position it agrees with and is 'nice' to everybody. But, probably more than for any other of the *miniscripts*, the strain of staying in the Please Me Driver is more than the individual can bear for very long, so he almost inevitably has vehement outbursts of the Vengeful Child position, usually taking the form of rudeness and lack of consideration for others, rationalized as his being sick of being put upon. 'Misunderstood' and 'embarrassment' are favourite *rackets* and 'Nobody lets me be myself' a favourite Final Miniscript Payoff. The outsider tends to feel he never knows where he stands with the Please Me player.

Try Hard defines the world's losers, and the phrase 'try hard' may reliably be used to infer that whatever it is the person using it is setting out to do, he will fail. Try Hard is often a response to an *episcript* which binds the individual to not making Mother's or Father's Witch or Ogre jealous by achieving something they wanted to achieve but never did. Manifestly, Try Hard is always putting all his eggs in one grandiose basket, forever being about to make the 'big time' in whatever realm his essential need to fail is focused. In his head the Try Hard player is forever competitive and forever comparing himself to others as either 'superior' or 'inferior' to them on some dimension or other. The Final Miniscript Payoff of 'I'm not as good as I think' is a very close relative of Adler's 'inferiority complex' whose 'compensation' is found both in the Driver position of being 'about to make it' and the Vengeful Child position of opting out of all competition with a rationalization of 'I could be the Greatest if I could be bothered'. As Eric Berne put it, 'A winner knows what he'll do next if he loses, but doesn't talk about it; a loser doesn't know what he'll do if he loses, but talks about what he'll do if he wins.'[3] In reality the Try Hard player is neither as great as he believes in his Driver and Vengeful Child nor as incapable of achievement as his Final Miniscript Payoff tells him. His cure resides in his gaining *permission* to succeed but — analagously to the Be Strong player who needs *permission* to be rejected *sometimes* in order to be accepted sometimes — Try Hard needs to learn that nobody succeeds all the time and that he will have to risk and be able to accept some failures in order to achieve the successes he is actually capable of. To the outsider Try Hard — especially in the Vengeful Child position — seems conceited.

Hurry Up manifests a cornered position. It is usually a response to two separate *injunctions*, 'Don't think' and/or 'Don't belong'. Typically, the child is called upon to obey Mother or Father instantly. Either he complies and foregoes thinking for himself *or* refuses to jump to it and finds that when he does arrive nobody has waited for him and he is left out of things and feels he does not belong. (There is a curiously relevant relationship between 'Don't belong' and 'Don't be long'.) In its third-degree manifestation the *payoff* to Hurry Up is some form of schizophrenia. Hurry Up always contains — at least implicitly and often explicitly — a strong death wish at the deepest level of the personality. In this it is the polar opposite of Be Perfect. When Hurry Up serves a less than psychotic purpose in the personality the individual manifests characteristics such as always being in a hurry; being late; rejecting others' invitations to closeness and warmth (cf. Be Strong, who *is* rejected); being unable to be contentedly alone (they may chronically shout across rooms to fill the space around them); being unable to sit still (they will at least continue to take notes if forced to sit still and listen); being tired (sometimes to the point of falling asleep in company). The cure for Hurry Up resides in gaining *permission* to use Adult, and to belong (manifest in a capacity to say 'We' as well as 'I'). Outsiders tend to feel tired or 'driven crazy' or have a headache in the presence of Hurry Up.

Tips for Diagnosing the Miniscripts

Once the diagnostician has established in his own mind the essential nature of each of the five syndromes, he will have little difficulty in observing in any individual an abundance of concordant symptoms in the forms of words, tones, gestures, facial expressions, and postures. The 'bits' of sensory data which exist in even the briefest *transaction* between people are multitudinous, yet the brain's capacity to translate the data into conscious perception is limited. Each diagnostician will automatically filter the available data through his own preferred mode of perceiving, the usual modes being broadly divisible into hearing and seeing. But whatever the focus of perception, a practised diagnostician will be able to discern the miniscripts of a stranger in a maximum of five minutes conversation — even about the weather!

The table that follows represents the most reliable diagnostic clues I have accumulated to date. Since my own perceptual bias is very much towards words, I leave it to the more visually-oriented reader to elaborate and differentiate the language of the body more fully for himself. Note that the symptoms include Stoppers, Vengeful Childs, and Final Miniscript Payoffs as well as Driver behaviours.

Miniscript	Words	Body language
Be Perfect	perfect/worthless; clean/dirty; tidy/untidy; should/shouldn't; obviously; as it were; believe; of course; depression; exactly; actually; precisely; It's not my fault; . . . for my sins . . .	precision; over-qualification; won't be interrupted; itemizing and numbering of points while talking; purses bottom lip between forefinger and thumb
Be Strong	strong/weak; boring; pull yourself together; I don't care; no comment; vulnerable; It's no good getting upset/crying over spilt milk; You don't appreciate what I'm saying	over-straight back; legs crossed; (apparently) continually in Adult (actually in Adapted Child); has moustache (to hide vulnerability when upper lip slackens); pulls socks up
Please Me*	Dear; Really? nice; pleasant; bastard; Y'know; I mean; Please yourself! embarrassed; Super; You misunderstand me.	nods head; raises eyebrows; looks away; (men) runs fingers through hair; horizontal lines on forehead; questioning inflexion
Try Hard	try; could/couldn't; impossible; superior/inferior; fail/succeed; I don't know; It's hard; lucky/unlucky; I'm better than/not as good as you/him/her	sitting forward, elbows on legs, chin in hand; puzzled look; asks more than one question at a time; does not answer question asked; stutters
Hurry Up	Hurry up; panic; anxiety; quickly; energy; tired; crazy; time; it's pointless; it's futile	brows knitted into vertical lines between the eyes; speaks rapidly and interrupts himself and others; fidgety; breathless; eyes shifty; taps fingers or feet

* Paradoxically, beginning a request with 'please' is a sign of *not* being in Please Me, since it forces the user actually to state his wishes.

The Miniscripts in Action — Everyday Examples

Be Perfect. I am painting a wall with meticulous care (Driver). When I have finished, I notice an imperfectly covered spot, feel guilty (Stopper), keep the spot carefully in focus as I approach it, wielding the paintbrush, fail to see the tin of paint on the floor, trip over and spill the paint all over the floor (Vengeful Child), and I weep at the 'worthlessness' of all that I have done (Final Miniscript Payoff).

Be Strong. I have just missed the bus, but it is stopped just ahead of the bus stop at the lights where I am standing. (It is a bus with a door which the driver opens and shuts.) The driver does not see me and I think of knocking on the door but fear he will refuse to open it, so don't ask (Driver) and walk away believing the driver knew I was there but purposely ignored me (Final Miniscript Payoff).

Please Me. I am visiting a friend and she asks me if I would like a cup of tea or coffee. I say, 'That would be very nice'. She says, 'Which would you prefer, tea or coffee?'. I say, 'Whichever's easier'. She says, 'It's all the same, a teabag or instant coffee'. I say, 'Whatever you're having'. She makes tea, I would have preferred coffee.

Try Hard. My local church is having a fair and a Beautiful Baby Competition. I think my baby is the most beautiful baby in the world and I'm sure she'll win, but afraid she will not. I decide to enter her, but when I get there and see all the other babies, my fear of my baby not winning increases. I don't enter her. I compare my baby with the winner, and think mine much more beautiful.

Hurry Up. I have invitations to three parties on New Year's Eve. I accept them all. I get to the first very early and leave, just as things are warming up, to go to the second. Soon after I arrive at the second party the hostess serves supper, but I refuse, thinking I'll want to eat at the third party. I feel left out while everybody is eating. I go on to the third party. Most of the drink and all of the food is gone and everybody is paired off.

Summary of Miniscripts

The table that follows summarizes what has been said about the *miniscripts* so far. Typical Stoppers, typical Vengeful Childs, and typical Final Miniscript Payoffs are identified for each of the Drivers, together with essential needed *permissions* enabling people to avoid the whole process, including the unconsciously sought-for Final Miniscript Payoff. The 'needed *permission*' column represents the antithesis (in general form) of the original existential *decisions* (reflected in the Final Miniscript Payoff) made in response to an *injunction* (reflected in the Stopper). By definition, these *permissions* are not part of the individual's Free Child as long as he is using the relevant antithetical *miniscript*. The curative *permissions* need to be *learned* in the same way as *permissions* are acquired in childhood, by Free Child to Free Child example. Thus new *permission* learning is one of the core functions of psychotherapy, and the therapist's own *permissions* are of crucial relevance in determining his capacity to cure any particular patient of his psychological ills. This issue is elaborated in Chapter 9.

Table of miniscripts

There are five Drivers in all of us. They are *pseudo-Parent*, that is, they look like *counterinjunctions*, but are actually in Adapted Child. They all say, 'I'm OK so long as I . . . .', but all lead to 'I'm not OK' payoffs

Driver	Typical Stopper (i.e. *racket* response to injunction)	Typical Vengeful Child (*antiscript*)	Typical Final Payoff (existential script decision)	Needed Permissions
Be Perfect	Guilt	Makes a total mess of things	Worthlessness, depression	To appreciate the variety of human attributes and values
Be Strong	Unappreciated	Invulnerable to others, boredom	Cannot get close, unlove—worthiness	To be rejected — and accepted, to ask for things for own Child
Please Me	Misunderstood, embarrassed	Wilfully lacks consideration for others, rudeness	Inauthenticity, nobody lets me be myself	To please oneself (and let others please themselves) and freely like and dislike others
Try Hard	Fear of failure	I could be the Greatest if I could be bothered	I'm not as good as I think	To fail — and succeed, to get on with things
Hurry Up	Panic, can't think, tiredness	Lateness, immobility	Not belonging, craziness	To use Adult and say 'We' (as well as 'I')

Counselling Through the Miniscript

Tips for getting on with different types of people

The miniscripts are so pervasive in everyday life and are so easy to recognize that only a little self-conscious awareness and sensitivity to the 'hang-ups' associated with them may vastly enhance good feeling in our *transactions* with others. That is, by knowing the *not OK payoff* another person is (unconsciously) seeking we may positively help him avoid it. Furthermore, since the *miniscripts* are contagious — one person initiating a *transaction* with his favourite Driver invokes a very high probability that the other person will respond with *his* favourite Driver — helping another person avoid his *payoffs* is almost certainly also helping ourselves avoid our *payoffs*. The trick is to *stroke a person for the antithesis of his Stopper*. Tell a Be Perfect person he is *not responsible*. Express *respect and appreciation* of a Be Strong person. Tell a Try Hard-er '*You can't win 'em all*', thank Please Me for *what he has done for you*, and tell Hurry Up you've *got loads of time*.

But however positive such social manipulation may be, it is limited by the fact that, without the therapeutic intervention which would enable an individual to disobey his relevant *injunctions* and gain needed new *permissions*, people will eventually *insist* on getting their *payoffs* by however devious a route they are forced to find. Thus, in everyday life, we have a better chance of coaxing others away from their *payoffs* in our brief encounters with them than we do in the continuing *transactions* of our more intimate relationships.

Finding OK displacements for the Drivers

In the long run, it is only ourselves we can change. Disobeying *injunctions* may be the ultimate answer, but this is easier said than done and is a long-term project for the individual. In the meanwhile, I believe a great deal can be gained by displacing the energy consumed by Driver behaviour into adaptive alternatives, that is, using behaviour phenomenally similar to the Drivers to gain *positive* rather than *negative strokes*. These displacements seem to correspond to

Driver	OK Displacement
Be Perfect	organization
Be Strong	resilience
Please Me	flexibility
Try Hard	persistence
Hurry Up	efficiency

elements in Kahler's and Caper's 'OK Miniscript', although I maintain, as at the beginning of this chapter, that the Parent *ego state* is not involved. Where they see 'not OK Parent', I see Adapted Child, where they see 'OK Parent', I see Free Child. It is noteworthy that even getting people merely to use the *words* of the *OK* displacements in their speech seems to provide an immediate sense of increased *OKness* for them.

But it is the jobs of work people choose that provide the most obvious outlet for *OK* displacements of Drivers. Such occupations as accountancy, law, or being a filing clerk may give Be Perfect people a great deal of satisfaction through the *organization* demanded by their jobs, as well as diminishing their need to play out the Be Perfect *miniscript*. The degree of psychological distance and emotional *resilience* required of me in my job of psychotherapist is a very adaptive outlet for most of my Be Strong impulses. Be Strong would also do well on a 'Complaints' counter. Please Me people are usually happy in jobs dealing with the public, through which they turn inauthenticity into *flexibility* and are thereby freer to be authentic outside their working lives. Try Hard is warded off in any occupation where *persistence* inevitably accomplishes. Jobs requiring physical effort and stamina are particularly apt, and I often set Try Hard people the task of learning to type, where failures (mistakes) are inevitable along the path to equally inevitable overall success. Hurry Up people enjoy and do well in jobs requiring *efficiency*, and especially in jobs involving the idea of or actual physical movement. Travelling salesmanship and working in the travel industry are jobs which often appeal to and are good for Hurry Up.

Dynamic Relationships Between the Miniscripts

As a practical generalization, we all use each of the *miniscripts* sometimes. However, it is also true that each of the *miniscripts* serves certain kinds of *script payoffs* more efficiently than it serves other kinds. So each individual — with efficiency in mind — has his own hierarchy of *miniscripts*, ranging from most-used to least-used. Some people manage to achieve most of their *script payoffs* with their favourite *miniscript* only, and some people seem to make frequent use of all the *miniscripts*, but most of us tend to get by most of the time with our first and second favourites. Thus the core content of an individual's Adapted Child can usually be inferred succinctly by naming his two favourite *miniscripts*. The five *miniscripts* provide ten pairings, which opens up the theoretical possibility of ten sub-types of Adapted Child. So far, the relationships between Be Strong and Hurry Up and between Hurry Up and Be Perfect are clear. The following observations concern the dynamic relationships of these pairs *within* a given personality and *between* individuals.

Be Strong and Hurry Up

When both Be Strong and Hurry Up are characteristic traits of an individual, the overall existential position served by them seems to approximate, 'People cannot be trusted to give me love for very long, so the best way for me to control my life is not to ask for, and to reject all offers of intimacy'. In my clinical experience I have found many prototypes for the Be Strong/Hurry Up combination amongst young men who have had a typical British upper-class childhood. Rejected by their 'busy' mothers and deposited in the care of paid nannies from infancy or early childhood, Hurry Up is well established by the time they are sent off to boarding-school at seven or eight years of age, at which time their sense of desolate aloneness probably reaches its peak. But thereafter, if not before, Be Strong is continuously and heavily imposed by teachers and caretakers as a moral imperative, with the aim of producing a stiff-upper-lipped gentleman, ready to 'serve the community' with impermeable emotional invulnerability. Usually this aim is successful, that is, Be Strong wins over Hurry Up (which gets suppressed out of awareness), though at enormous cost to the free energy resources of the individual. I see those for whom Hurry Up has won on balance, individuals tragically bound in a Dr Jekyll and Mr Hyde existence, oscillating wildly between Be Strong plus (genuinely) morally upright, giving Parent, and a crazy, rejecting, and often drug-addicted Hurry Up. When Be Strong and Hurry Up meet as two separate people, *relatedness* is the key issue between them. Hurry Up *racketeers* from a Victim position and flips into a Persecuting, rejecting *payoff*. Be Strong *racketeers* from a Rescuer position and flips into a Victim, rejected *payoff*. Be Strong and Hurry Up are very bad for each other.

Be Perfect and Hurry Up

Be Perfect and Hurry Up are polar opposites on the psychoanalytic Libido/Thanatos dimension. Be Perfect is, at core, a manifestation of the fear of death, and Hurry Up manifests a deep-seated wish for death (as the only guaranteed quietude). In combination they seem to be used adaptively to hold each other in check. However, as in the case of Be Strong and Hurry Up this equilibrium binds energy and the individual may report feeling that he has not enough energy to fulfil his potential in life.

As protector against the most self-destructive aspects of Hurry Up, Be Perfect is often manifest as religiosity, and many patients have told me of times in their lives 'when my religion stopped me from going crazy'. On this basis, I often counsel people purposely to organize or ritualize (*OK* displacements of Be Perfect) some aspects of their daily lives as a device for warding off the fear of craziness in Hurry Up. Conversely, I will urge Be Perfect people to 'speed up' and make their lives more efficient (*OK* displacement of Hurry Up) in order to ward off the madness incipient in Be Perfect. The more one looks at Be Perfect and Hurry Up the more paradoxical their relationship seems. It is as if they are right-wing and left-wing political parties, manifestly opposites and capable of holding each other in check, yet meeting in an explosive collision when each becomes extreme. Be Perfect, which, in small degrees often masquerades as highly organized rationality, in extremis turns into obsessive-compulsive psychosis and becomes as crazy as the schizophrenia which is an extreme form of Hurry Up.

When moderate degrees of Be Perfect and Hurry Up meet in two separate people the relationship is often harmonious and stable in their complementarity. A happy counterbalancing of these two *miniscripts* can be observed in some manifestly successful partnerships and marriages.

Love and friendship and the miniscripts

This is also an area where I am still very much in the process of collecting data, but a few generalizations are in order. We all tend to feel empathy for and like best people exhibiting our own favourite *miniscripts*. Although they may lack some of the spark between 'opposites' (see also Pam Levin's Two Types of People, Chapter 6), friendships and marriages between people who have the same *miniscripts* are likely to be harmonious. An exception may be between Try Hard and Try Hard, where each will probably constantly be seeking to 'put down' the other in order to boost his or her own self-esteem. Be Strong and Hurry Up are anathema to each other; Be Perfect and Hurry Up may make a happy couple of opposites; Be Strong and Please Me seem bad for each other (though they are often married in England).

National stereotypes and the ambivalence of the Anglo-American relationship

The (animal-loving) English are Be Strong and Please Me. (Cats are Be Strong, dogs are Please Me.) Roman Catholicism lends a decided Be Perfect flavour to most of Europe. The French seem wholly Be Perfect (focused on sex and food and the pronunciation of their language). The Italians and the Irish are both Be Perfect and Hurry Up. In Italy Be Perfect wins — just; in Ireland Hurry Up wins. The Germans are Be Perfect (focused on order) and Try Hard (although economically they have very successfully turned Try Hard into persistence in the last thirty years). The Japanese are hugely Please Me and — like the Germans — Try Hard transformed into persistence. Americans are Hurry Up and Try Hard (to make a million dollars and be loved). Herein lies the rub between us and them. So long as only their Try Hard and our Please Me meet, we are 'nice' to them and they, in return, Try Hard to deserve our niceness. But lurking in the background always are their Hurry Up and our Be Strong. Our inefficiency 'drives them crazy', and their loud impatience with what is leaves us feeling deeply hurt, but masked by being 'invulnerable' to and 'bored' by their 'childishness'. (The assumption that if we became more efficient we would necessarily also take on Hurry Up seems to be at the root of much of the British resistance to increased efficiency in everyday life. Whether this presumption is justified is an open question.)

Summary

Kahler's and Capers' *miniscript* is another major description of the ways in which we reaffirm our *scripts*. The *miniscript* is defined as a sequence of behaviours, occurring in seconds or minutes, which reinforces early *decisions*.

There are four parts to the *miniscript*: the Driver, a Stopper, a Vengeful Child, and a Final Miniscript Payoff, corresponding to Franklin Ernst's four existential positions of $I + U +$, $I - U +$, $I + U -$, and $I - U -$. Stoppers and Vengeful Childs and Final Miniscript Payoffs vary amongst individuals, but there are only five possible Drivers. These are Be Perfect, Be Strong, Please Me, Try Hard, and Hurry Up.

Five personality types are sketched in terms of the five *miniscripts*. These types may be diagnosed very quickly by attention to key-words and behavioural signs symptomatic of each of them.

Everyday examples of the *miniscripts* in action are given and also a table summarizing typical Stoppers, Vengeful Childs, and Final Miniscript Payoffs and needed *permissions* for each of the *miniscripts*.

Tips are given for helping people avoid the *payoffs* of their *miniscripts* through *stroking* the antitheses of their Stoppers, and *OK* displacements of each of the Drivers are defined.

Dynamic relationships between Be Strong and Hurry Up and between Hurry Up and Be Perfect are postulated, both *within* the individual personality and *between* separate people.

Some generalizations are made concerning good and bad relationships between people in terms of their *miniscripts* and some national stereotypes are also proposed. It is suggested that the difficulties inherent in the Anglo-American relationship reflect Be Strong interacting with Hurry Up.

Notes and References

1. T. Kahler with H. Capers, 'The Miniscript', *Transactional Analysis Journal*, **4**, no. 1, January 1974. Taibi Kahler won the 1977 Eric Berne Prize for his article on the Miniscript. Taibi Kahler has contributed an (up-dated) account of the Miniscript to G. Barnes (Ed.) *TA After Eric Berne*, Harpers College Press, 1977.
2. F. Ernst, 'The OK Corral: the Grid for Get-on-With', *Transactional Analysis Journal*, **1**, no. 4, October 1971.
3. E. Berne, *What do you say after you say hello?* Bantam, 1972, p. 205.

CHAPTER 8

The Art of Diagnosis

What Are We Looking For?

Defining a person

There is no such thing as a single or 'correct' definition of a house or a horse, let alone of a human being. Everything depends on the frame of reference used. Some popular frames of reference used by human beings to define themselves and other things are mathematics, physics, chemistry, biology, philosophy, psychology, anthropology, sociology, political theory, history, economics, religion, cosmology, art, drama, music, and poetry. The number of 'facts' from which meaning may be extracted is infinite, so the choice of frame of reference for any particular purpose depends on a *judgement* (Parent–Adult collaboration) concerning which synoptic view focuses with greatest clarity on those facts we deem to have greatest significance. To find out even one thing necessarily involves ignoring or devaluing something else.

The most satisfying revelations are usually those made when the Little Professor 'sees' the meaning of a fact within two or more frames of reference at the same time. When validated by the Adult in each of the separate frames of reference this then becomes 'original thought'. Within the framework of psychology, Transactional Analysis leaps the boundary between existentialism and behaviour modification in defining a person as a *product* of his consciousness *and* the feedback mechanisms operating on him.

Individuals and types

The two most interesting things about human beings are their differences and their likenesses. TA accepts the underlying sameness of the Freudian Unconscious in all of us. It also sees sameness in our need for *strokes* and sameness in the ways we develop *script* and in our compulsion to live out the life plan of the *script*. TA sees individual differences in the contents of our *ego states*, in the distribution of energy between *ego states*, in the quality of our *scripts* ('winning', 'losing', or 'non-winning'), and in the degrees of boundness-to-*script* versus *autonomy* in our lives.

How Do We Find What We Are Looking For?

The selectiveness of perception

There is no such thing as 'neutral' or 'motive-free' observation. Our frames of reference provide the categories into which we sort the data and these influence our perception in two ways: first, we ignore data that do not fit any of our categories, and secondly, we probe for data to fill as many as possible of the categories of our frame of reference, in order to make our perception comprehensive. The categories a TA therapist uses include Parent, Adult, Child, *injunctions, counterinjunctions*, skills, Drivers, *rackets, impasses, contaminations, exclusions, permissions*, and *script decisions* (including *payoffs*).

Dimensions of experience

Many different frames of reference — from Psychoanalysis to Zen Buddhism — testify to the importance of *opposites* in human experience. George Kelly is especially convincing in proposing that an individual may be defined existentially in terms of a finite number of dichotomous constructs.[1] Kelly's theory is particularly compatible with TA in as much as it incorporates the idea that 'a person may successively employ a variety of construction sub-systems which are inferentially incompatible with each other'.[2] Thus we have another way of saying that different *ego states* contain and express points of view which are not necessarily consistent with each other.

In drawing out an individual's 'dichotomous constructs', which are important elements in his *script*, it is very important for the diagnostician to pay particular attention to the extreme versatility and ambiguity of words. Without due regard to the many possible 'opposites' of nearly any word, the therapist will *project his own constructs on to the patient* and risk failure in attempting to understand the meaning the patient is conveying. (For elucidation of this principle see Roget's Thesaurus.) If, for example, in response to my question, 'What sort of a person was your mother?' a patient says, 'She was very strict', I immediately — and I believe legitimately — infer that he is referring to some of his mother's *injunctions*. But what are these *injunctions*? It is the easiest thing in the world for a therapist (or anyone else) to impose a mental construct of his own on such a statement and make a completely mistaken inference. For me, 'being strict' might imply being punctilious about cleanliness, or not allowing me to play with the kids next door, or not allowing me to 'answer back', or . . . . . any number of things. But it is only what it meant to the person who so refers to his mother that counts. So the next question I ask is, '*If your mother had been the opposite of strict, what would she have been like?*'. Then, for example, if he says, 'She would have been more cheerful' I will infer 'Don't be cheerful', or if he replies, 'She would have had more time to play with me and talk to me' I will infer 'Don't be close'. (All *injunctions* need to be phrased as beginning with 'Don't' since they are all *restrictions* imposed on the Free Child.)

Translating metaphors

Man is a metaphorical being, and all languages are full of universally understood metaphors which express wisdom accumulated by mankind over aeons of time. Language itself may be thought of as the ultimate metaphor for experience. Many metaphors do us the service of counterbalancing much unwisdom contained in the often invalid dichotomy of mind-body. Thus when a new member of one of my therapy groups commented (*à propos* her Please Me Driver), 'I always feel I should swallow my bad feelings', I asked, 'Do you get indigestion?'. She replied, 'Oh yes, I've always suffered terribly from in-digestion'. The other members of the group smiled in recognition of the holistic truth she had just expressed about herself, but she herself needed to have explained the significance of her answer as well as how I had come to ask my question. It is at this point that diagnosis blends into therapy, since the revelationary 'I never thought of it that way before', when such a reconciliation is made, in itself often provides much relief from 'dis-ease'. Freely mixing and generally playing with metaphors in the Child to Child freedom of a therapy group is, for me, the single most enjoyable and powerful technique associated with both diagnosis and therapy.

Drawing Up a Script Matrix

For every person coming to me for help, I usually choose to spend the first hour we meet in an individual session, drawing up a *script matrix*. At this first meeting my perceptions will be minimally *contaminated* by 'knowing' him. Not having met him before, I have the best chance of 'getting inside his skin' as close to 'objectively' as my *executive* Adult will allow, with minimal interference from my Parent *beliefs* and Child *feelings* towards him, which inevitably accumulate as our relationship develops. With this maximum objectivity in mind, several different formal questionnaires have been drawn up by various TA therapists to facilitate this procedure. However, there are two objections to such questionnaires. First, they impose a structure on the responses the patient feels free to give, and thereby distort the gestalt of his *script*. Secondly, they impose a structure on what one hears, and deny one the full use of the Little Professor's 'third ear'. Ideally, if there were no time limit, I would give the greatest *permission* possible for expression of *script* by simply saying, 'Tell me about yourself' — then sitting back and looking and listening. As it is, I usually do begin this way and am sometimes fortunate in that the patient accepts the fullness of the invitation and gives me a wealth of *script* data. But, more often than not, people need prompting in order for me to get the information I am seeking in the course of an hour, and I have some standard questions to intervene with when *script* is not forthcoming. These are usually,

When you were a child . . . . .

What did your mother/father tell you about life? (*counterscript*)

What do you remember your mother/father being good at *doing?* (Adult skills)

What did your mother/father *enjoy?* (*permissions*)

What was the one thing you knew would most upset your mother/father if you did it? (a major *injunction* often expressed in terms of a Driver)

And what did you feel/think about this? (a *script decision*)

If your mother/father had written her/his autobiography, and it was given to you to give it a title, what might you call it? (*episcript*)

What was the story told in your family about the day you were born? (Evokes a profoundly believed myth about the meaning of the person's whole life *in relation to other people*, although it is often expressed as a metaphor which needs translating.)

When you feel bad, what kind of feeling is it usually? (*racket*)

If you were prime minister, what would be an important problem you would want to solve? (the foreground *impasse* presently on his mind)

What will it say on your tombstone? (Driver)

What would you *like* it to say on your tombstone? (contravention of destructive *script* and *episcript*)

Giving plenty of free rein to my Little Professor as well as to my Adult I can usually accumulate a large amount of data in between half and three-quarters of an hour. I will then spend the rest of the hour communicating to the patient the meaning I make from all that he has given me, as well as getting him to correct the mistakes of my Little Professor, which is especially responsible for hearing *script decisions* interpolated amongst all that the patient has spoken. The patient is always the final arbiter of the precise wording of the elements in the *matrix* — it is *his script*, not mine.

At the end of such a session the patient has available to him an explicit, though necessarily skeletal picture of the structure of his personality. I am often gratified by people's frequent expression of the usefulness to them of this analysis in itself, regardless of whether it is followed up by subsequent therapy. In particular, many people seem to be enormously helped by the new-found *permission* they gain from structural analysis to be *inconsistent* — that is, to recognize the normality of having different parts (*ego states*) in themselves, which do not necessarily agree with each other. An example will indicate how well an even brief analysis may clarify the meaning of dominantly felt experiences in a person's life.

Two Cases

(1) A good-looking young man of twenty-three came to see me recently with a view to 'possibly joining a group'. He seemed nervous in having come at all so I did not immediately ask him why he might want to join a group, but asked him to tell me about himself and his family and what sort of relationships they all had with each other.

He told me he was the younger by four years of two brothers. He had recently graduated from teacher training and was employed as a Physical Education teacher at a comprehensive school. His childhood had been materially stable, but there had been constant bickering between his parents, usually concerning his father's making passes at other women and, in fact, having had several brief affairs. His mother seemed to him to have been constantly in tears and threatening to leave his father — which she had never done — in response to which his Father either coldly defended his 'innocence' or, alternatively, overtly courted his mother, to which behaviour she always succumbed. This information, together with answers to some supplementary questioning on my part, enabled me to draw up, in the course of half an hour, a *script matrix* which included the elements below.

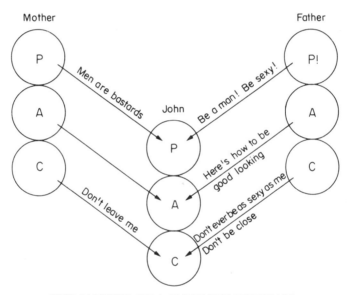

THE MAKING OF A MALE HOMOSEXUAL

Drivers: Please Me + embarrassment *racket*. Be Strong + misunderstood racket.
Decisions: Men make women suffer. Being sexy is the most important thing. I will be a man, like Father wants me to be, but I won't hurt Mother.
Episcript: Whatever happens I must never be sexually content.

By this point I was betting my bottom dollar that he was having clandestine homosexual relationships which caused him a great deal of misery and that he was probably desperate to feel normal heterosexual impulses. Bearing in mind his 'misunderstood' and 'embarrassment' *rackets*, I put it to him that 'Whatever else, *messages* like these must almost certainly create sexual problems. *Is* your sex life OK?'. This gave him the *permission* he needed to acknowledge his homosexuality and its problematic nature to him, and we proceeded from there to make a *contract* 'to explore the meaning of his sexuality and to decide whether to be homosexual or heterosexual'.

I chose the above example because, it represents in broad outline, one prototype *script* for the making of a male homosexual. For this young man — and probably many others with a similar *script* — his homosexuality represents obedience to *injunctions* from both Mother and Father. As a homosexual he will not 'leave Mother for another woman', nor will he threaten Father's precarious sexual *OKness*. The *counterinjunction* to 'be a man' is fulfilled in his 'manly' physique and good looks, epitomized in his choice of occupation as a PE teacher.

Sometimes I am fortunate enough to meet the parents of people who consult me. When this is the case I am usually awestruck by the validation I am presented with of the profoundly continuing effect of *script* through the generations. An example, of this is my second case.

(2) Before I met the forty-year-old 'drop out' I mentioned in Chapter 6, I was consulted by his mother, a woman in her sixties, who sought my help in coping with her seventy-two-year-old husband who had become, consequent on a minor stroke, deeply depressed, and sometimes delusionally obsessed with the thought that he had fraudulently obtained his few thousand pounds life-savings.

She came from a high-principled and highly intellectual Quaker family with moral principles tending to Be Perfect. The most shattering event in her life occurred when she was seventeen and her father, whom she deeply respected and adored, suddenly left his wife and family and ran off with his secretary. Her mother never recovered psychologically and remained bitter for the rest of her life. She, his daughter, forgave her father and continued to love him but was *deeply disappointed* by his behaviour.

My patient's husband also came from a highly intellectual family, but with rather more worldly ambition as well. The crucially determining event in his life was his father's death, in his forties, while his son was an undergraduate. At the time of his death, the father was showing promise of soon becoming a High Court judge. His mother was left penniless, and the family became dependent on the charity of relatives.

For the couple I came to know the crucial *script* determinants in their relationship were as follows:

Husband:
Script decisions: I am shamefully dependent on others for the money I need to live. Great intellectual accomplishment is the only thing that makes life worthwhile.
Episcript: My father died before he achieved the greatness he was capable of. So must I.
Drivers: Try Hard (to win the Nobel Prize), Be Perfect.
Rackets: guilt, depression.
Final script payoffs: My life has been worthless. My wife and children will not be able to survive materially when I am dead.
Wife:
Script decision: The men I love will deeply disappoint me, but I will not show this.
Drivers: Be Strong, Be Perfect.

Racket: 'If you say so, dear'.
Final script payoff: Life might have been much better.

For forty-three of the forty-five years they had spent together when I met them, this husband and wife had been essentially contented. He had been Trying Hard to Win the Nobel Prize (for his work in electronic speech transmission) and she had refrained from ever confronting his grandiosity of which she was privately aware. His *script* crunch came when, after several postponements, he was finally forced to retire at the age of seventy, and about the same time suffered two minor strokes. He was no longer able to evade the fact that he was not going to win the Nobel Prize and he went into a deep depression and *script payoff* which insisted that everything he had done in his life was worthless. Two things seemed to keep him alive. One was his delusional obsession that his few thousand pounds savings did not, in fact, belong to him. He was convinced that, fifteen years ago, when he had sold his house and bought another he had not paid the residual mortgage on the first house. His dependence on this *delusion* to *structure his time* and provide his *script payoff* of 'shameful poverty' was underlined by the fact that he resisted all suggestions on the part of his wife and others to check out the facts once and for all by reference to the building society with whom he had had the mortgage. Realizing his desperate need for his ruminations, I took him 'seriously' (and urged his wife to do the same), while at the same time maintaining and expressing my Adult's *near*-certainty that he was mistaken. For this combination of attitudes in me he rewarded me with 'You've got your head screwed on right', and I was able to provide some relief for him from his desperate misery.

The other thing that kept him going was that his son was a 'no hoper' who 'thought he was a great inventor'. The son had, in fact, made some innovative design changes renovating a clapped-out old car he had bought. When I met him he was convinced that, if and when he met the appropriately influential people, he would 'revolutionize' the small-car industry. His father admitted that he, the father, twenty years ago had invented a device for transmitting voice which, for many years, he had hoped was going to oust the telephone! Meanwhile the son was demonstrating that it was *perfectly* possible to live on £2 a week (he refused to accept social security) and was living in a very squalid squat—which his mother visited him in and enthusiastically admired.

Summarily, this family *script* may be diagrammed (see opposite). For Jeffrey, his *script* only began to make itself felt in his early thirties. Until then, in his *counterscript*, he had obtained an engineering degree and was conventionally employed. But for about ten years, up until the time I met him he was basically living in *antiscript*—that is, in the Vengeful Child position of Try Hard, 'I could be the Greatest if I could be bothered'. He was carrying his father's 'hot potato' of failure (while denying it) and getting covert *strokes* from his mother for being 'a disappointment to her'. Deep down, like his mother, he was deeply disappointed in himself and manifestly longing for *authentic strokes* from the

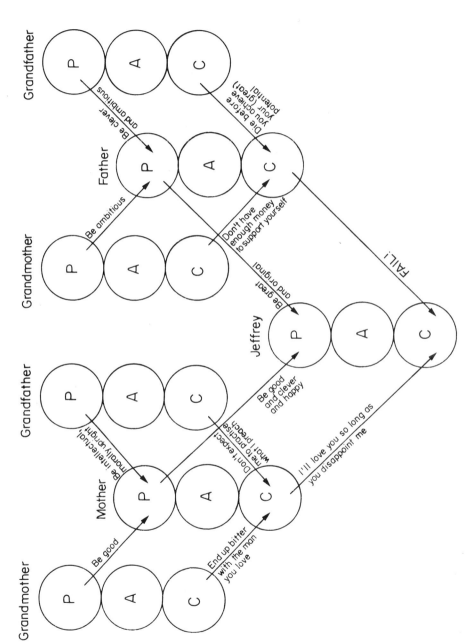

THE MAKING OF A FORTY-YEAR-OLD DROP-OUT

world. The *authentic* aspect of his personality for which it was possible to give him some straight *strokes* was his *counterscript*. He was intelligent, kind, and, above all else, scrupulously honest in word and deed. He came to a group of mine for a couple of months and we achieved some *stroking up* of a realistic sense of self-esteem in him, but unfortunately he got very scared when things began to get a bit close to the bone, and he left the group before we were in any radical sense able to lift the burden of his *script*.

Thus — if proof be needed — 'the sins of the fathers are visited upon the children and upon the children's children unto the third and to the fourth generation'.

Transcript of a Diagnostic Interview With Commentary

Therapist: Please sit down wherever you'll be comfortable.

Patient: [as she is sitting down] Is there any way you think you could possibly help to take away this, this anxiety?

Th.   Everybody in the world feels anxiety sometimes. I'll tell you what, let's talk about your anxiety after you've told me a bit more about yourself. Tell me, have you read *I'm OK, You're OK*?

P.   Yes, but recently I haven't been able to take in much. I don't have any drugs at the moment.

Th.   Let's talk about yourself as a whole person first. I suggest you sit back and relax as much as you can.

P.   [on edge of chair] I'm better here.

Th.   Are you? OK. After we've talked for about half an hour, I think I'll be able to give you some feedback and tell you what I think your problems consist of and how I might be able to help you. Tell me your date of birth.

P.   18/1/42.

Th.   And have you any brothers or sisters?

P.   Yes, I have one sister, she's younger than me.

Th.   By how much?

P.   Two years.

Th.   And did you grow up in a normal family, in the sense of Mother and Father and sister and you all living together?

P: Yes. It was very happy, a very happy family. [Does she protest too much?]

Th.   Tell me about your childhood. Mother and Father — are they alive?

P.   Yes. My mother is Spanish. She came over here when she was eighteen. I think I was born when she was twenty-four.

Th. Aha.

P. My father is a schoolteacher. He used to go and visit these Basque refugees, and my mother was a sort of secretary to them. And they married, but they were very clever. My mother said, 'I wonder if this man's marrying me out of pity'. [*Script decision* 'It's clever to be suspicious of people's motives'.] Because she was a refugee, you see. So they waited a year. And then she married him, knowing that — my father had told her — he had had a sort of breakdown in his twenties. [*Permission* to have a 'nervous breakdown' in her twenties.]

Th. Tell me about your childhood — where you lived.

P. Well first of all I lived in a semi-detached house in Ipswich and my sister and I, we first went to private schools and then to grammar school and my father taught at the grammar school next door, so we were teacher's daughters [she smiles] and we were very happy, I think. [*Decision*, 'I like being my father's daughter'.] Because of this foreign situation, my mother always made us go back to Spain every year — ever since I was five years old — to her relatives. [*Injunction from* M. 'Do as I say'. *Please Me* Driver, probably] That was the order of the home. I mean you wouldn't slip off to the seaside. [*Decision*, 'I must do as Mother wants, not as I want'.] You went back to your mother's culture. Oh, I forgot to tell you, we were made to be bilingual [*Decision*, 'I am forced to be torn between two cultures'], because when we were at home we swopped from English into Spanish. I think that continued till I was about nineteen, when my sister broke away from the set-up.

Th. What sort of family life did you have?

P. I think we were very coloured by the Spanish values. We were made to be different in school. My mother refused to give up her Spanishness. She was not prepared to integrate.

Th. Did you not feel half-Spanish yourself?

P. I did feel half-Spanish at one stage.

Th. Did you not talk to your mother or father about this problem?

P. No, I couldn't. My father's dead now. He's been dead fifteen years.

Th. You said before that your parents were still alive?

P. I'm sorry, I meant to say, I made a mistake, I'm sorry, I misunderstood you. My father's dead.

Th. Did that misunderstanding mean something to you?

P. No. You see, if my father hadn't have died I wouldn't have had any of my health problems. Ever since he died I have had, I think, four breakdowns. He died when I was about twenty-two. I was in Sheffield doing my teaching year, when I found I couldn't . . . . . Till I was twenty-two I was all right. I showed no signs of illness, but I had a sort of slight illness — I didn't have to have drugs — when I was twenty-two, when he died. I was a bit ill, and he became ill. I was very lonely and I simply didn't know how to look after myself correctly. [*Decision*, 'My dependency needs cause others' illness and death'. *Be Perfect*?] I'm quite old now, I'm thirty-six, but I still have big problems. [*Permission* to have breakdown in her twenties only.]

Th.   What did your father die of?

P.   Well, he had a sort of depressive illness. He was taken to the local hospital and he died. My mother immediately looked round for things for me to do, which would keep me occupied. She's a very recovery-type person — she's had to recover. [*Decision*, 'In order to recover, I have to be like my mother' *Be Strong*]

Th.   So when your father died there was a part of you that died?

P.   Yes, because I wondered if it was through me not being able to cope that helped cause his death.

Th.   What sort of a man was he, your father?

P.   He was very organized, very clever, very methodical. [*Be Perfect* confirmed.] He was able to do a *lot* of things — a skilful man — not just teach.

Th.   What were his chief skills?

P.   Languages and he was also very practical. He was an intellectual man. [*Permission* to combine practicality and intellect] And my mother was a very good cook and kept the girls very nice and neat [*Please Me* confirmed] and the house beautiful and invited people in [*Permissions* to be good cook, housewife, and hostess] because she gave to the marriage a lot of brightness, which my father didn't have in his life. [*Decision*, 'Women should bring brightness to men's lives'.] He was a very humble man. We were like a cone.

Th.   What do you mean, 'a cone'?

P.   A protective cone — a Spanish-English family.

Th.   You mean a half-cylinder shape?

P.   Yes.

Th.   I don't quite understand the metaphor. I don't quite understand how you saw your family as a cone. What does a cone do?

P.   Well a cone's got a base, hasn't it? And yet it sort of comes to the top, and I think it stands out a lot, with a sharp edge at the top. It's not a square, strong thing [I'm *not Be Strong*, like Mother] it's weak towards the top. [*Decision*, 'I'm physically strong, but psychologically vulnerable'.]

Th. So your weaknesses have all been psychological?

P. Yes, I've never had any other illnesses. I don't know what's brought it on. It's very boring [i.e. to M's Be Strong!], but it hampers me.

Th. What sort of values did your father give you?

P. I think I'm trying to find someone quite like him — sort of humble and able to do things and able to give you a lot of strength. The best aim in life would be to be very self-sufficient. He was very self-sufficient. [*Counterinjunction* and *permission* to be self-sufficient, but contaminated with decision *not* to Be Strong, which she confuses with self-sufficiency.]

Th. When you were a little girl, growing up, was there anything that if you did it would have really upset your mother?

P. I suppose sex. We weren't normal in our time, my sister and I. We never had a friend from eleven until we were eighteen or nineteen.

Th. You mean a boyfriend?

P. Yes. I felt that things were unfair, that I was being deprived of something human.

Th. If your mother had written her autobiography and it was given to you now to give it a title, what would you call it?

P. 'I fought a losing battle.' [*Episcript*, 'Life is a losing battle'.]

Th. And if your father had written his autobiography, what would you call it?

P. 'I did the best for my family, but the children have to go at some stage.'

Th. What was the story told in your family about the day you were born?

P. It's a terrible story. Either one of us was going to die. I don't know which of the two, but one of us. She might have exaggerated. When I repeated this to her she denied it. [*Decision*, 'In my relationships with others, either they or I nearly die'.]

Th. It might sound very far-fetched, but the answer you gave to that question is a reflection of how you see yourself in relationship with other people. That's pretty terrible.

P. But my boyfriend's a very sane man. He's got very good qualities. He's intelligent, he's perceptive, he's got no money . . . . . [laughs] But my anxiety might stand in the way of our marriage. [*Decision*, 'My dependency needs stand in the way of my happiness'.]

Th. What do you think it will say on your tombstone?

P. I would say — I would once have said — 'She tried, she tried to. . . . but now I'd say 'She became determined'. [She has been reading some TA.]

Th. Is there anything else you'd like to talk about?

P. You mean that's not good enough? [*Decision*, 'What I am is not good enough for others' — for Mother?.]

Th. It's as if by saying that you're reflecting that very perception of yourself that says that other people are not going to find you good enough for them.

P. Yeah, that's right.

Th. One last question. If you were prime minister, what would be a very important problem you'd want to solve?

P. I'd be interested in making psychiatric help more open and better and more tolerated.

Th. I'd like to say something now about your anxiety. Anxiety is a very positive sign to a psychotherapist, because what it represents is your repressed impulses refusing to be held down any longer. It represents a battle between the forces of expression and repression. When the forces of repression were overwhelming you, you didn't have any anxiety, and as the forces of expression win, so will your anxiety go away. Your anxiety exists because the forces are about equal now. I know what a horrible feeling it is, but the best thing you can do about it now is to decide that you will have to live with it for the time being. I can assure you that slowly but surely, as your problems are solved, your anxiety *will* go away.

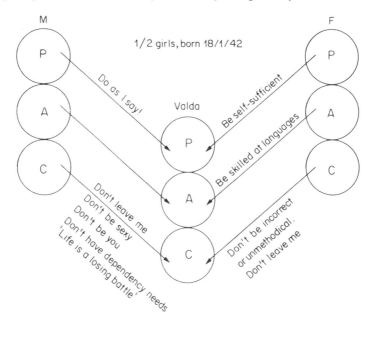

(I spent the rest of the session discussing with her the implications of the *script matrix* I had drawn up in the course of our talk, as below.)

Drivers: Be Perfect, Please Me, Try Hard (to win the battle of life)

Decisions: It's clever to be suspicious of others' motives.

I am forced to be torn between two cultures.

I like being my father's daughter, but in order to recover (from my psychological problems) I need to be Be Strong, like Mother.

I must do as Mother wants, not as I want.

My dependency needs cause others' illness and eventual death.

Women should bring brightness to men's lives (not needs).

I am physically strong but psychologically vulnerable.

In my relationships with others either I or they nearly die (not necessarily literally).

My dependency needs stand in the way of my happiness.

What I am is not good enough for others.

Episcript (from Mother): Life is a losing battle.

Permissions: To have a nervous breakdown in her twenties; to combine practicality and intellect; to be a good cook and housewife and hostess; to be humble and self-sufficient.

Core existential problem: Dependency versus self-sufficiency.

At first blush, this looks like a nasty losing *script*. And, indeed, my patient had been living out the pain of it all for fifteen years. However, her anxiety *was* an encouraging sign — it seemed to be a manifestation of disobedience to Mother's *injunctions* 'Don't leave me' and 'Don't be you' and also to Mother's *episcript*, 'Life is a losing battle' — and the number and quality of her *permissions* was also favourable to her prospect for overcoming the destructive elements of her *script*. Subsequent to this diagnostic interview she came to see me with her fiancé and my prognosis for her became enormously more optimistic. She had managed to find in her fiancé as ideal a complement to her as could be imagined. He had a very stable, OK-nurturing Parent, and his own *script* included the need to have a woman depend on and be basically obedient (Child to Parent) to him, but he also wanted and expected his wife to 'have a mind of her own'. So, through him, she will have a way of fulfilling her core need — to be both dependent *and* self-sufficient at the same time. She will be her father's daughter again. Like her father, she is marrying a foreigner (he is Turkish) and, like her father, she will submit herself to a half-foreign, half-English way of life. Furthermore, her fiancé shares with her Be Perfect and Please Me and also has a (minimal) Try Hard in association with a *script decision* 'I fear failure, but I know I will succeed'. Overall, his childhood gave him unconditional love and he understands with compassion the suffocation that his fiancée has suffered. At the time of writing, they were planning to be married in a few weeks. Her mother only barely acknowledges his existence, although she seems finally convinced that her daughter is going to get married. With her other daughter already married, Mother is making flamboyant plans to return to Spain to live.

Summary

All definitions depend on frames of reference. For any particular purpose, a frame of reference is chosen which seems to focus with greatest clarity on the facts we judge to have the greatest significance. TA amalgamates the frames of reference of existential psychology and behaviour modification in seeing human beings as products of consciousness *and* feedback mechanisms. TA assumes the universal validity of the Freudian Unconscious and of the human needs for *strokes* and for *script*. It sees individual differences in the contents of *ego states*, in the energy distribution between *ego states*, in the qualities of *scripts*, and in the degrees of *autonomy* with respect to *script*.

TA categorizes the data of human beings into *injunctions, counterinjunctions*, skills, Drivers, *rackets, impasses, contaminations, exclusions*, and *script decisions*. In diagnosis it is important to include 'opposites' when discovering existential dimensions expressed by a patient. Playing with metaphors can be a very enjoyable and potent technique in both diagnosis and therapy.

A transcript of a diagnostic interview, with commentary, is presented.

Notes and References

1. See G. Kelly, *A Theory of Personality*. W. W. Norton & Company, 1963.
2. *Ibid.*, p. 83.

PART III

Therapy

CHAPTER 9

Theories and Therapies

Psychological Theories in General

Theory as vested interest

A psychological theory tends to define its adherents as vehement enemies of the adherents of any other psychological theory. Certainly there are factions within other disciplines, but less often than in Psychology do theoretical differences exert a powerful enough divisive influence to compete with the natural sympathy between people of like interests. All too often Psychoanalysts and Behaviourists, Humanists and Experimentalists despise each other, and even Freudians and Jungians and Adlerians or Eysenckians and Skinnerians keep a coldly respectful distance from each other. Thus it is clear that psychologists — of whatever (Parent) school — often have very strong *script* investments in their chosen profession, and tend to defend against any perceived threat to their relevant *script decisions* with primitive Adult/Child and Parent/Adult *contaminations*.

Theory as language

More positively, different theories may be thought of as different but concordant languages. Within very broad limits, any language is capable of expressing any thought that any human being may wish to utter. From China to the Azores we are all one species. However, environmental conditions, both physical and psychological, have created differences in the *relative* importance and pertinence of various elements in different peoples' experiences of life. And these differences are reflected in the vocabulary of any given culture-language. A centrally important issue will have invoked the creation of minutely discriminating words to match the *need to perceive* such differences. Thus the Eskimos, I am told, have about twenty words for our one word 'snow', and Yiddish enables me to describe varieties of fools with subtlety and gusto.

Such, I believe, is the most valid spirit in which to view various psychological theories. Though we will each, inevitably, be most fluent in our native tongue, a degree of multi-lingualism in the form of appropriate interpolations of 'foreign' words and phrases can do nothing but enrich our experience and our expressiveness. However, amongst the 'languages' of psychology, no one theory does seem to do sufficient justice in its enunciation, on its own, to both the unconscious and conscious realms of human experience. So a psychotherapist who claims to treat the whole person needs to be at least bilingual. (TA assumes the validity of the Psychoanalytic Unconscious, but does not explicate it. So a TA therapist really needs to be familar with Psychoanalytic theory before coming to TA.)

TA Amongst Theories

TA and psychoanalytic theories

TA is a child of psychoanalysis. Eric Berne remained, throughout his life, committed to the central tenets of traditional Freudian personality *theory*, but he parted company with psychoanalysis as *therapy*. TA as personality theory may be thought of as a spin-off from TA as therapy, which evolved out of Berne's dissatisfaction with the *slowness* of psychoanalysis in curing people of their problems. The slowness of psychoanalysis resides in the time it takes to develop and work through the 'transference' relationship — a form of falling in love of the patient with the analyst — through which the patient projects onto the analyst all the unresolved conflicts of his early years (*protocol*), and through the analyst's interpretations of them makes new sense of the present. The basic assumption of psychoanalysis is that, without this process, no cure is possible. Berne questioned and found wanting this basic assumption. He decided that patients could, in fact, be made better *first*, through direct confrontation of the conscious parts of the ego, and have their unresolved deeper conflicts dealt with *later* — if necessary. Furthermore, Berne asserted, it *is* possible for therapists efficaciously to give advice to patients.

Out of TA therapy, TA theory developed as an elaboration of the Psychoanalytic Ego. Although Freud never represented it this way, there is no theoretical objection to representing the psychoanalytic model of the structure of personality as in the diagram opposite. With the psychoanalytic concept of the structure of personality so represented, we may now superimpose the TA structure to form a compatible whole (as shown on p. 112).

As may be seen, allowing for Freud's understanding that parts of the ego are unconscious, parts of P_2 and C_1 are unconscious. It is also worth pointing out that, as this diagram indicates, psychoanalysis, contrary to popular belief, does not actually deal, in therapy, with 'unconscious' material, which is, by definition, always inaccessible to consciousness. As therapy, however, psychoanalysis does make propositions about the nature of the unconscious elements in personality, whereas TA limits its propositions to the realm of the conscious ego. In its theory, TA takes for granted the psychoanalytic theory of the Unconscious, but restates and expands psychoanalytic ego theory. In diagnosis and therapy, the stuff that TA tackles incorporates much Adult as well as more sophisticated

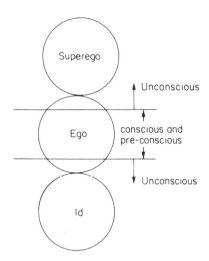

THE PSYCHOANALYTIC MODEL OF PERSONALITY

Little Professor material than psychoanalysis does. Psychoanalysis deals nearly exclusively with *protocol* material, whereas TA deals nearly exclusively with *palimpsest* material. In this, TA is further than psychoanalysis from the roots of personality in the Id which, Freud inferred, ultimately determine our destinies. However, the Id and our ultimate destiny, death, is the same for all of us. Our egos shield us from this ultimate 'pessimism' by 'making the most of life'. TA, in being a little further removed than psychoanalysis from the Id, is a little more 'optimistic'.

In his own creative blend, Berne certainly knew he was using many of the ingredients of psychoanalysis, and he repeatedly praised Freud's original recipe for understanding human nature. Although he mentioned him less frequently than Freud, Berne also acknowledged Adler, and he saw Adler's 'individual psychology', in its emphasis on the unique existential decisions each individual makes, as a close relative of *script* theory. In his widespread reference to myths and fairy-tales throughout his writings, Berne also pays implicit tribute to the influence of Jungian 'analytic psychology'.

TA and operant conditioning

Probably no two schools of psychology are generally considered more fundamentally opposed than Freud's psychoanalysis and Skinner's operant conditioning. True believers in the former dismiss the latter as dangerous, mechanistic, simplistic, dehumanizing, trivial nonsense, whilst the committed experimentalists of the latter school go to considerable lengths to prove the former to be pernicious, unscientific, tautological mythological rubbish.

And yet, it seems to me that the essential genius of TA as theory resides in the reconciliation of these two languages into a whole that overcomes the limitations of each of them in their separateness. Surprisingly, Berne himself seemed to be

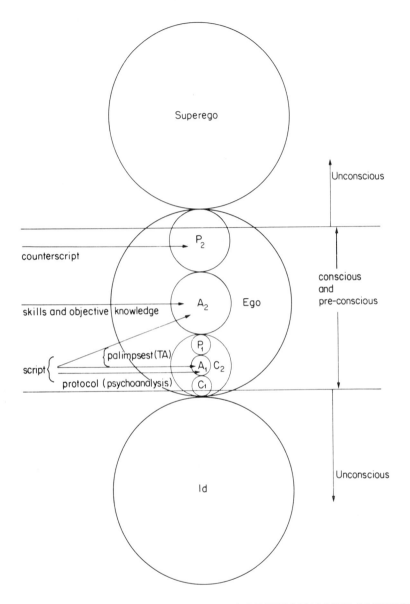

THE PSYCHOANALYTIC AND TA MODELS OF PERSONALITY COMBINED

quite oblivious of TA's links with Skinner's theory. Paul McCormick, a TA therapist who is doing research for the California Youth Authority, comparing (Skinner's) Behaviour Modification and TA as therapeutic modalities, confirmed this in personal correspondence with me. He wrote, 'Berne was probably not at all influenced by Skinner. I never heard him mention the man in five years of weekly seminars . . .'.

Yet if we examine the core premises of psychoanalytic theory (which are also the core premises of TA) and the core premises of operant conditioning they can be seen to be not at all opposed but, on the contrary, complementary aspects of a single model of human reality — aspects perfectly synthesized in the theory of Transactional Analysis.

Freud's core understanding is that all the meaning we give our lives derives from the dilemma inherent in our biological nature. Instinctually (Child) we are wholly self-centred; factually (Adult) we are all always desperately dependent on each other. Our life-long struggle (Adult–Child) is to find a meaning (Parent) which will justify us (Parent–Adult) in our best possible adaptation (*script*) to our biological dilemma, whilst soothing us (Parent) into accepting the compromises (Parent–Child) we are willy-nilly bound to make.

Skinner's central position is that (whatever our core ontology) the patterns of our behaviour (overt manifestations of *script*) are learnt and maintained through being reinforced (*stroked*) by rewards (*positive strokes*) or punishment (*negative strokes*). Punishment (*negative strokes*) only inhibits undesirable (*not OK*) behaviour while the punishment is actually being inflicted (Final Miniscript Payoff). (*Not OK*) patterns of behaviour (Drivers, *racketeering, games*) are only eliminated when they are systematically ignored (neither *positively* nor *negatively stroked*) over an extended period of time (which is the central behavioural tenet of TA therapy).

Berne's overlooking the relevance of operant conditioning theory is TA's loss. Given Skinner's experimental findings, the *stroking* concept of TA is too general. TA does recognize the core Skinnerian concept that *negative strokes* have the same reinforcing power as *positive strokes*. But much could be gained, both theoretically and in clinical practice, from a differentiation into various patterns of *stroking*, by borrowing from the 'interval', 'ratio', and 'intermittent' schedules of Skinner.[1] Armed with this explicit knowledge, the TA therapist as 'stroker' of new, adaptive behaviours in his patients, might enormously increase his curative potency.

Therapies in General

What is therapy?

Therapy is helping people find out what they want and then helping them get it. The former task is almost always by far the more prolonged. Finding out what people want involves discovering the *meanings* of their symptoms — symptoms being both bodily and psychological. The pursuit of meanings involves microscopic analysis, that is, what in everyday life would be called 'making mountains out of molehills'. Thus therapy consists in large measure of the continuing refinement of diagnosis. Revelation is the goal.

Once people know what they want therapy becomes oriented to the behaviour modification necessary to fulfil their wants. Psychoanalysis stops when revelation is considered complete. Purely behavioural therapies discount the necessity of revelation. TA and most other contemporary ego-centred therapies pursue meaning and adaptive behavioural change hand-in-hand.

Any therapy which recognizes the centrality of meaning is more art than science. Highly personal validity rather than publicly demonstrable reliability is the measure of therapeutic success. Accuracy rather than precision is the target, since qualitative as well as quantitative truths can be accurate, whereas precision refers to measurable exactitude — which is irrelevant to subjective reality. (Furthermore, even when exactitude is relevant, a high degree of precision is spurious and misleading if accuracy is lacking. For example, no matter that a micrometer screw gauge measures to within a thousandth of an inch if, unbeknown to the experimenter, the screw gauge itself is warped.) The criterion of 'repeatability' which would gain therapy the status of 'science' is impossible to achieve because each human being is unique. And yet, absurdly, we go on Trying Hard to make a science of human nature. I. A. Richards puts it beautifully:

We worship the test for fact, in the scientist's framework of assumptions, and when we go beyond it, as we incessantly must, we tremble with guilt and shame, or pretend, if we can, that we are not doing so.[2]

But the long-entrenched implicit assumption in society at large that scientific truth is *the* truth is losing ground. Subjectivity is becoming fashionably acceptable.

Varieties of therapy

All therapies assume that the conditioning of the individual in infancy and childhood is an important determiner of the individual's lifelong propensities to respond to life in the ways he does. And all therapies assume the necessity for — one way or another — undoing faulty conditioning. All therapies also propound — at least implicitly — principles of conservation and flow of energy. Somewhere in every therapy is the notion of energy flowing freely in health and being 'blocked' in pathology. As a functional being, man is likened to the rest of the universe. These assumptions are the heritage of Freud.

The vast majority of contemporary therapies are extensions and elaborations of psychoanalysis into the realm of the ego. Exceptions are Jungian and Meditative therapies (which 'transcend' the ego), behaviour therapies (which discount the relevance of subjectivity), and primal therapy (which reduces the ego to a single experience). My own view is that 'transcendence' of the ego, though a meritorious ultimate life-goal, is only truly possible *after* the ego has been faced and lived in adaptively. I have yet to see behaviour therapy, on its own, without reference to conscious experience, enhance anybody's life. I am sceptical but open-minded concerning the validity of primal therapy.

Amongst ego-oriented therapies, differences are essentially of focus. My own bias is firmly towards those which do *not* dichotomize thought and feeling in the therapeutic process itself, but I am prepared to concede this to be a matter of

	Terminology	Mode of therapy	Curative focus
Psychoanalysis (Freud)	concepts in analyst's head	transference of unconscious conflicts (patient's P_1 to therapist's A_2)	new adaptations to reality through clarification and understanding
TA	concepts shared between therapist and patient	therapist's and patient's A_2 against patient's P_1	concrete goals achieved
Analytical psychology (Jung)	thinking, feeling, intuiting, sensing, shadow	balancing and transcending these functions	transcendental harmony
TA	A_2, P_2, A_1, C_1, P_1	balancing these functions and applying them pragmatically	worldly happiness
Individual psychology (Adler)	life-style, inferiority complex, compensation	positive encouragement; stresses sibling relationships and creative problem-solving	self-mastery of the environment
TA	script, Drivers (esp. Try Hard and Be Perfect)	positive strokes; stresses all family relationships; creative (use of Little Professor)	separate selves (ego states) each gaining own gratifications
Gestalt (Perls)	here, now, feel, want, do, top dog, under dog	stresses emotional acting out; disallows A_2 interpretations; de-emphasizes group process	changing 'can't' into 'won't' into 'will' through feelings
TA	P, A, C, racket, script, etc.	discourages emotional acting out; emphasizes A_2 interpretation and group process	making new A_2 decisions in the light of P, A, and C
Client-centred (Rogers)	self-actualization, self-regard	support of client's frame of reference	contentment through high self-regard and self-actualization
TA	contentment through positive social interaction	challenges frames of reference	same plus high regard of others

	Terminology	Mode of therapy	Curative focus
Psychodrama (Moreno) TA	roles	role play	solving problems through their redefinition
	ego states	intellectual analysis	solving problems through analysis and action
Existential (May et al.) TA	uniqueness of the individual	shared experience; minimizes the value of explanation	achievement of uncontaminated consciousness
	same	shared experience, but also emphasizes explanation	same plus social facility through operational understanding
Primal (Janov) TA	Actual Pain	extreme acting out of single primal trauma	catharsis of pain
	many pains (and pleasures)	thinking out many experiences	making sense of all one's experiences
Biofunctional (Reich and Lowen) TA	bodily functions and energy flow (esp. sexual); body types	freeing bodily blocks; self-referring	OKness manifest in the life of the body
	psychological functions; psychological types and individual scripts	freeing psychological and social blocks; interactional	OKness manifest in life of mind and social interaction
Encounter groups TA	emotional expressiveness towards others	vehement emotional expressiveness is demanded	'I'm OK'
	transactional analysis	emotional expression is analysed	'I'm OK, You're OK'
Meditative TA	transcendental feelings	self-referring	awareness and serenity
	ego feelings and thoughts	interactional	awareness and action
Behaviour modification (Skinner) TA	reinforcement	changes behaviour through positive reinforcement	new behaviours giving new satisfactions
	strokes	same plus existential understanding	separate ego states each gaining its own satisfactions

taste or individual need. The table on pp. 115–6 compares TA with other post-Freudian therapies in respect of terminology, mode of therapy, and curative focus.

Who needs therapy and for how long?

The people who need therapy are the people who are unhappy in their lives and are either unable to understand why or else understand why but feel themselves in an *impasse* with respect to changing things.

The time needed in therapy is very difficult to predict. It depends on how radical are the changes the individual needs to make and how enthusiastically (that is, with how much Adult–Child collaboration) he embarks on the task. Furthermore, the goals the individual is seeking will very often change during the course of therapy. Quite often the appetite grows whilst eating, and the original desperation that may have prompted a person to seek help is transformed into a positive desire to enjoy the *intimate* and revelationary pleasures that therapy affords. Generally speaking, my experience is that important *script* issues cannot be resolved in much under about two years of once weekly group therapy. However, most patients in TA therapy report an immediate and continuing increase in their sense of wellbeing right from the start of therapy.

Inevitably, *script analysis* and treatment are fraught at every moment with deep resistance, since *script* change is concerned with renouncing the most profoundly held beliefs of the individual. Parent control, Adult argument, and Child manipulation by the therapist are all called into play in persuading a patient to stay in therapy at crucial turning points, when his deepest *script* impulses make him want to flee. Naturally, and sometimes legitimately, the patient suspects the therapist of having vested interests in keeping him in therapy, and in this it is of the utmost importance that the therapist be scrupulously honest with himself as well as the patient.

Satisfactory termination of therapy occurs when patient and therapist and the rest of the group concur, in an 'I'm OK, You're OK' spirit, that the patient's *contract* has been achieved. The evidence for this achievement is the patient's reporting on his achieved state of mind, combined with the group's and therapist's awareness of changes in his overt behaviour which are relevant to his *contract*. By these criteria, most experienced TA therapists claim a 'success rate' in excess of 80 per cent.[3]

How to choose a therapist

All good therapists are alike, but a bad therapist is bad after his own fashion. Good therapists *cure* people of their ills, bad therapists do not cure them — and, unfortunately, may exacerbate their ills. Two characteristics go to make a good therapist: he or she has personally endured psychological suffering *and* is now a well-integrated, happy person. Without the former characteristic — no matter how great his formal knowledge — a therapist lacks the insightful sensitivity needed for essential (Child to Child) empathy with his patients. Without the second characteristic his patients cannot become weller than he is himself. Even if he knows how to enable people to achieve wellbeing he has not achieved for himself, at a profound level he will sabotage their happiness out of *jealousy*. Most people who choose to become psychotherapists *have* suffered themselves, but too many have not yet achieved their own integration.

Unfortunately there is no way of being absolutely sure that a therapist is a good one, but it is worth checking his credentials. Although it is no guarantee, if he has acquired professional credentials in a particular school of psychotherapy chances are he has been a patient himself, as part of his training, and is more likely to have dealt with his own problems. Credentials also refer to *competence*, which makes the difference between a wise friend and someone who has the *objective skills* to help you change in the ways you need to.

From then on trust your own feelings — especially your very first feelings when you meet him. Has he got a pleasant face? Is he open and ready to answer your questions about himself as therapist? Do you find the room you meet him in pleasant? Does he seem to have the personal characteristics (*permissions*) you yourself want but have not yet achieved? Aim for a positive answer to all these questions before committing yourself.

If the above process of elimination still leaves you with a choice of therapies, go to the one you feel you would *enjoy* most. The language may vary, but the substance is essentially the same from one therapy to another. People's problems and their 'human nature' have been around for a long time.

In general, though, choose group rather than individual therapy. People live in the world as social beings, not just in intimate relationship to one other. And the closer the analogy between you in relationship to therapy and you in relationship to the world, the more you will gain from it. However, there are circumstances when individual therapy is more appropriate than group therapy — at least to start with. For example, someone who starts therapy in a state of acute anxiety can make no positive use of the group until the therapist has worked with him individually to achieve a sufficiently energized Adult that he can function *transactionally* with some degree of *autonomy*. Furthermore, there are times when a TA therapist sees fit to refer a patient to another therapist or therapy for supplementary treatment. For example, a male patient who — amongst other therapeutic needs — particularly needs *permission* to establish his gender identity, may be referred by his female therapist to a male therapist for some individual sessions. And a patient in a verbally-oriented TA group, who would clearly benefit from some cathartic 'acting out', may be encouraged to join a Gestalt, Psychodrama, or Encounter group, etc.

Summary

Psychologists tend to have strong vested *script* interests in the theories of human nature they espouse. Different theories may also be thought of as different, but essentially concordant, languages. Multi-lingualism is an advantage to a psychologist.

TA is a child of psychoanalysis. In its underlying assumptions about human nature it is completely congruent with psychoanalysis, but it parts company with psychoanalysis in its theory of therapy. TA as therapy reconciles the behaviour modification of operant conditioning with the existentialism of psychoanalysis. Therapy is helping people find out what they want and then helping them get it. All therapies assume the need to undo faulty conditioning of childhood and to enable energy to flow freely in the individual. The vast majority of contemporary therapies are elaborations and extensions of psychoanalysis in the realm of the ego. Differences between therapies are essentially differences of focus. These differences are summarized in a table comparing TA with various other post-Freudian therapies. The time people need in therapy varies, but radical *script* change usually takes a minimum of two years. TA therapy is 'successful' when a patient achieves his *contract* before leaving the group. Generally, the choice of therapist is more important than the choice of therapy. Therapists should be chosen for their personal OKness, their competence, and their relevant *permissions*. After these criteria are satisfied, choose a therapy you feel you will enjoy, but prefer group to individual therapy, unless you and the therapist you consult consider there are particular reasons why individual therapy would be more suitable for you.

Notes and References

1. See B. F. Skinner, *Science and Human Behaviour*. Macmillan, New York, 1960.
2. I. A. Richards, *How to Read a Page*. Routledge & Kegan Paul, London, London, 1967.
3. See also 'The Uniqueness of TA Therapy', Chapter 10, and 'Rules of Conduct for Group Members', Chapter 12.

CHAPTER 10

TA As Therapy

The Origins, Aims, and Limitations of TA Therapy

TA as therapy arose out of Eric Berne's dissatisfaction with the slowness of psychoanalysis in achieving effective and discernible cures in patients. TA aims to cure people of their *dis-eases as quickly as possible*. Cure is recognizable as the achievement of *a concretely specified goal*, agreed upon at the beginning of therapy by therapist and patient.

Berne made one exception to his general observation of the superior efficiency of TA over psychoanalysis and that was in the treatment of hysteria. TA is essentially group therapy, but hysterics have so profoundly repressed awareness of the meanings of their symptoms and their behaviour as to be invulnerable to the social feedback which plays so important a role in group therapy. On the other hand, individual Psychoanalysis as therapy was primarily developed by Freud as the appropriate treatment for hysteria, and no other effective method has yet been found to treat hysterics. The 'defence mechanisms' of the *palimpsest*, which the TA therapist uses as his wedge, are often entirely absent in the hysteric. The 'repression' of his conflicts into the *protocol* is so nearly complete as to make him inaccessible to any form of therapy less than profound psychoanalysis. The 'repression' of the hysteric may be thought of as 'fourth-degree' pathology. (Cf. 'third-degree' *exclusion*, Chapter 5.)

For all other categories of psychological disturbance Berne saw the aim of TA in group therapy as 'to carry each patient through the progressive stages of *structural analysis, transactional analysis* proper, *game analysis*, and *script analysis*, until he attains social control'.[1] Many thousands of people who, over the past fifteen years or so, have had first-hand experience of TA therapy, can testify to the validity of Berne's premise that effective work *can* be done with the *palimpsest*. With the exception of Berne's acknowledged limitation for hysterics, objective research has shown TA to be significantly effective in treating the most diverse psychopathologies, including psychoses.[2] A delightful, subjective accolade for TA as therapy can be found in Solon Samuel's 'Games Therapists Play'.[3]

In general terms, a healthy person is defined as one who is:

(1) *Autonomous*, i.e. aware of *who* he is, *what* he is, *where* he is, and how he *feels* about it.
(2) *Spontaneous*, i.e. neither calculating for effect nor impulsively driven by his Adapted Child, but having all his behaviours freely at his disposal.
(3) *Authentic*, i.e. *game-free* with those with whom he wants to be *game-free*.

The Uniqueness of TA Therapy

Language

The first and foremost advantage of TA is its incisiveness as language. TA speaks the truths that psychoanalysis and the greatest writers have always known, and it speaks these truths with enormous clarity, precision, and concision and without any loss of meaning. And, as a language rather than an exclusive belief system, it also happily descriptively encompasses any of the eclectic wisdoms people may bring to it from a wide variety of sources.

Although it is clearly advantageous for a patient joining a TA therapy group to have some fluency in the language of TA, this is not necessary. In my experience, about half the people who come to TA therapy specifically choose TA therapy, the other half are just seeking psychotherapy, and happen to end up in the consulting room of a TA therapist. Those who specifically seek TA therapy have often been prompted to do so by a favourable impression they have gained from attending an official '101' or other brief introductory, didactic course on TA theory. Such courses are frequently advertised in the press and are attended by members of the general public interested in gaining psychological knowledge, as well as by students, by practitioners in the helping professions, and by personnel managers in business and industry. Those who simply 'happen' to consult a TA therapist — usually by the personal recommendation of a friend — are usually totally unfamiliar with TA theory. For them, it is valuable, before they join a group, for the therapist to explain the concepts Parent, Adult, and Child, since the existence of these *ego states* is the basic assumption of all TA theory and therapy.

Once they are members of a group, most people pick up the more advanced vocabulary and grammar of TA, according to their needs, through the teaching of the therapist, although those with a taste for theory often also ask for reading lists. Most TA therapists recommend James' and Jongeward's *Born to Win* or Harris' *I'm OK You're OK* to start with, followed by any of Berne's books, but particularly *What do you say after you say hello?*

Contracts

Secondly, TA therapy is unique in being contractual. Each patient in TA therapy has at least one major *contract for change*. TA *contracts* are hard *contracts* in being insistently concrete and specific. For example, 'To get and stay out of debt', 'To feel easy and comfortable in social situations', 'To be in harmony with my husband/wife in bringing up our children', *not* abstract and vague, such as 'To improve my self-knowledge'. No *contracts* are accepted unless it is clear that their achievement will be able to be validated both subjectively and objectively. Thus TA therapy is geared for each individual to his own highly idiosyncratic needs. The fulfilment of his needs through the fulfilment of his *contract* will be both felt in himself and clearly observable by others in behavioural changes.

Self-determination

Thirdly, TA is unique in holding each person responsible for his or her *script decisions*. No matter how inhibiting and destructive his *injunctions*, it was the recipient of them, not the sender, who made the existential *decisions* he did around them. Therefore it is the recipient who can change the *decisions*.

Uses the whole ego

Fourthly, TA gives credence and value to the whole personality of both therapist and patient. Unlike psychoanalysis, and many 'supportive' and other therapies derived from it, it is not symbiotic. That is, it does not rely on — and in fact positively discourages — the Child to Parent 'transference relationship', which is the essential *raison d'être* of psychoanalysis. Such a symbiosis implicates therapists as Rescuers $(I + U -)$ to their Victim patients $(I - U +)$. Instead, the TA therapist encourages the dignity and *autonomy* available to the patient in the use of his Parent, Adult, and Child in a relationship which is essentially and reciprocally 'I'm OK, You're OK'. However, TA is fully aware that anyone seeking therapy is fundamentally in his Child and is seeking an omnipotent Parent to wave a magic wand and 'make it all better'. For most people, some degree of transference is inevitable, no matter how explicitly both patient and therapist seek to evade it. My own approach is to acknowledge it and allow it whilst also openly analysing it (Adult to Adult) and asking the patient to allow himself to have an Adult understanding of the nature of his transference even while experiencing it in his Child.

Levels of TA Therapy

In the ongoing experience of therapy, levels of therapy are often not discrete. *Structural, functional, transactional, game,* and *script* analyses easily blend and overlap. However, for the purpose of exposition, some differentiation of levels of therapy is in order.

Structural analysis

Structural analysis begins with the drawing up of a *script matrix*, which highlights the core contents of a person's *ego states* (as well as revealing the essential paraphernalia of his *script*). *Structural analysis* continues as an integral part of ongoing therapy, as more and more elements in the *ego states* are revealed in the *transactions* of the group. The flesh is added bit by bit to the skeleton of the original *matrix*.

Once a *script matrix* has been drawn up and a person has decided to join an ongoing therapeutic group, a *contract* for change is made between patient and therapist. In clarifying the issues and articulating the *contract* satisfactorily I find Muriel James' standard five questions useful. They are:

(1) 'Is there anything you want that would enhance your life?'
(2) 'What would you need to change to get what you want?' (The emphasis here is on taking responsibility for oneself.)
(3) 'What would you be willing to do to effect the change?' (Here the therapist makes it clear that he has no magic wand.)
(4) 'How would other people know when the change has been made?' (This makes the *contract* hard.)
(5) 'How might you sabotage yourself?' (This reveals *games* that the patient is likely to play with the therapist and group.)[4]

Additionally, I ask, 'If I had a magic wand to wave, what would you want me to do?'. (From his answer to this I am able to clarify what is and what is not possible.)

Transactional and game analysis

Transactional analysis proper concerns tne analysis of the social interactions between people in their various *ego states*, including *contaminations* and *exclusions*. Some useful *transactional analysis* can be done in individual sessions with anecdotal material from the patient providing the substance analysed. However, *transactional analysis* within a group setting is usually a great deal more productive, the group *transactions* themselves providing much more reliable and easily validated material than second-hand accounts from one person to another. *Transactional analysis* proper, irrespective of it being related or not to each individual's *script decisions*, enables people very rapidly, in the course of even a few sessions, greatly to increase their social control.

Game analysis is a specialized form of *transactional* analysis in which the vested interests of each of the players in their *payoffs* are examined as well as the *transactions* themselves. This is the level of therapy where resistance of the *not OK* Child to change is first encountered, and the therapist needs to be skillful in offering the patient alternative *stroke* sources through new behaviours in order to enable him willingly to give up his *games*. Jack Dusay enumerates four possible ways in which a therapist may respond to *game-playing* that he observes.[5]

(1) Expose the game.

(2) Ignore the game.
(3) Offer an alternative.
(4) Play the game.

Therapists may effectively choose all of these options on different occasions. The therapist's choice on any particular occasion will depend on a summation of his Adult's and Little Professor's opinions as to the most productive way to treat the patient in the context of the present moment as well as taking into account the patient's overall readiness to accept any or all of the options offered.

Rackets and trading *stamp collections* are also dealt with at this stage of therapy. In dealing with them the therapist has on his side the fact that, for most people, some parts of their *rackety* behaviours are based on needless habit as well as some parts still serving a dynamic—that is, *scripty*—need. Once aware of their *rackets* many people can gain very rapidly a feeling of enhanced *OKness* by dropping a large proportion of their *rackety* responses by a simple Adult *decision* to do so. I often liken *rackety* behaviour to cigarette smoking (although the feeling of 'need' for a cigarette is more like a Driver). Most smokers, no matter how addicted, agree that by the simple act of being self-conscious about the cigarettes they smoke they can, without any 'willpower', significantly reduce their consumption. The comparative easy accessibility of *rackets* to treatment is probably due to the necessary verbal component in the transmission of them (see Chapter 4) compared with other *injunctions* which *may* be wholly non-verbal and therefore require new and harder-to-achieve articulation.

Script analysis

Actually changing *script decisions* is very radical surgery of the soul and, should only be attempted when all other treatment is insufficient to achieve a satisfactory sense of wellbeing for the patient in his life. Almost always it is possible for patient and therapist alike to gain a great deal of gratification from knocking their Little Professors together and deriving ways of literally obeying *script decisions* whilst cunningly serving only the spirit of the Free Child. Rabbis and priests have always been particularly skillful in resolving life's agonizing dilemmas along these lines, as is evidenced in the happy outcome of the rabbi's ruminations in Jack Rosenthal's television play 'The Barmitzvah Boy'. I knew a recidivist thief with a love of fishing who found a socially acceptable adaptation to his *script* in becoming a river policeman; and a woman with a *counterscript* to be clever and a *script* which called on her to 'get encyclopaedic facts right or be humiliated' immensely enjoyed her job as a Latin teacher. There can be no argument about the ending of the third person singular future subjunctive of *cogitare*. Such also are the nature of the choices made by the Little Professor in the first place in constructing the *protocol* and later the *palimpsest*, and the difference between life's 'winners' and 'losers' is largely a matter of how socially adaptive the Little Professor's choices originally were. Berne exemplified this in his story of the two brothers who, as children, were always threatened with 'ending up in the mental hospital'. They both did—one as a chronic schizophrenic, the other as the chief psychiatrist.[6]

Patients in the process of overthrowing *injunctions* or *script decisions* will inevitably experience periods of stagnant despair and wonder if, after all, therapy has done them more harm than good. At this stage, elucidation of the nature of 'learning curves' and the unobservable but important assimilation that takes place on 'plateaus' may be some reassurance. Remind them that it is as dark at 2 a.m. as just before dawn.

Styles of TA Therapy

Styles of TA therapy are as multifarious as the number of TA therapists. Style is the total manifestation of the structures and functions of the therapist's Parent, Adult, and Child. However, despite the fact that TA therapists exhibit enormously various overall styles, there are three specific functions of personality which all TA therapists are required to exercise. They are called 'the three P's of the TA therapist' —*potency, permission*, and *protection*. *Permission* and *protection* were first described by Pat Crossman, for which she won the 1976 Eric Berne Memorial Scientific Award.[7]

Potency refers to the capacity of the therapist, through means generalized as principles in his Parent, to cure the patient. Within limits, it also refers to his power to attract and keep in the 'winning' therapy of TA people whose *scripts* would otherwise lead them to therapies and therapists who simply help them keep their heads above water while giving them the *delusion*—usually over many years—that they are 'making progress'.

Permission, according to Pat Crossman, refers to the licence given by the therapist's Parent to the patient, when the patient is ready, to disobey an *injunction* and choose instead to behave *autonomously*. Whilst I agree with Pat Crossman as to the nature of *permission* in the patient, I do not agree that it is transmitted from the therapist's Parent, but rather from his Child. For me, *permissions*, like *injunctions*, are given by essentially non-verbal, covert *transactions* from Child to Child (see also Chapter 4) and, in so far as the giving of new *permissions* is one of the most vital tasks of therapy, the characteristics of the therapist's own Free Child will crucially determine his effectiveness with particular patients. Unless the therapist has more *permissions* than his patients in the areas in which he is treating them he is bound to fail. No matter how much Parent and Adult counsel and 'permission' he may offer, it will not work unless his Free Child also gives its sanction. This was brought home to me very pointedly recently concerning one of my patients, a young woman of twenty-seven who was nearing completion in the group of 'unfinished business' with her father. Due to the postponement until her twenties of that adolescent rebellion which she needed to experience in order to achieve full maturity she was still a virgin at twenty-seven and beginning to be obsessed with the fact. I sensed that a tendency to Be Perfect with respect to sex and love was holding her back so I, and other members of her group, gave her good Parent advice and Adult counsel over a period of weeks, telling her it was quite OK to choose a man in a fairly arbitrary way and simply get losing her virginity 'over with'. It did not work, and she quite rightly accused me of not really helping her. That is, my own Child inhibitions about casual sex shone through all the Parent and Adult blarney — and this was the most powerful *message* I was actually giving her.

Conversely, when I gave up smoking in my groups, there was a very significant diminution of smoking amongst my patients — without any admonitions or pleas whatsoever on my part.

From such evidence it is clear that patients get better in accordance, above all, with the *permissions* in their therapists. So, generally, the more *permissions* a therapist has the better therapist he is. And this also makes clear the legitimacy of patients 'shopping around' for the right therapist for them, and for therapists having the appropriate modesty and goodwill towards a prospective patient to refer him elsewhere if their own *permissions* do not match his needs.

Protection from the therapist's Parent for the patient's Child is required at certain stages in therapy when the patient's Child feels particularly vulnerable. Such occasions most often arise when the patient has just recently, for the first time, disobeyed some important *injunction* or *script decision*. At such times the patient is likely to feel a combination of *despair* (at being unable to conceive of *alternative stroke* source) and anxiety for the anticipated wrath of his Witch or Ogre for his disobedience to them. When *protecting* a patient in such a crisis the therapist needs to demonstrate a potency in his Parent capable of overpowering the patient's Witch or Ogre. Appropriate *protection*, includes being readily available on the telephone between group sessions to anybody in one of my groups who feels the need for some brief reassurance when in a state of existential crisis.

Schools of TA Therapy

As well as in style, TA therapists differ from each other specifically and definably in their (Parent) views of the nature of the *therapeutic process*. In the last few years three quite distinct 'schools' of TA therapy have emerged. Yet the therapists of each school remain TA therapists and share with all other TA therapists the TA theory of personality and the basic principles of therapy expounded in this chapter so far. Graham Barnes[8] suggests that the different schools share the same *psychology* but espouse different *sociologies*. My own view — somewhat more cynical, perhaps — is that each therapist, in fact, chooses a modality that most appeals to his Free Child, which he then rationalizes with his Adult and justifies with his Parent.

TA/Gestalt

Probably the most popular school of TA therapy is that which joins forces with Gestalt therapy (based on the work of Fritz Perls). Bob and Mary Goulding are the best known exponents of this school, and between them have trained hundreds of TA therapists. In TA/Gestalt therapy individual patients, within a group, get in touch with the content of *impasses* between their Parents and their Childs and, especially, between their Adapted Childs and Free Childs. The confrontation of the *ego states* is accomplished by precipitating the warring *ego states* into vociferous battle with each other. The resolution of this battle provides an enormous catharsis of affect for the patient and, consequent on this catharsis, his Little Professor and Adult are called upon to choose new *permissions* and make new *decisions*. Gestalt therapy is particularly appealing to many TA therapists because it shares a core assumption with TA that the personality consists of discrete parts, inconsistencies between which parts are the prime cause of people's suffering. Reconciling the parts into a harmonious whole is the overall aim of both therapies. The 'top dog' Gestalt concept is sometimes the Parent and sometimes the Adapted Child; the 'underdog' Gestalt concept is sometimes the Adapted Child and sometimes the Free Child.[9]

Bob and Mary Goulding have differentiated ten basic *injunctions*: Don't be; don't be you (the sex you are); don't be a child; don't grow; don't make it; don't; don't be important; don't be close; don't belong; don't be well (or sane). Subsidiarily, they have distinguished, 'Don't think about X'; 'Don't think what you think but what I think'; 'Don't feel X'; 'Don't feel what you feel but what I feel'. For their work on *redecisions* and *injunctions* Bob and Mary Goulding won the Eric Berne Memorial Scientific Award for 1975.[10] By contrast with Eric Berne's original emphasis on the inter-personal, the TA/Gestalt approach stresses, almost exclusively, the *intra-psychic structural (content) problems*.

Confrontation

By contrast with the TA/Gestalt school, which emphasizes Parent and Child expressiveness, the approach of Jacqui Schiff and her followers emphasizes Adult confrontation of *discounting* and *passivity*. A *discount* is a kind of *negative stroke*. It is defined as the functional manifestation of either a *contamination* or an *exclusion*. Stimuli, problems, and options may each be *discounted* by means of denying their existence, their significance, the possibility of change, and of one's own or the other person's abilities. *Passivity* represents a person's attempts to maintain a symbiotic personality structure because of unresolved issues left over from childhood relationships. The four *passive behaviours* are 'doing nothing', 'over-adaptation', 'agitation', and 'incapacitation or violence'. Jacqui Schiff insistently confronts these behaviours with more energy than the patient can muster in their defence.

Jacqui and Aaron Schiff won the 1974 Eric Berne Memorial Scientific Award for their work on *passivity*.[11] Jacqui Schiff has also written an account, in narrative form, of her and her husband's living experience of taking schizophrenic patients into their home. It is published as a book, *All My Children*, by Jacqui and Lee Schiff (with Beth Day), Pyramid, 1972, and it is for this remarkable work that Jacqui Schiff is best known. In treatment programmes lasting up to two years patients are regressed to early infancy and *re-Parented* by progressive nurturing through all the normal stages of child development to healthy maturity.[12] This school of TA therapy retains Eric Berne's emphasis on the *inter-personal* but also stresses *functional intra-psychic problems*. Jacqui Schiff insists on the theoretical (as well as practical) necessity of inflicting *negative strokes*. She argues that in as much as many schizophrenic patients received only *negative strokes* from the significant people in their childhoods, they can — at the beginning of therapy, anyway — only perceive a therapist as significant to them if he or she gives them *negative* as well as *positive strokes*.

Interaction

The third school of TA therapy is the modality within which Berne himself worked, that is, that which emphasizes *transactions* within the group in the here-and-now. The group itself is taken to be a microcosm of the world at large, and the individual's *transactions* within the group are taken to be a match for his *transactions* outside it. The emphasis in this modality is in bringing *ego states, rackets, games*, and *scripts* out into the open in a 'life-like' environment which is yet uniquely enabling of change through the totally non-critical, purely analytical orientation of the process. Claude Steiner, Muriel James, and Jack Dusay, who were all close colleagues of Eric Berne, are very well-known practitioners of this school. It is the style of therapy that I practise also.

Eric Berne, in his lifetime, resisted all pressures to allow sociological issues to have any bearing on his theory or therapy, disdaining such as 'cop-outs' from individual responsibility or (at best) irrelevant. He derisively referred to sociological justifications as a kind of *game*, which he called Arse-Society. Claude Steiner is notable in radically rejecting Berne's judgement in this, and he has broken away from the mainstream of 'classical' TA therapy to form his own 'Radical' approach. He insists that present-day (American) society *is* oppressive, and he exhorts therapists actually to *do* something about it, including in their work with patients.

The Asklepieion Foundation, on the other hand, though equally 'sociologically' oriented, holds a contrary view to Claude Steiner's, in as much as it specifically trains the prison population better to adapt to society's norms.

Summary

TA therapy evolved out of Berne's dissatisfaction with the *slowness* of psychoanalysis to effect cures. In TA therapy patients have *concrete goals* and the therapist helps patients to achieve these as quickly as possible. TA is not suited to the treatment of hysteria. In general terms, a person is defined as healthy when he is *autonomous, spontaneous*, and *authentic*.

TA therapy is unique in its *language*, which is singularly precise and concise, without sacrificing profundity of meaning. All patients in TA therapy are required to accept the basic assumption that Parent, Adult, and Child *ego states* exist. TA is also unique in its use of *'hard' contracts* for change, and in holding the individual responsible for his *script decisions*, and in using the *whole personality* of both the therapist and the patient.

After an initial individual session, in which a script matrix is drawn up and a *contract* made, a person usually joins an ongoing therapy group. Group therapy consists of *structural, transactional, game, racket,* and *script analysis.* The therapist's and patients' Little Professors add creativity to *script* work, enabling the *script* to be obeyed to the letter whilst actually serving the interests of the Free Child.

TA therapists vary enormously in their personal styles but all fulfil the *roles* of providing *potency* over the patient's Witch and Ogre, *protection* for the patient in existential crisis, and in giving the patient new *permissions.*

Three are different 'schools' of TA therapy, each of which expresses its own (Parent) view of *the nature of the therapeutic process.* These schools include *TA/Gestalt* therapy, best known through the work of Bob and Mary Goulding, *confrontation* therapy, best known through the work of the Schiff family, and *interaction* therapy, which was the style used by Eric Berne and is currently used by — amongst others — Claude Steiner, Muriel James, Jack Dusay, and the present writer. Claude Steiner and the Asklepieion Foundation represent sub-groups of the interaction school, and both emphasize sociological as well as psychological issues.

Notes and References

1. E. Berne, *Transactional Analysis in Psychotherapy*, Grove Press, 1961.
2. See the *Transactional Analysis Journal*, **5**, no. 3, July 1975, which features a special section on objective research into the validity of TA concepts and the effectiveness of TA therapy. See also J. Schiff (with Beth Day), *All My Children*, Pyramid, 1972, for an account of some of TA's successes with 'incurable' schizophrenics, which features a special section on objective research into the validity of TA concepts and the effectiveness of TA therapy.
3. S. Samuels, 'Games Therapists Play', *Transactional Analysis Journal*, **1**, no. 1, January 1971.
4. M. James and contributors, *Techniques in Transactional Analysis*, Addison Wesley, 1977, pp. 106–107.
5. J. Dusay, 'Response', *Transactional Analysis Bulletin*, April, 1966.
6. E. Berne, *What do you say after you say hello?* Bantam, 1973.
7. P. Crossman, 'Permission and protection', *Transactional Analysis Bulletin*, July, 1966.
8. In a paper delivered at the Fourth European TA Conference in Helsinor, Denmark, July, 1978. See also G. Barnes (Ed.) *TA After Eric Berne*, Harpers College Press, New York, 1977.
9. See F. Perls, *Gestalt Therapy Verbatim*, Bantam, 1972, for a good explication of how Gestalt therapy works.
10. An article by Bob and Mary Goulding elaborating on their work can be found in the *Transactional Analysis Journal*, **6**, no. 1, January 1976.
11. Their work on *passivity* is reported in the *Transactional Analysis Journal*, **1**, no. 1, January, 1971. An extended account of the Schiff's elaboration of TA theory can be found in *The Cathexis Reader*, by Jacqui Schiff and Cathexis Staff, Harper & Row, 1975.
12. See also 'Reparented schizophrenics', *Transactional Analysis Bulletin*, July, 1969.

CHAPTER 11

Individual Case Histories

The Limitation of 'Case Histories'

Case histories are the accumulated record, made by the therapist, of the changes which take place in patients during therapy. An individual's notes are freely available at all times to the people concerned. But these notes inevitably can only refer to what is *observable*. A great deal may be 'happening' in a silent person's mind, and such 'happenings' are very often as valuable a form of 'work' or 'progress' as that which is revealed in overt *transactions*.

Efficiency in Therapy

Although, ultimately, our primary need for *strokes* can only be fulfilled through *transacting* with others, there are periods in each person's experience of group therapy when he or she *needs* to be silent — sometimes to 'take' in order later to be able to 'give' and, very commonly, to assimilate the meaning of accumulated active experience. The traditional psychoanalytic approach insistently makes the patient wholly responsible for his own silence or talkativeness. While TA recognizes that rescuing people from silence very often denies them the *reflexive* insights their discomfort will eventually lead them to, TA therapists are often willing to compromise these gains in the interests of the *pragmatic goals* of their *contracts*. The pursuit of an optimum mixture of gratuitous giving and insistent demanding on the part of the therapist is the quest for maximum *efficiency* in therapy. For each patient, at every stage of therapy, this quest calls on the therapist to be alert to the over-changing balance of giving and demanding which is most appropriate to any moment.

   The notes that follow are significant extracts from the total therapeutic histories of four patients in one of my therapy groups. At the time of writing, two had been in the group for between two and three years, one for a little over a year, and one for eight months. Each set of notes begins with the very first group session attended and concludes with the session of 26 July 1978. Chapter 12 will be concluded with a transcript of the group session of 2 August 1978, at which

130

were present the four people whose histories are detailed in this chapter. It seems appropriate to preface what follows about others with a relevant note about myself as therapist.

The Author

For me, being a TA therapist is an enormously gratifying *script* fulfilment. In the midst of all the psychological suffering that surrounded me in my childhood, I decided that 'When I grow up and *understand* all this I will make them (Mother and Father) happy'. I have not made them happy, but I've stopped Trying Hard to, and I now earn my living helping lots of other people who give me the *permission* I need to promote their happiness.

For a time, as a child, while I still felt impotent in my lack of understanding, I made a *palimpsest decision* to escape from it all to the ultimate distance it was possible to go. Between the ages of about eight and eighteen my answer to the question, 'What are you going to be when you grow up?' was 'A famous astronomer'. But I failed A-level Physics, so my original *protocol decision* won, although it was not until about ten years later that I realized the meaning of that burning childhood ambition to be an astronomer. Only in the last few months, since I have become aware of people I do not know having 'heard of me' have I also remembered the 'famous' part of that *palimpsest decision*. That, I now believe, was a consolation prize I awarded myself in my *script* for the rejection I felt as a child. In fact, it is my hunch that all those people who seek fame have the same aim in mind — to 'prove' their love-worthiness to their parents. Is that why I have written this book? If so, I thank them.

My *permission* to love words biases me towards a strictly verbal therapy. My *script decision* to enjoy life (rather than be miserable) biases me towards valuing laughter both as 'the best medicine' and as the chief manifestation of curative insight. (As a TA therapist I must, of course, distinguish between laughter which represents the triumph of the human spirit over despair and *gallows laughter*, which represents the triumph of the Witch or Ogre in the Adapted Child. Although this distinction may seem, in the abstract, a fine one, in practice it is usually very easy to make.) My rationalization (Adult/Child *contamination*) of my preference for words (over non-verbal therapy) is that the words (of our *script decisions*) were our undoing in the first place, so it is words which will mend us. My argument in favour of laughter (rather than tears) as the best catharsis is that, though both are uniquely human manifestations of that nether state between Adult and Child where truths are really known, given the choice, laughter is much more fun.

Within the context of the group experience, I project myself more as sister than Mother (or Father). My own younger and only sister tells me she experienced our childhood in a quite different way to me. Though we each longed for 'togetherness' with the other, our innate differences, which were reflected in the differences in our *scripts* and associated differences in our behaviour patterns, seem to have made it inevitable that we were a disappointment to each other. Out of this, and out of the fact of having no brothers, I project onto my groups my quest for an escape from the constant suffering of Mother's and Father's realities into the comforting, empathic company of brothers and sisters, who all share in each others sadness and joys.

Martin

Martin is a twenty-eight-year-old man, the only son in a family of five children. He is unmarried and at present is a semi-self-employed carpenter. The chief burden of his *script* is a huge Try Hard 'inherited' from his father, who has been an explicitly unhappy employee for most of his life, but now ekes out a living as a self-employed farmer. Martin's chief manifest problem is that, for him 'work' and 'pleasure' are incompatible. In relation to the group, Martin exhibits Hurry Up behaviour.

27/8/75 Contract: To dialogue between his Adult and Parent in order to reconstitute his Parent in the interest of being able to make judgements about people and situations.

He talked of the *guilt* invoked in him by transactions with his mother, and awareness of the *rackety* nature of this response. He referred to the repeated message he receives from her, 'Remember you can always come back home if you fail in London'. I pointed out the ambiguity to the Little Boy in this statement and the probable resultant conflict he felt — that is, *not daring to succeed, lest he be unwelcome at home.*

3/12/75 He asked to check up on his *contract*, which revealed we had done little work on it. His Adult–Child collaboration continues very strong, Parent–Child OK, Adult–Parent virtually non-existent. He seemed unconvinced of any need for a Parent in his life, seemingly having dissociated his Adult and Child from a very heavily *prejudiced* Parent a couple of years ago, still insisting on *discounting* the baby he has thrown out with the bathwater. Homework: to list Parent characteristics.

23/12/75 Some work leading to recognition that his choice of girlfriends so far has been either of two extremes: (1) clinging vines or (2) those who reject him as 'too demanding'. Present girlfriend is type-1. *Script-freeness* would be choosing a girlfriend who was neither (1) nor (2). The problem, he agrees, is to know on what *other* basis to choose a girl if *not* in *script*.

25/2/76 Read us his fairy-story he had written — beautiful in its capacity vividly to evoke the nature of *not-OKness* and the *OKness* of TA, through the metaphor of various thicknesses of blankets of fog. Pursuing the Don't Belong theme of last week, he revealed an occasion when his mother was very angry with him as a teenager when he 'knew more than her' in precisely naming a particular kind of rat, which she insisted was just a rat. Thus he seems to have concluded '*I can either have superior knowledge or belong*'. I gave him explicit *permission* to demonstrate superior wisdom/knowledge to me in the group *and* belong *and*, moreover, get extra *strokes* from me for the intellectual stimulation he would provide me with.

25/5/76 He revealed that he '*never really gets angry*'. This was presented as *OK*, but exploration revealed that he uses 'super-reasonableness' to defend against anger (which he doesn't express) *to defend against a more primitive fear*, which derives from a remembered incident when he was very young of being petrified by his father, who insistently held him in water, despite his terrified protestations. He also revealed a very *OK* lusty, open sexuality in all his family, which seems to include a total lack of inhibition — in talk at least — between Mother and Father, parents and children, and brothers and sisters.

1/8/76 Contract for session: to discover his vested interest in having a girlfriend who 'clings' to him. Some very good work in which he was glad to be 'pinned down' to discovering that 'taking the plunge' towards fearless independence implies drowning himself or someone else drowning. The *payoff* for his girlfriend's 'clinging' is the vicarious excitement/satisfaction of having his own fear exhibited by someone else while he can 'coolly' keep his own anger covered and covering his own fear.

1/9/76 More water metaphors emerged. Father keeps his head above water, Martin is held under.

10/11/76 No explicit work but, in response to Francine's wanting to leave the group, he offered her his own experience in the group of overcoming a big Don't Belong by continuing to come to the group even when he went through prolonged periods of not wanting to. He gave a very clear and convincing account of the qualitative change that takes place when people stop 'wondering' if they are part of the group and just *know* the existence of the group as all around them and themselves an integral part of it.

8/6/77 Said he related my 'dormouse' description of him to his 'bull' image of himself. It is as if he is being a dormouse until the time is ripe for the expression of the great (constructive) bull power and strength in him. He sees his residual *not OKness* as fearing jumping in the deep end, but he feels he holds this fear very much in check by swimming slowly towards the deep end from the shallow end.

4/1/78 In response to Richard's work about his 'stuckness' at the age of fourteen, Martin told us about his response to his mother's having given birth to a stillborn son when he was fourteen. Consequent on this he felt obliged, by his father, to take on the burden of 'carrying on the family name' and also being immensely *angry* with his mother for not having given him a brother. In toto, this experience gave to his script the dimension *angry frustration-resigned disappointment*. The partnership of feelings around this (between him and his parents) was somebody stubbornly frustrating the other, the other being disappointed. Thus he is actually not far from his girlfriend in her position of 'It's your fault or my fault, but I'm not sure which'.

11/1/78 He identified his Child as being a nine or ten-year-old, and thus recognized that this is what we often misconstrue as Adult. However, he also became aware of an angry two-year-old in himself, remembering being ducked in a swimming pool by his father. He said the *anger* he experienced tonight was a direct remembrance (rather than the nine- to ten-year-old recollection he has expressed to us previously?).

8/2/78 He expressed the feeling that after two years of duping me and the others, he was only now *'just beginning to get down to work in the group'*. There was certainly evidence of a change in his softer tone of voice. We began to explore his overwhelming *scare of jumping in the deep end* in all the things he would enjoy doing in life, and also his conviction *'No one would listen to my thoughts and feelings if I did tell them'*, which to some extent accounts for his having held back for so long in the group from *authentic* expression of his Child.

15/2/78 Towards the end of the session, he expressed two Little Professor perceptions he had: (1) that there was a special attraction between Francine (another member of the group) and Richard and (2) that I was being 'duped' by Richard's 'charisma'. I asked him to check out the validity of these perceptions. (1) proved true, (2) false. But much more important than the content of these fantasies was the fact that he *dared to utter them and check them out*. He now wants a *New Contract: to express and check out the validity of his fantasies*. Until now, it is clear, he has cherished his Little Professor insights and given himself *strokes* when they proved valid, but has basically so much feared being 'wrong' that he has denied himself many *strokes* from others as well as many more opportunities to *'guess' and be sometimes right and sometimes wrong*. (Is this a displacement of the fear of jumping in the deep end and drowning?)

8/3/78 We pursued the meaning of our discovery (last session) that his greatest fear seems to be of *not* being *discounted* by others. I arrived at the tentative conclusion that *being discounted is the price Martin feels he has to pay for maintaining a relationship to others*. Thus, the *script* position is something like, 'I want to be related to others. If I express my insights and they are hurtful to others, they will leave me. If my insights are acceptable and true they will accept me so overwhelmingly that I will feel *suffocated* and I will have to reject them — and be left alone'. The protection against this whole process is to maintain a 'just right' distance from others by *fantasizing his superiority to others* (Vengeful Child of Try Hard) but keeping *silent* about these fantasies. It is thus important in future for me to confront Martin's silences and check out the thoughts and feelings he is having.

15/3/78 We assessed the work of the last few weeks in order to formulate a *New Contract: to (dare to) express his thoughts and feelings in the here-and-now of the group to differentiate reality and fantasy. To (dare to) drop Vengeful Child of Try Hard outside the group, manifest as daring to succeed in his work and daring to mix with 'winners' socially.*

24/5/78 He revealed a crucial occurrence in his life. When he was four he was hospitalized for an eye operation. The girl in the bed next to him got a model house as a present (from her parents), 'just for being', Martin got nothing (from his parents). Conclusions: 'I am unloved'. 'Girls can just be, boys have to do.' Exploration of the implications of this experience revealed that Martin's *curse* is *living life inexpediently* and *without much pleasure*. His *script antithesis* is to make *his parents recognize and love him through making lots of money and then vengefully breaking Father's curse by living life expediently ('eccentrically') and with pleasure.*

14/6/78 We identified a communality between Martin and Sally (new to the group tonight) in their use of Try Hard. Each of them witholds expression of their intuitive hunches until somebody else expresses the same idea, then they say — aloud or to themselves — 'I knew that all along'. (I.e. 'I am superior'.) In confirmation of this, Sally revealed that she had felt relatedness to Martin as soon as she came into the room.

26/7/78 In group talk about everybody's physical symbols of their psychological stresses, Martin preferred his as 'chest pains', the significance of which he immediately *discounted* (that is, self-diagnosed as 'just tension', which he rids himself of with running). I insisted that the 'natural' reaction to such symptoms would be *fear*, which he again *discounted*. However, later probing enabled him to admit to experiencing a *chronic state of non-specific fear* and his *chief longing being to 'overcome loneliness'*. He then admitted that he *had* been defensively 'bullshitting' earlier, but also expressed his feeling of immense difficulty in offering himself intimately to the group.

Keith

Keith is a twenty-four-year-old man, and an only child. He is engaged to be married, and is currently a post-graduate research student in Philosophy. His chief *script* burden is his only-childness, which makes Child to Child *transactions* very difficult for him and is behaviourally associated with Please Me. He also feels alienated from his parents' working-classness, but hostile to many middle-class values. This is manifest in his studies as Try Hard.

29/10/75 Contract: to drop Please Me and become 'real'.

26/11/75 At the end of the session I pointed out that he had said very little since he had joined the group, in accordance with his Witch and Ogre messages to stay in the background. He told us that at the dinner table in his house *nobody talked*. Since he is an only child, I asked him to pick someone in the group whom he would particularly like for a brother or sister. He chose Maggie (at the time of writing no longer a member of the group), who immediately expressed reciprocal feelings of wanting to hug and Rescue him. I asked her to be his sister in the group, and asked Keith to let us know, when he was ready, how we could best help him to get out of his *scripty* position of silence in the group.

14/1/76 Read out the fairy-story of his life so far, very much appreciated and *stroked* by the group. The little boy was a *Prince* who escaped from the Queen (having won hands down over the King in winning the Queen, but then was asked to pay the price of never leaving her), by going incognito as a *troll*. This not being satisfactory either he *wanted to become 'ordinary'* and went to the Fairy Godmother (who told him how to do this). (But the Fairy Godmother cannot do this yet because she did not get from the story what it really means to be either a Prince or a troll.) *Homework: to list characteristics of princes and trolls and 'ordinary people'.*

18/2/76 Reported that his experience in the group so far has achieved for him two out of three of Steiner's criteria of *OKness*: awareness and creativity as reflected in his university work and his internal feelings of *OKness*. Says he has not yet achieved the third criterion, that is the capacity *to give and receive strokes by transacting with others*. I felt reassured by this statement from Keith in the light of his almost total silence in the group so far. When I asked, he said the essential element in the group which had enabled him to achieve what he had done so far was that it was a 'reality trip'. I take this to be as *OK* a *stroke* as I could receive from any member of my groups.

10/3/76 Expressed difficulty in cathecting readily into Child to Child in casual encounters with people.

5/5/76 He opened the session by reporting his success in his relationship with Anne (his girlfriend) in *coming out of his Withdrawal*. Even though there are plenty of unresolved problems in the relationship, he now realizes that he does not *have* to respond to *not-OK transactions* from Anne (or others). His reward from Anne has been a lot more Adult from her. He sees his relationship with her as preventing him from getting back into *being a hermit* — a response to his *fear of the world-at-large*, but which leaves him desperately *stroke-deprived*. I pointed out that, as well as in *intimate* relationships, he could also get *strokes* from *rituals* and *pastimes*. He says that this is what he most wants to learn to do. I pointed out his increasing *OKness* in this respect as manifest in his initiation and continuing participation in *transactions* in the group.

25/5/76 Maggie opened the session by referring to her discomfort that Keith talks so little in the group. This led to some very productive work with Keith, which revealed that — deriving from his early experiences at school compared to his only-childness at home — (1) '*Transactions* with others means *competition* for what I want'; (2) 'I am entitled to what I want without competition'; (3) 'All other people are competitive and thus *not-OK* shits'. Thus '*competition*' is the single frame of reference Keith has for peer-group *transactions*. But we pointed out the many other percepts involved in Child-to-Child *transactions*, such as fun, fighting, sharing, antagonisms, jealousy, etc., and that though a lot of these feelings are bad at the time they are very valuable in providing us with reality information that other people's moods are not always due to what *we* have done (which only children presume because of the singularity of their relationship to their parents). Keith agreed that this self-centred feeling of being wholly responsible for others' moods was a self-conscious problem for him. He agreed to check out such fantasies in the safety of the group and also to allow me to facilitate his interactions with the group by asking him (if he has not spoken during a session) to give the group a *stroke* for what he has received, at least once at the end of the session.

24/6/76 He asked to check his *contract* and said he feels he has completed it and would like to make a new *contract* next week.

7/7/76 Reported that he has achieved some *OK transactions* outside the group, for which we all *stroked* him. Says he has not yet thought of a new *contract* for himself, but will make one next week.

11/8/76 New Contract: to drop Try Hard and Make It (get his degree).

12/1/77 Some very good work through which was revealed:

(1) He has essentially gained control over *injunctions* which, in the past, prevented him from interacting with others. But he is left with a practical inability (through sparsity of Adult *messages*) to *pastime* easily.
(2) He *contaminates* Adult statements with Child feelings, manifest in his over-quiet voice. That is, he 'can't get away from himself'.
(3) He is aware of his *self-image being of 'a failure'*, whereas the facts (of his academic record) speak clear-cut success.
(4) He gets by in most of his work with his Little Professor, but finds great difficulty in translating these thoughts/feelings into Adult.

23/3/77 Group reference to my suggestion (last week after Keith had needed to leave early) that members of the group expressed (silent) hostility to Keith's lack of inter-activeness in the group, led to analysis of Keith's self-perception as well as others' projections on to him. What was particularly revealed was his only-child's position of *having to incorporate all that both his parents gave out* (not being able to share them out with siblings) being lived out in the group, where he is treated as the blank wall against which everybody else's self-images are projected. However, group members observed a much increased inter-activeness by Keith lately, and I suggested he was beginning *to feel like a brother for the first time.* Keith agreed.

24/8/77 *He has shaved off his beard*, which greatly increases the expressiveness of his face. Said he had been planning to do so for some time, but only now felt ready. He has got a grant for next year, so will be doing his M.Phil. at University College. He is presently looking for a flat for him and Anne to live in London.

26/10/77 He announced that he and Anne became officially engaged about three weeks ago. Later on in the session he expressed empathy with Colin in his difficulties (as Keith perceived them) in differentiating between *what is the case about another person and what is projection of his own feelings of the moment.* I pointed out that this difficulty consisted of two separate issues:

(1) *What does the other person feel?* — easy to find out, by asking him.
(2) *What is 'the case'?* — *about the other person's behaviour.* More difficult, requiring Adult consensual validation (with the person in question's Adult being the final arbiter).

7/12/77 Apropos Alan's complaint that there were not enough feeling *transactions* in the group, I asked Keith if his Parent ever nudged him to talk more and if he felt comfortable being as silent as he usually is. He answered, 'Yes and no respectively', but claimed that he had withdrawn in the last few weeks consequent on having talked about himself and having felt that no response was forthcoming from others in the group. I suggested that he is probably including *some covert transactions which block others from responding.*

11/1/77 He identified his Child as about eleven and thus enabled us to understand that what we often perceive as strong Adult in him is actually a *latency Child.* I asked him if he identified with the eleven-year-old in Hilary. He said no, but he identified Hilary with his girlfriend, Anne, so supposed that he and Anne have Childs of the same age.

25/1/78 He opened the session by announcing that he was thinking of leaving the group. Exploration revealed that this impulse arises out of a feeling of 'waiting indefinitely for himself to gain permissions from the group to 'relate' to it' — that is, to be able to give and take *positive strokes* of a superficial kind. He is now beginning to feel that this may not be a possibility from this group. Most notably he is dissatisfied with this lack of *permission* in himself because

(1) he is still feels largely in a Parent/Child *contamination* felt as *confusion* and
(2) he *wants to relate to people in superficial as well as intense ways.* (For example he finds it difficult even to smile readily at people.)
(3) He *wants to have fun.*

Many hypotheses sprang to my mind and Keith agreed that we would explore the possible meanings of his impulse to leave the group in the month that he has given himself to make up his mind.

(1) Was the announcement that he wanted to leave a *way* of beginning to give and take *strokes* to and from me and others in the group?
(2) Is he waiting yearningly for 'relatedness to happen', analogously to the way he must have waited for brothers and sisters to 'happen'?
(3) Was tonight an expression of a new-found energy source which he wants to use to relate to others with? This might very well be the case, now that he has achieved, by the group, '*permission* to be himself', including being comfortable being silent.
(4) Is there some reality in his not being able to get what he wants from the group? For example, are there too many chronically depressed people in the group to provide the external energy source he needs to initiate his relatedness to others?

He took his notes to read this week, with a view perhaps to finding some answers.

1/2/78 I read him my notes of last week, and we continued where we left off. Keith confronted me with having, in a sense, 'neglected' him in the last few months, and suggested I was being 'anti-Rescuer' to him, which I agreed was probably at least partially true. However, in exploring all the possible explanations for his feelings in the group, he *increasingly acted out the antithesis of his negative feelings* — that is, his face was *transformed by mobility* and a continuous *dialogue* was occurring between him and me and the others. He confirmed that he felt he was getting very much from tonight. All this led me to hypothesize that, above all else, the *process began last week* was of paramount importance and that most of the content was essentially redundant. Thus I suggested that what it probably all amounted to was that his experience in the group so far may be summarized as:

Stage I Learning a great deal and notably *gaining permission to be himself.*
Stage II Felt like he was '*getting nowhere*'.
Stage III Begun last week. *Learning to relate to others.*

22/2/78 He reported perceiving himself to set himself up to be '*misunderstood*' and '*discounted*', just as he did in childhood towards his mother. In childhood he made the (rational) *decision* that the *only free space was in his mind, therefore it is best to withdraw* from all expression of the contents of his mind, since expression would inevitably be *discounted*. But, of course, it is impossible to go through life without *transacting*. I invited Keith to do two things: (1) dare to *transact* in the group and (2) be aware that, inevitably, he will *transact*, in the first place in such a way as to invite *discounts*, therefore, knowing this, whenever he feels *discounted* to *say so* there and then so we can pinpoint the *behavioural elements* which are keeping his script going. He accepted these invitations.

1/3/78 He identified with Martin in Martin's description of his parents, and exploration revealed an identical *script* position in Keith as in Martin; a Parent belief that if he expresses himself he will be *trampled on* and a *decision* therefore not to risk this, but to *withdraw* instead. Although manifest behaviour in the two of them is dissimilar, Martin is just Keith plus a façade of talk.

22/3/78 I expressed my awareness (which came after last week's session) that Keith and Alan had in common that they '*never know how to tell what is going on in other people's minds*'. Examination of the meaning of this complaint led to an understanding that what they both mean is that they rarely (if ever) openly project on to other people *because they cannot clearly articulate their own feelings to themselves* (Please Me). Thus, I insisted, the only possibility for *anybody* confidently to infer what is going on in anybody else's head is being knowing (Adult) about the contents of the other's *script*. However, it is true that *some of the time* our projections of our own feelings on to others *do* fit them, and it is this pleasure that Keith (and Alan) presently deprive themselves of.

12/4/78 The group as a whole was pleasantly *pastiming* for about the first half of the session, during which time Keith was *easily* (and nearly continuously) participating. He recognizes that his silences are *Trying Hard to be sociable*, the 'grandiose' element being something like '*I can only say something if it's really significant*', and then does say something significant or particularly insightful, only to *fail* (to get a response from others) through the *brevity* of what he says, which leaves others bemused and non-comprehending, yet feeling it inappropriate to ask for elaboration (since Keith's manner of expression suggests he believes his observation is self-evident in its meaning).

3/5/78 I insistently urged him to elaborate on some of his very brief statements of opinion, and thus underlined for him the way his Try Hard works and he has explicitly given us *permission* to confront it (both in its overt form and its silent manifestation).

12/7/78 Some elucidation (in conjunction with Richard) of the meaning of Please Me as it relates to his only-child difficulty with *Child to Child play fighting*. He was able to see (in Richard) the crossing of Child to Child with

Parent to Child, which results in the bad-feeling withdrawal of the other's Child. I offered him the behavioural tip — a paradox — that *saying 'please' is a way of avoiding Please Me*. He understood this and explained (to me) that if you say 'please' *it forces you to follow it with a statement of what you want*.

19/7/78 He announced that he was planning to leave the group 'in two or three months' and had some issues he wanted to deal with before then. In response to 'why' he was planning to leave the group, his chief answer seemed to be that 'he has been in the group for nearly three years now'. This led me to retrospect to 25 January this year, when he also gave notice of leaving. Although some of the meanings then may also apply today, it does seem more straightforward now — especially as this time he is giving himself and us time to confront and deal with residual issues, which seem to be essentially around *giving more to others transactionally*. He recognizes and acknowledges this and wants to focus this on bringing to the group knowledge and wisdom he has acquired through his Group Analytic experiences of the last year. He also says he wants to *take* more concerning the *miniscripts*, which he does not yet understand to his satisfaction. Subsidiarily, we also dealt tonight with an aspect of Please Me in him that enables him to 'get away with it' more than others do. That is, by his head-nodding and other non-verbal forms of assent he is better able to avoid being confronted with his inauthenticity than if he were to indulge in more obvious verbal 'yes-yessing'.

26/7/78 He offered us something of his Group Analytic experience by enquiring why, when he arrived at 7.30, the group had already started. (I came in about a minute early as a return *stroke* to Richard, who was about fifteen minutes early. Keith was not interested in the 'why' of this.) Later on in the session I confronted his *'yes-nodding'* and insisted that he speak instead, which he did and, in speaking, expressed how much better he felt in the group when he felt the group was *interacting*. (It was clear that his greatest pleasure is when *he* is an active participant.) He expressed awareness of Richard's sometimes Rescuing him into talking, but enquiry revealed that he likes rather than resents this in Richard, so we redefined Richard's 'Rescuing' as 'helping'.

Alan

Alan is a twenty-three-year-old man, the second of three children. He has an older and a younger sister. He is unmarried. He graduated from university a couple of years ago, since when he has been in a more or less constant state of non-specific anxiety, sometimes acute. His chief problem derives from his relationship to his mother, who is an (unacknowledged) alcoholic, and whose emotional dependence on Alan has fixated his emotional development at mid-Oedipal stage. That is, he is *torn* between emotional identification with his mother and gender identification with his father. 'Masculinity', at the moment, means Be Strong to him, 'femininity' means Please Me. In his job he Tries Hard to be 'manly'.

27/4/77 Contract: to learn from the group about the impact he has on other people. He introduced himself to the group in terms of his manifest problem of getting on with his immediate boss. The group quickly saw the boss as Father, and suggested that 'doing something' about his relationship with his boss would be bound to lead to some *not-OK-payoff*. The most *OK* thing to do, for the time being, is to put the man completely out of his mind and deal instead with two immediate issues:

(1) Getting his overdraft paid off.
(2) Learning about himself in *transactions* with others, through the group.

11/5/77 No explicit work. At the end of the session I suggested that, in the interest of his particular *contract*, he really needs to talk — that is, provide data for the group to interpret in terms of the effect he has on others. He said he is impatient with his overdraft, which is diminishing 'too slowly'. I asked him to make sure he brings up the subject of *money* next week.

1/6/77 Some productive, continuing analysis concerning *script* issues around money. Based on Father having sent him less pocket money at school than most of his friends' fathers sent them he concludes — 'Why shouldn't I have what those around me have? No reason. So I will have'. So, in accordance with Mother's Witch, urging him on to be a *money-holic*, he overspends money hugely 'on trash', gets into debt, and invokes the wrath of Father's Parent. However, Father's Parent doesn't mind spending money '*on serious things*', and he has no prohibition on actually having lots of money. So the most adaptive Little Professor solution seems to be *to make lots of money and spend some for Mother thoughtlessly and some for Father 'seriously'*. His problem at the moment is that, in paying off his overdraft (which he dares not tell his father about) his Child is frustrated in its wish to spend and is not even getting any *negative strokes* (for admitting to Father that he got himself into a financial mess). We made various suggestions about getting some energy cathected into Adult about this, since only by combining Adult and Parent would he have energy on the side of continuing to pay off his debt. He also seems to have received a message from Father, '*If things get too bad, it's not worth bothering any more at all*'.

15/6/77 He is feeling desperately *not-OK* in his job, and is clearly setting things up to leave or be sacked. We did some role play with David (who is a personnel officer) and Alan was totally *confused, meandering, aggressive, defensive, frustrating, and boring* in the way he presented his dissatisfaction. He openly acknowledges the *scriptiness* of *his* thoughts and feelings in the situation, but, at the same time, is insisting on the essential *not-OKness* of people around him at work. We urged him to hold on at least until we *clarified the nature of the transactions that are going on between him and others* so that we can help him avoid simply reiterating the whole experience under a different guise elsewhere. *Homework*: to write a clear statement of exactly what his complaints are in his job.

20/7/77 Not unexpectedly he expressed his wish to leave the group on the grounds that it was getting him nowhere and, anyway, he couldn't take the *negative strokes* — for example, 'Bullshit!' — that he felt he was continually receiving from us. In exploring the meaning of his feelings it became clear that he has spent his time in the group so far obeying Mother's *injunction, 'Don't think, but hide the fact from others'*. In this he has been talking bullshit non-stop, but singularly *failing* in the group (compared to elsewhere) to *hide* the fact that he is *not* thinking. Hence his feeling that we simply pile on *negative strokes*. I then realized that he needed to be given the *permission* appropriate to Hurry Up players, just to sit back and relax and not worry about 'giving' or 'taking' or anything but just 'being' and letting the group experience 'wash over him' until such time as he *spontaneously* feels like responding to something somebody else has said. In the light of his present lack of conviction, despite much positive coercion by other group members, I proposed that he stay on till the end of August, at which time we would review his thoughts and feelings again. In the meanwhile, he has a short-term *contract to be actively alert to what the group has to offer him, whilst giving himself permission to be physically passive, that is, make no demands on himself to 'do' anything.*

24/8/77 Some extremely productive exploratory work based on a crucial anecdote from his childhood. When Alan asked his father for money (or anything else) his father would indicate where the money was *without looking up from his paper*. This created the impression in Alan (1) that he was *disturbing* his father, who made this eminently clear, whilst at the same time refusing to be disturbed, and (2) it was up to Alan to take as much as he (Alan) thought fit, since his father *never explicitly stated* how much he should take. These two percepts have been transferred to all Alan's *transactions* and the following dimensions are continuously enigmatic to him.

(1) How much others *disturb* (are a nuisance to) him and how much he to them.
(2) How to *ask for or offer* from and to others without being aggressively rejecting or rejected or humbly and ingratiatingly accepting or expecting humble ingratiation from others.

Furthermore, his father gave him a very explicit Parent value to be *aggressively 'masculine'*, and Alan uses this dynamically to attack his own Free Child via his Adapted Child. The cycle goes:

(1) Please Me Driver in all dealings with others.
(2) Resentment collected in Adapted Child.
(3) Adapted Child joins forces with aggressive Parent in kicking Free Child for not being aggressive to others.

All the above seems to me to provide a critical and core understanding of Alan which will provide a reference for all future work he does in the group.
19/10/77 Two issues seemed to be *contaminated*:

(1) Alan's wish for some Free Child *transactions* with his father.
(2) Alan's ambiguity in Try Hard between *not* succeeding as well as his father and putting his father down by succeeding more than him.

In as much as (2) *contaminates* (1), Alan is looking for some Child achievement which will make his father envious of him. We pointed out that the only *real way to 'win'* over Father's *episcript* that he *not* succeed, is to cop out of the Try Hard superior/inferior dimension altogether. Anyway, the Free Child to Free Child *transactions* he wants are a separate issue to be sought on a different and non-competitive level.

7/12/77 He is still basically exhibiting a Parent/Adapted Child *confusion* around *Trying Hard To Pay Off His Overdraft* and rationalizing this with the 'need' to leave the group (which he says is 'too *authentic*') while he does so. I did my best to persuade him to stay whilst avoiding invoking his rebellious Adapted Child or his Parent. Eventually he acknowledged he was leaving for *not-OK* reasons, but still wanted to. However, he agreed that the advantages he expected to gain from leaving must, at this stage, be hypothetical, so he agreed to take leave of absence (on an experimental basis for two months), coming back on 8 February to report on how he's going and to consider rejoining the group.

8/2/78 He returned to the group tonight and, at the end of the session, said he had felt *comfortable* tonight and wanted to return on a permanent basis. Some exploration of his feelings towards and perceptions of his father, which led me to hypothesize that his father wants him to be a *happy* (*Parent wish*) *failure* (*Adapted Child 'Don't compete with me'*.)

15/2/78 He reported a 'difficult' relationship with a man he works with, which he and the rest of us recognized as another instance of him always *managing to find Persecuting Father wherever he goes*. He still seems to be *Trying Very Hard to live in Counterscript* — that is, to block out *script* and be *happy 'in an office job'*. Fortunately, however, his awareness of his *script* need to fail keeps breaking through, so I urged him to bear in mind that he is *never* going to get the kind of approval from Father that he most longs for and that I was determined to give him a 'kick up the arse' (1) *to get his overdraft paid off much more efficiently* and (2) *to realize that there are many more 'middle-class professional' occupations open to him other than 'working in an office'*. In view of (1) being first priority, he accepted the *homework* of finding out about the conditions and wages for being a milkman.

15/3/78 Keith offered the hypothesis — which seems to fit — that he and Alan share the characteristic of choosing to mix with 'ordinary' ('tough guy'-type) men in their working lives in order to get a *fail payoff* to *Trying Hard to-get-on-with-people*. Alan also expressed a discomfort (expressed by Keith about himself in the past) of not being able to 'figure out' what motivates other people and generally what goes on in other people's minds. I pointed out that *none* of us knows what goes on in others' minds. We simply project ourselves on to them and hope for the best. However, given the awareness through the group that *people's motives are idiosyncratic to their scripts*, Alan could achieve a head-start over the vast majority of 'ordinary' people if he trained himself to discern *miniscript* clues in others, thereby having a very powerfully insightful tool for psyching others out, which is not available to the vast majority of people (who remain essentially totally ignorant of the realities of others).

22/3/78 He expressed a great deal of identification with Hilary in her sense of being Persecuted by me when I insistently confronted her with her unwillingness to be *authentic*. He said that though he now appreciates that there was a good purpose served in having his resistance 'battered down' (several months ago), he still feels that I unfairly accused Hilary (and him) of being *unwilling* when actually incapable. He also revealed — a propos of the period when he felt Persecuted by me — that he had experienced a lot of *hatred* towards me (which he now perceives as 'transference of Father' on to me), which he could not bear, at the time, to express. I assured him that if he *had* openly expressed hateful feelings towards me I would certainly not have been 'hurt', but would have understood the anguish he must have felt and would have hastened to reassure him that it was *OK* by me. He said that, be that as it may, he would probably then not have been able to accept anything I offered him in the spirit in which it was offered.

19/4/78 He told us of his current relationship to two of his workmates, which is currently 'pissing him off'. The three of them are a team and have equal responsibilities, but Alan is technically a subordinate to the other two, who have two 'blue stripes', whereas Alan has as yet none. The whole situation and Alan's responses to it exemplifies Try Hard in many different ways.

(1) The other two guys *asked* for their 'blue stripes'; Alan says *he* should be offered them and not have to ask for them. (Grandiosity and fear of failure.)

(2) Alan objects as much to the 'unworthiness' of the others as to his own lack of recognition. (Competitiveness aiming to put down others to increase self-esteem.)

(3) His idea of asking for his own 'blue stripes' was to ring up and *demand* them. (Ensuring failure.)

We analysed all of this and I asked Alan to see the whole situation through the eyes of Gulliver (as well as a Lilliputian) and to go in there (seeing the absurdity of the whole set-up in reality) and ask for his 'blue stripes' in an *OK* way, that is on the grounds that he and the others are doing an *equal* job, and that his formal subordination is a handicap to all of their relationships and shared work.

26/4/78 New Contracts: (1) to get into Child to Child more often and less often into Try Hard to Try Hard; (2) to be successful in his work (organization versus Try Hard/Be Perfect). He got his blue stripes, but has, since then, been put down by one of the others, who claims superiority over him for having had his longer! Alan is now aware of how the job continuously offers him the options of *either* being his *not-OK Parent (of his father)*, as when he is 'boss' to his workmates, *or not-OK* Child (himself to his father), when he is subservient to others. Although the opportunity has arisen for him to be boss amongst the three people he works with and to practise at being *OK* Parent, Alan prefers at this time not to accept this challenge, but instead to work at improved Child to Child with the others.

24/5/78 Early in the session he bombarded Francine (another member of the group) with *negative strokes* concerning her only sharing her Child feelings through her Adult and never really giving what others wanted, straight Child to Child. The vehemence of his outburst was striking and, all the while, he seemed consciously to be evading looking at me whilst accusing Francine. This led me to hypothesize (1) that his complaint against Francine was a complaint against himself in the group and (2) he was displacing felt anger towards me on to Francine. I confronted him with my inference that he was covertly saying to me '*I've stopped hating you and started loving you instead and you don't give me any strokes for loving you. I'm angry and hurt*'. His smile confirmed my hypothesis. At the end of the session I told him I thought he had been great in his outburst in 'really having said something'. (I asked him if he felt this to be a *stroke* from me. He said yes.)

21/6/78 Some productive exploratory work using anecdotal material from childhood, which enabled me to infer a core gestalt of some of Alan's internal dynamics. In relation to his mother he seems to have acquired a position of '*Strokes from women involve me in reflecting their feelings rather than my own and are also associated with my being sick in some way*'. From Father, whom he *feared and envied*, he *aspires to Be Strong*, but feels he cannot quite manage. His *moustache* manifests this aspiration and also serves to keep away the Parent-type women he really wants to love his Child. Another way of looking at the same dynamic is that he perceives being 'a sick little boy' or being a 'tough invulnerable Be Strong man' as the only alternatives open to him. It is important for him to learn to be both or neither of these.

28/6/78 He has shaved off his moustache — great! No explicit work, but he continues to relate well to what goes on in the group.

26/7/78 He reported some *transactional* difficulties he is having at work with a man who is clearly 'getting a rise out of him' (with various cynical-type remarks). Alan's response is a self-conscious inhibition of an impulse to respond with a Parent to Child 'put down'. We offered him some other possibilities. He rejected reporting his Child with his Adult as 'not him', so we asked him to consider Parent to Parent, Adult to Adult, Adult to Child, and Child to Child as possible other alternatives. (He rang me after the group very distressed at the '*teasing*' way in which I referred to 'stripping bare' his social façade last year. Exploration revealed a lot of *unfinished business* around his relationship to me at that time, which still needs to be dealt with in the group.)

Richard

Richard is a twenty-three-year-old man, unmarried, an only child. His mother bore him when she was thirty-five. His father died, at the age of seventy, when Richard was fourteen. His only-childness makes Child to Child *transactions* difficult for him, a difficulty which is manifest in Please Me. He is burdened with a Try Hard from his mother, which makes 'likeableness' and 'success', in a man, incompatible. This is reflected in his having twice failed, the third year of his Law degree. He is at present oscillating between the Driver and Vengeful Child positions of Try Hard, with respect to finishing his degree. His father's death when he was fourteen, put him in the (guilt-ridden) position of having won the Oedipal battle. That is, his (unconscious) wish to kill his father and have his mother to himself was realized. In his everyday life, this is reflected both in his propensity to form 'triangular' relationships and to feel burdened by girlfriends he doesn't want (Mother).

21/12/77 Contract: (1) *to choose a future career;* (2) *to know and express what he feels when he feels it.* Says he feels his Child to be about fourteen-years-old.

11/1/78 Some productive analysis through which we were able to define with increased clarity the nature of the consequences of the death of his father when he was fourteen. He openly admits to *smiling (in triumph)* at having 'won' his mother from her closeness to Father, but he is increasingly aware of this as a Pyrrhic victory, since, at the deepest level he longs for a man to stop him (*extricate him*) from attachments to women. He achieves these attachments all too easily and cannot 'get out of' them long after he has lost interest in the relationship. Sadly, at a social level, his problem is scorned by others as something they 'envy' in him, and this superficial response of others adds to his burden by making him feel *sorely misunderstood as well as trapped.*

1/2/78 He told the others about himself and his *script*, particularly revealing the Try Hard elements which lead him to begin all ventures with *speed and great promise*, which then justify him into flipping into the Vengeful Child position. I likened him to *the hare rather than the tortoise*, which analogy he said he did not like. In considering his Try Hard, I encouraged him to remain in his present (meaningless) job until such time as he had analysed and overcome his Try Hard sufficiently to *make any goals he sets himself likely to actually be attained* (before Try Hard intervenes). He agreed. He reported having found useful my Parent advice about girls, that as they get older they tend—notwithstanding their overt protestations to the contrary—to prefer primarily to be 'desired' rather than 'respected'. He said that, since this kind of data was *not* given him by his mother, he thought of it (coming from me) as *para-Father*. Thus, *whatever Parent I can offer him different from his mother may serve the purpose for him of filling in the blank left by Father's death.* (In this, I suspect sexual advice will be paramount.)

1/3/78 He reported having experienced considerable *sadness* (which he said he experienced again in the telling) when he walked through Grays Inn one day last week and was reminded of his *failure* in his final exams. This *authenticity* of feeling seems to me to bode well for his eventually repeating—and this time succeeding in—his exams.

29/3/78 He 'confessed' to having been 'inauthentic' with the group so far and asked, for the future, to be confronted when he was. This led us to explore what he meant by 'inauthentic', which turned out to be closer to *unspontaneous*—that is, characterized by *Try Hard (to be one of the group) and Hurry Up (to get his problems solved*). I pointed out the commonplaceness of people being in these Drivers in the first stages of being in a group, but suggested he consciously drop them and just 'come without any plan' to each session, in which case, he need not worry, all his problems *would* get aired and dealt with of their own accord. He also seems very much to be caught up in relatedness problems in the group, which reflect his *only-childness*, and I suggested that it would be helpful for him to consciously talk of *the group as brothers and sisters*, thus facing and dealing with these, to him, *'foreign matters'* as they arose.

5/4/78 In taking up our suggestion of last week that he learn to type in order to be able to get better paid and possibly more gratifying jobs, he fell into Try Hard by enquiring of *one* typing school, discovering a fee of £90 for a lengthy course and feeling depressed and 'a failure' for the rest of the week. I tonight recommended another place to try and he fell into Try Hard again by saying 'OK, I'll try that one', but clearly indicating that he had no thoughts whatsoever of what he would do next if that one proved too expensive or in any other way not suitable. However, he was immediately positively responsive to my confrontation of this and agreed instead to plan to make many enquiries, using his own initiative (and the telephone) to make himself a winner in this enterprise. He also revealed that at least part of his Try Hard derives from a perception he has that his father was *'very nice but unambitious'*. Thus 'niceness' and 'ambition' are incompatibles to him, but I suggested that inasmuch as his concept of *'niceness' is mostly Please Me*, he may happily maintain the polarity of these concepts but drop 'niceness' in favour of ambition.

26/4/78 He reported an incident at work, in which he responded with considerable anger to some teasing behaviour from a workmate. It seemed, by his reportage, that he had responded from the Vengeful Child of Please Me rather than Child to Child *play-fighting* (which would have been appropriate). I urged him, for future similar occurrences to (1) express anger (and other bad feelings) in small doses, as they occur, rather than accumulating them for an outburst, and (2) accept that 'teasing' is 'play-fighting' and respond in kind.

17/5/78 He reported that he is currently on holiday from work and doing his two-week typing course. His Try Hard was fed right at the start by *'An excellent beginning'* comment on his work by his teacher, but he self-consciously took himself in hand and changed it into *persistence*. (Typing as a task seems to be excellent therapy for Try Hard inasmuch as every error — of which there are inevitably many — is a failure, but accepted as a necessary concommitant of the inevitable overall success gained by persistence.)

28/6/78 He reported a *good feeling* in himself deriving from his having confronted (albeit a bit Vengeful Childishly) my Be Perfect over-explaining of something to him. He says it feels to him now that he has knocked me off my 'magical pedestal', which frees him to get on with an *OK* 'human' relationship with me.

12/7/78 We explored the meaning of the Hurry Up he came to the group with tonight. It turned out to serve the *payoff* of *'not belonging'*, which, in turn, was revealed as an inability to tell me (or anyone else) that *he* wanted something (in

148

an *OK* way). Thus, when I was taking a lot of time talking from my Child, Richard, feeling *controlled by me* attempted to reverse roles by *controlling me* (from his Parent). I demonstrated how much more *OK* both he and I would feel if he *told me to shut up Child to Child*. He appreciated the meaning of this, but expressed difficulty in 'knowing how to'. I agreed to teach him by example, whenever such inappropriate Parent to Child instead of Child to Child *transactions* occur between him and the group in future.

19/7/78 He reported that he has effectively been practising saying *'please'* as a way of getting out of Please Me, and this was evident in a brief *transaction* with me tonight which was straight Child to Child. He also sat on the floor for the whole session.

26/7/78 No explicit work, but in a very *OK* relationship to the group.

Summary

Case histories can only record *obervable* material. Much that is valuable to the patient may be 'happening' in his mind while he is silent.

There are times in group therapy when patients need to be silent. A therapist needs always carefully to balance the *insightful* gains of making the patient wholly responsible for his own silence against Rescuing him from silence in the interests of the *pragmatic* goals of his *contract*. An optimum mix of giving and demanding on the part of the therapist achieves maximum *efficiency* in therapy.

A summary of the *script* of the author, as therapist, is presented, followed by selected extracts from the case histories of four patients in group therapy.

CHAPTER 12

Group Therapy in Practice

The Role of the Group

A reflection of the world

Few therapists would dispute the efficacy of group treatment compared with individual treatment — not to mention the fact that group treatment earns the therapist a better living. All would probably agree with Berne's contention that

> Psychiatric disorders and patients tend to be uniform throughout the world. One universal is the therapeutic value of groups.[1]

The group is a microcosm of the world, in which the patient can play out his *games, rackets*, and *miniscripts* in the presence of insightful but totally accepting and non-critical witnesses. Man is a strictly group animal, and solitary confinement is always the harshest punishment. Moreover, although the therapist is always attributed the greatest (magical) power, for each patient in a group of eight patients and one therapist there are actually eight therapists ready and willing to help. Eight Little Professors and eight sets of *permissions* must always be more *potent* than one.

The universal dimensions of experience

Freud taught us that each human being, in his Id, believes he is omnipotent, supremely attractive, and immortal. Out of this universal trilogy in the Id, each person in his Ego has to come to terms with the opposite poles of helplessness, ageing, and death. Sharing lightens the burden a little.

It is through the sharing within a group that a patient can also experience the harmonious reconciliation he so often needs to find between 'being' and 'doing' and 'giving' and 'taking'. I often feel that amongst many TA therapists there is too great an emphasis on the masculine principle of 'doing' to the neglect of the equally needed feminine principle of 'being' (both of them being aspects of the

149

Free Child). Many men, in particular, benefit from the *permission* given in my groups simply to 'be' for a couple of hours each week, if they feel so inclined. Nobody gets harassed to 'do some work' until they are ready and — so long as it is clear they are comfortable — people are given every encouragement to take weeks at a time, if necessary, comfortably to digest and assimilate previous 'doing'.

For each patient 'giving' and 'taking' also find their balance within the setting of the group. Very often people begin therapy with a *contamination* of the concepts of 'giving' and 'taking' evidenced in apologies they are prone to make for 'taking too much of the group's time' in airing and seeking help for their own problems. Implicitly, they tend to divide two hours by eight and only feel entitled to 'take' a quarter of an hour. They are quickly persuaded that very much of their 'taking' is in fact 'giving' to others of themselves, and that in free and *spontaneous transactions* with others the polarities disappear in a blend that is equally gratifying to all the participants.

Claude Steiner's Four Rules for Co-operative Living[2]

Claude Steiner's four rules for co-operative living succinctly summarize qualities which apply equally to a TA therapy group as to interpersonal life in general. They are:

(1) *No Rescuing.* When one person purporting to help another does more than half the work and both 'helper' and 'helped' end up with bad rather than good feelings, the 'helper' has been Rescuing.[3] Rescuing is an occupational hazard in being a psychotherapist, and an acceptable *role* for a therapist to play in many therapeutic systems. It is not acceptable in TA.

(2) *No secrets.* This probably distinguishes the quality of TA therapy from other therapies more than any other factor. As a TA therapist, all my thoughts and feelings concerning my patients are freely made available, either spontaneously or on request, exposing, when relevant, elements in my own *script* which may be interfering with my therapeutic *potency* in certain transactions with certain patients.

(3) *No power-play.* Power-play is quickly dispelled in a TA group by an implicit *I'm OK, You're OK* feeling emanating from the therapist and insistently sustained by him at all times towards every member of the group. The covert message is 'We're all equal in this business of understanding the nature of being human'.

(4) *Loving confrontation.* When each member of the group has experienced for as much time as he needs the basic trust in the therapist and the other members of the group, derived from the *unconditional positive stroking* for 'being', loving confrontation is possible. In the *OK* TA group each member of the group knows that any other's suggestions for changes in his behaviour will either be generally validated by the group and the therapist and therefore be worth his consideration, or else will be a manifestation of the commentator's

script projection which will, in turn, be confronted by the rest of the group and the therapist. In the context of basic trust, if a loving confrontation is offered before a recipient is ready to appreciate it, the OK therapist withdraws gracefully for the time being.

The Conduct of Therapy

General considerations for therapists

There are no generally laid down 'rules' in TA concerning the formation of groups or the running of them. However, most TA therapists seem to operate fairly conventionally with respect to the empirically determined generalizations agreed by most group therapists of whatever theoretical persuasion. For me the following (commonplace) generalizations hold true.

(1) There is something magical about six to eight people. Fewer than six people tends to make the group cohesiveness feel precarious. More than eight people is a crowd.

(2) The best selection procedure for group membership is no procedure at all (although, of course, a great deal of selection — of the therapist — has gone on already by the time a person asks to join a group). The problems that people bring to a therapy group transcend age, gender, education, social class, etc: the more heterogeneous a group is, the closer a match to the world. But I do have two criteria of selection for my groups. I attempt to balance the numbers of men and women in order for us all to enjoy some sexual aliveness in the general atmosphere, and I will not take people into group therapy who are so disturbed that their general *reliability* (in coming to the group regularly) cannot be counted on. Such people gain little or nothing for themselves from the group experience and often disturb the cohesion of the group without any positive compensation.

(3) Once a week is a minimum frequency of meeting for individuals to sustain their achievements from one session to the next. Two hours is a good length of time for a group session.

(4) My groups are 'open' in the sense that individuals leave when they are ready to do so and newcomers take their place. These events in the life of the group parallel the normal family events of adolescent children leaving home and siblings being born.

(5) My groups are 'closed' in the sense that visitors or observers are not welcome, since their non-participatory presence is open to the charge of being mean, 'one-way intimacy'.

(6) Group members pay for every group session, irrespective of their absence for any reason (although I am always willing to reduce my sessional fee in cases of hardship). Any less stringent arrangements concerning the payment of fees is inevitably fraught with unavoidable *game-playing* as well as making the therapist's livelihood uncertain.

(There are a number of TA therapists in this country who are employed by the

NHS as social workers, psychologists, psychiatrists, and general practitioners and who, within the context of their general duties, use their TA knowledge in their counselling and treatment of their clients and patients. However, none of them is employed by the NHS *qua* transactional analyst. It is to be hoped that the time will come when TA — like psychoanalysis — will be found a niche of its own within the NHS.)

Rules of conduct for group members

As in the case of the general considerations listed above, the rules of conduct which I ask people to agree to before joining a therapy group are commonly accepted by group therapists as based on sound empirical generalizations. My rules are:

(1) There are no rules except as follows.

(2) No sex or physical violence is allowed in the group. Experience leads me to warn against — though I do not yet make taboo — sex outside the group between group members who are not already in a relationship before joining the group. Sexual bonds formed in the group run a very high risk of being based on intense but unstable and mutually damaging *scripty* issues. In some respects, such sex may be likened to sex between brothers and sisters.

(3) In order to resign from the group, members agree to come to the group and talk over their reasons for wishing to leave before actually doing so. No resignation is considered in the first six weeks of membership of the group, since it takes at least this time for a new member to appreciate the potential of the group to meet his personal needs.

This rule is particularly emphasized as a preliminary to any individual being offered a place in a group. It is especially important because, almost universally, everybody, at some time or another during the course of therapy, feels an Adapted Child impulse to flee, when continuing in therapy makes painful new awareness feel inevitable and imminent. So the explicit agreement required of patients that, no matter how they feel, they give notice, in person, of their intention to leave the group, protects the patient against those parts of his Adapted Child that seek to sabotage the therapy. The rule also enables the therapist to exercise his or her most valuable skills — *protection, permission*, and *potency*. Many people, including friends, can give people with problems good counsel at superficial levels of functioning, but the Free Childs of most people who undertake therapy are usually seeking profound changes in their lives, which only a therapist's skills can help them gain. Of course, some people do break this rule and leave without notice. These people must be counted amongst the therapist's failures, but since the patient knows he has broken the rule, he has at least learnt a lesson about the need for himself to accept some responsibility for the changes in his life that he wants.

(4) Any *transactions* which take place between a group member and the

therapist outside the group (on the telephone or in an individual session) are the 'property' of the group.

Transcript of Group Session With Commentary and Notes

With a command of the theory and language of TA now his own, I hope the reader will sit back and enjoy some of the reality of a live TA therapy group through the transcript of the following pages. I hope, too, that in witnessing (at least the words of) the group in action he will form for himself hypotheses about meaning that I have missed. For at any moment in any therapy group an incalculably large number of 'events' are occurring in words and body language and in the minds of all the people present. When therapist and group are in top form, they may be able to make conjoint use of two — or perhaps three — simultaneously occurring different levels of 'happening', but by and large what gets analysed is (for reasons which must be infinitely multifarious and complex) what makes the greatest impact on the therapist's consciousness.

In order not to disturb the flow of the experience nor to interfere with the reader's own frames of reference I have added commentary to the dialogue (in brackets) only when necessary to clarify some 'in-group' allusion or to indicate some 'large' piece of non-verbal behaviour. My notes for the session (which I write after the session is finished) conclude this chapter.

Present: 4 out of 6 members of group. (Martin, Alan, Keith, and Richard) *time*: 7.30–9.35 p.m.

Therapist: I think, Keith, I ought to make a point — since you're planning to leave the group soon — of making sure every week of expressly drawing you in — especially as you expressed appreciation last week to Richard for doing so . . . So what are you going to give us tonight?

Keith: I don't know. Will you read my notes? [I read him my notes of last week — see Chapter 11.]

Th: I was interested in why you weren't interested in *why* beyond that. Is that all your Group Analytic group does? [Keith was until recently a member of a Group Analytic therapy group at the same time as being a member of this group]. Do you just state a cause and not look behind it? It does seem a typical way in which you cut conversation off.

K: I just wasn't interested.

Th: I know. I hear you, and my Adult accepts that. Fair enough, but there's a kind of abruptness in your thoughts that comes across. [Keith starts nodding his head continuously.] Don't nod! [Therapist laughs.] You seem to be saying, 'I'll offer this' or 'I'll give my opinion' and then, when it's said, full-stop, end of paragraph, end of chapter, as if to freely associate into another thought is somebody else's business to initiate or. . . .

K: I don't see why this area of why Richard arrived early is of any interest.

Th: Well why did you ask the question, 'Why did the group start early?' instead of saying to me, 'Why did you come in early?'

K: Because the group started early and that was all that was significant.

Richard: Wasn't it more that you maybe felt a bit left out, since you were on time, but it had started without you?

Alan: You are restricting your attention to the group.

K: No, I'm not saying that.

R: OK, how did you feel, then, when you came and you knew you were on time but it had started?

Th: And what did you think?

K: I thought, 'Hello, hello, hello, what's going on here?'.

Th: What do you mean — 'What's going on here?'? C'mon, elaborate, tell us what you really mean. Give! I mean what kind of hypotheses did you have? Did you look at your watch? Did you think, 'Oh I thought I was on time'?

R: Well, you knew you were on time.

K: No. I looked at my watch and thought my watch is not right, which it wasn't, anyway, so perhaps it's just me. Then I checked the time [on the electric clock in the room]. But that wasn't terribly significant, but you see I was saying the kind of thing that in Group Analysis would be noticed. [I had previously suggested that Keith could 'give' a lot to the group by telling us about his experience of Group Analysis.]

Th: OK. Fair enough. But what do you *do* with that information?

K: Do with it? Nothing, necessarily.

Th: What kind of criteria would determine that you *would* do something with it?

K: No criteria. Just the same as transactional analysis, except that you analyse different things.

R: From what you said, you came into the group and thought, 'Hello, hello, hello, it's started early and I may be late'.

K: But then I checked the time and realized I had been on time. I think this is hair-splitting.

Th: The hair-splittingness right now is, in a way, a feeling that comes across from you. You're now projecting, calling it hair-splitting, because when I responded to something you said last week with a smile, your response to me was 'Well, you might *discount* that . . .'.

K: Mm.

Th: I wasn't *discounting* it at all. What my smile represented was, 'Well, that's an interesting, abstract statement, but so what?'. I wasn't *discounting* it in itself, but you didn't give enough — and you're still not giving enough — to make it feel to us like something.

K: I gave what I had to give at that point and that was it.

Th: OK. Anyhow, the important thing tonight is that you've already talked.

K: Yeah.

Th: Talking is giving and it doesn't really matter what the content is.

K: I don't necessarily agree.

Th: What do you mean, 'necessarily'?

K: Because I don't necessarily think this kind of dialogue's constructive.

Th: Constructive to what end?

K: To getting me out of my *script*.

Th: That word 'necessarily' that you keep using, what does it mean?

K: I'm uncertain. I'm not sure whether it's getting me out of my *script*.

Th: All right. Let me suggest to you that it, in itself, is not working on your *script*, in the sense of thinking anew about your *script* decisions, but it's behavioural therapy . . .

K: Yes.

Th: Which is saying 'Keith, you are behaving in a way which will get you feedback from the world different from the kind of feedback your *script* gets. So whether it *feels* different in you, or not . . .

K: Yeah, but I'm *not* getting feedback different from my *script*. I am getting *script* feedback . . . You're getting very frustrated with me.

Th: No, no [mildly].

R: I was [getting frustrated]. Probably because you [to Keith] didn't want to go any further with the analysis, you therefore didn't give or didn't play along with Mavis's questioning and therefore it was frustrating for me watching you.

K: Yeah. That's the feedback that I'm getting.

R: So that means that because you don't necessarily want to do it you won't play the game.

Th: [to Keith] Your *script* is entering into the very *transactions* we're having here now by saying, 'I don't necessarily see the point of this'.

K: I see the point, but I'm not getting any new feedback.

Th: OK. If we go on like this for long enough, you'll relax and we'll relax and we'll stop thinking about content and you'll simply be talking.

K: Maybe.

Th: If you're willing.

K: What I was actually feeling was, 'If this goes on for much longer, everybody else will be getting so pissed off . . .'.

Th: No, no, no. We'll have fun, if you let us.

K: Yes, I suppose if it gets to that point, we will.

Th: I'm feeling more relaxed with you *now* [Keith starts nodding] . . . Don't nod! [Therapist laughs.] Say yes, do anything, but don't nod! I'm playing with you. I'm effectively saying to you, 'Come out and play'. I'm teasing a little bit as well. And every gesture I make you are still withdrawing as if I'm doing something horrible to you or not liking something about you.

K: That's the way it feels. Now we are getting somewhere. That is the way I actually feel, you see.

Th: That's the look you've got on your face, which is totally incongruent with the feelings in me as I'm talking to you, which are 'Come out and play, Keith'.

K: Yeah. I can't do it.

Th: Yet.

K: Yet.

Th: Well, can I offer you the behavioural suggestion that you make a point of doing what perhaps your *script* would call making a fool of yourself as often as you possibly can by interjecting *anything*, including nonsense, as often as you can possibly manage.

K: I don't know whether I can do that.

Th: Well can I ask your Adult to accept that if, for want of a better method, later on this evening, I tease you — in a way that is my wont — that you will know that your Child is actually being asked to come out and play.

K: How will I know if you're teasing me? At which point do you regard yourself as having started teasing me?

Th: Um. . . . When I say something that sounds like a Parent to Child put-down, like. . . .

R: 'Stop nodding!'

K: [to therapist] Every time you say that you get me back into my Adapted Child.

Th: I think this would be very good for Alan to know too, because Alan rang me up very distressed after last Wednesday. Subsequently we had an individual session, out of which, it seems the business of teasing is very important to Alan as well. [To Alan] It may be useful for you to see me teasing Keith and — from the outside — see that it's harmless play.

A: Yeah. Actually, it was what Sally [a member of the group absent tonight] said that I thought was a big put-down. I think that was more important than the teasing, which I think was merely irritating.

Th: [to Alan] Did she remind you of your mother?

A: Yeah, because it was as if she was saying, 'Don't be vulnerable, I don't want to see you vulnerable. . . .'

R: And that her feeling, right or wrong, was that, as a result of that, she wanted to mother you. She was making a comment about her own feeling.

A: She was also venting a bit. . . . I was feeling very vulnerable then. . . . venting something on me.

R: I think she was making a statement about herself, not you. What was there in that to make you upset? What's wrong with feeling vulnerable?

A: There's nothing wrong with feeling vulnerable. It's just that at that point I felt that. . . .

Th: There is something wrong with feeling vulnerable — from a Be Strong point of view.

A: Yeah. It's just that sometimes I feel *so* vulnerable that at that point I felt particularly vulnerable for some reason last week, that when she said that, I felt that that was just enough to say to me, 'Whatever you do, don't be vulnerable'.

R: What did you actually say in the group after that happened? You made a comment—'I didn't like that,' or something.

A: In fact she sort of went like that [arm outstretched] and I felt that was bad as well because it was preventing me from coming back again.

Th: [to Alan] I notice that we're talking about a *transaction* you had with somebody who is not here tonight, which is a way of not dealing with unfinished business in a way that can be done effectively. . . . It wasn't only Sally, was it? Your whole experience of the whole session was a bad one. . . .

A: Yeah, mm.

Th: And it also had quite a lot to do with me, as I recall.

A: Yeah.

Th: I remember saying to you on the phone that if there was unfinished business between you and me we could both benefit much more [than by just talking to each other] by having the group assess what happened between us. Can you recall what it was that upset you about me?

A: I dunno. Just a lot of things. I don't really want to talk about it, actually. It's so. . . .

R: Why don't you be vulnerable now?

A: I don't want to be vulnerable. I just don't feel like being vulnerable.

Th: [to Alan] Are you willing to have me read my notes? [of last week].

A: Yeah, sure. [I read my notes of last week. See Chapter 11.]

Th: It was at that point when I was asking Sally to bear the assault of me on her social façade and, in an attempt to lighten the intensity of my *transactions* with Sally, I remember saying, 'Come on, Sally, I'm not asking much of you compared to what I asked of poor old Alan last year' — something like that. And that was the trigger, as I understood you when I spoke to you on the phone, for you feeling absolutely terrible.

A: Mm. Well, you see, I dunno, I'm sorry to go off the subject, but I've got sort of. . . . I had palpitations as I was coming here for some reason, and I've only had three hours sleep in the last thirty-six hours.

Th: Why have you had so little sleep?

A: I've been on a long shift [at work].

Th: Were you frightened of coming here tonight?

A: Yeah.

Th: What of?

A: Frightened of revealing myself.

Th: Revealing which part of yourself?

A: Well I had a raw nerve in me struck last week and I felt it wasn't something I wanted to deal with.

Th: What about the analysis we achieved [in the individual session]— the relationship of what happened last week to your childhood experiences? Are you willing to share that with the group?

A: I'm sorry, I can't even remember what it was.

Th: Well, as I remember it, it seemed to be a kind of reiteration of your essential childhood relationship with your sisters, your *big* sisters, who always *discounted* you by teasing you.

A: Yeah.

Th: Either your big sisters taking the piss out of you — 'silly little boy'-type thing or — there was something I can't recall — some kind of *transaction* you had with Mother that was also represented last week.

A: I just . . . I mean I . . . Er . . . You know, I feel in a sense, there's no point in my being here tonight because I'm not prepared to go through with it at the moment and so we're really wasting our time, talking about it.

Th: You're not wasting anybody's time. I'm not going to push you if you wholeheartedly don't want to pursue the topic any more. But I don't want you to walk out of here, as you did last week, in a state of distress, without my knowing about it and without you giving me the chance to help you feel OK before you leave.

A: Yeah. No, I don't feel *not-OK* this week. I accept what you said about the teasing. It's just that — as a general comment about teasing — I'm not quite sure when it's ever going to stop and if, say, I take over at D——'s [the place where he works as a security officer] I won't know, I'm not quite sure how I'll know when to allow people to tease me and when to allow them to. . . . and when to say, 'Do some work' or. . . . It's that that concerns me.

Th: OK. Whether you, at this moment, realize it or not, this is a very protected environment. . . .

A: Yeah.

Th: And anything you want to know about your own personality in relation to other people you can practise here — experiment. . . .

A: That's the point. That's what I'm not prepared to do now.

Th: OK, you don't feel like it now, but for the future, bear in mind that you can try out anything here and you can get feedback from other people. . . .

A: Yeah, I know.

Th: And you can set us up as your work-mates and ask for our responses about how we feel. . . .

R: It could be a thing that if Mavis was teasing there might be a point when you'd really want to sort of cool it and get on with some work here. Or even if she was teasing someone else. . . . [to therapist] In the same way I did that when you were sort of *pastiming* and I sort of made a mess of it. . . .

A: Mm. I just felt last week that I was so vulnerable that. . . . I just didn't feel like being teased. It was just the exact opposite of what I wanted.

Th: Another thing that I can remember from our individual session was that you indicated to me a hyper-sensitivity to emotion in general. This came across when you referred to how protective you felt towards me when you felt Richard had attacked me a couple of weeks ago, when he spotted me manifesting Be Perfect, and more or less told me to shut up.

A: Mm.

Th: In the individual session we had, you said that you felt I'd been. . . .

A: You looked hunted.

Th: I looked hunted and you wanted to come out and protect me from the pain that I was feeling. You were quite right, Richard had caught me out in some *not-OK* behaviour, but from my point of view, although I had a momentary feeling of . . . . bad feeling inside me, primarily for having *been* in a Driver — not for Richard having told me to shut up — you grossly exaggerated, in your perception, the intensity of my response, which gave me a clue . . . . which led me to say to you, 'I think, Alan, you are grossly exaggerating your sensitivity to everything, to the point where it's no longer adaptive'. Your sensitivity's a lovely thing to have, but to magnify your emotional response to things that happen to that extent is. . . .

A: Well, I just mentioned it. I didn't make a big thing of it. I was trying to understand what your feeling was at that particular time.

Th: I know, but you perceived my feeling to be a helluva lot more intense than it was.

A: Yeah, probably.

Th: And I think your sensitivity makes you respond to everything with a much higher degree of intensity than is warranted, so that a lot of your problems at work with people are probably due to a quite different perception on your part and their part about the significance or intensity of *transactions* that happen between you. Things the others have forgotten five minutes later, you go around *feeling* the power of for a whole day.

A: Well, I know, yeah. I mean my sister said that last Friday.

Th: It could be turned to something very adaptive. It means also that when the stimulus is too small for other people to be aware of, you will be. You have an immense capacity for analytical understanding of situations.

R: [to Alan] Do you feel vulnerable now?

A: Yeah, but I've put a clamp on it.

R: I was just thinking your hand was being your moustache again. [Richard was referring to Alan's hand being over his mouth. A few weeks ago, Alan shaved off his long-standing moustache in response to the group's pressure. Alan had said that girls always seemed to be looking for a Parent in him — which he didn't like — and the group all agreed that his moustache was, amongst other indicators, inviting this.]

Th: I know what the moustache was about now. It was about hiding the fact that your upper lip stops being stiff sometimes. [Therapist smiles at Alan, Alan grins and then laughs.] Yeah?

A: Yeah. [Grins]

Th: Was that tease all right? Will you forgive me for that? [Alan laughs].

A: Well my problem with teasing is either to back down and not say anything, just to withdraw, or come on heavy Parent, which I'm afraid is just going to shut them up completely, which I don't want to do.

Th: Why don't you?

A: Well, I feel it's maybe. . . .

R: Maybe they'll catch you out. [Is this a *script* position of Richard's? — but I don't want to detract from Alan now.]

A: No, I don't think that.

Th: Are you saying you don't want to do that because you know they're really playing?

A: Yeah. I know on one level that they are. It's a sort of all-embracing personal prejudice — from my father, I think — that makes me want to stamp on them. I like it on one level, but I disapprove of it on another.

Th: Ah yes. It's Father's put-down or big sisters' indulgent patronage.

A: I mean when I was at school I use to quite often enjoy it. And I enjoy it at work as well a lot of the time. It's just sometimes. For instance, if I've got my mind on something else and someone says something in the wrong tone of voice, I'll respond sharply and they'll look hurt and I'll feel bad.

Th: And what do you *think* then?

A: I think they don't like me or something.

Th: You don't think, 'I must have responded inappropriately'?.

A: I think I was too intolerant of them.

Th: But what I think you think you're intolerant of — I hear the same words coming from you over and over again — it's as if you were saying, 'If I was a real man, if my Be Strong were highly enough developed, I would take their criticism like a man — stoically'.

A: No, no, not stoically. It wouldn't affect me.

Th: But the whole point is that you think they're criticizing you. You call it criticism when they are not intending it as such — quite the opposite.

A: Well I don't know that, you see.

Th: So you're in the same position as Keith?

A: Yeah.

Th: When I explained to Keith, did you understand what I was saying to him?

A: Yes.

Th: Well can't you apply that to yourself as well?

A: It doesn't work because it's just Adult. I mean you never know anything until you experience it.

Th: When I was teasing Keith before, did your Child go out to his Child in sympathy to his, as if I was doing something horrible to him? Did you feel 'poor Keith'?

A: I already felt like that for Keith. I didn't feel like that tonight. I just knew it with my Adult tonight. I wasn't particularly feeling sympathy, because. . . . I suppose I felt a bit of sympathy.

Th: Did you believe I was criticizing him?

A: No.

Th: Are you sure?

A: I suppose I did, a bit, yeah. Huh! I suppose I did, because I tend to feel my *script* so bad — that when you *start* buggering around with people's *scripts* it's a sensitive area. I mean the nod to Keith is an integral part of him.

R: No it's not. It's something I'd like to see him get rid of. It's an exterior so we can't get to see what's really in the Child.

K: Yes, that's right.

Th: [to Alan] It's not like telling him to change the colour of his hair.

R: Or give up Philosophy [which Keith is studying].

Th: Well obviously a useful thing for both of you [Alan and Keith] to do is that when I tease one and the other one is not vulnerable because it's not them who's being teased, if the other one says what they're thinking and feeling at the time, we can get somewhere.

A: But I sort of feel 'Ha, ha, look at him being teased'.

Th: Being got at.

A: Yeah.

R: [to Alan] Whenever you've made a comment that you felt like that, you've never brought it up at the time. It's always after you've stewed it over.

A: Can I just close sort of. . . . I've got sort of palpitations. I'm not quite sure what they are. I was talking to Martin about them at the beginning of the group [before therapist came in and the session began]. My heart feels it's sometimes turning over when I'm slightly frightened of something and I and I'm just wondering what what. . . .

Th: It's a symptom of anxiety.

A: Yeah. Well Martin says he gets a bit of a dull ache. I don't get that. It just feels as though it's missing a beat or jumping. It's being squeezed.

R: Well I do, too.

K: It's quite normal for people — especially our age group. [All are in their twenties.]

Th: You mean the identity crisis age?

K: Maybe, yes.

R: If you delay it till forty it kills you. [All laugh]

K: *Transactionally*, is this teasing Parent to Child or is it Child to Child?

Th: *Transactionally*, I think it's overtly a Parent to Child put-down and covertly a Parent to Child expression of affection. [Therapist draws diagram below on blackboard.]

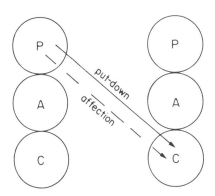

A: It can be a Parent to Child put-down. For instance, if you dislike someone — it depends how you say it, doesn't it?

Th: Well let me tell you how you can read that I'm teasing. Very occasionally, I overtly express Parent to Child anger to someone in the group. It doesn't happen very often, but when I do you can rest assured I won't be smiling.

R: With Joan. [Joan is a member of the group, absent this evening, with

164

whom I am inclined to play 'Why don't you. . . . ?' 'Yes, but . . .', a *game* which is very common indeed in the world at large. One party to the *game* nominally seeks advice from the other or others. The other(s) respond with various 'Why don't you's?', to which the instigator consistently replies, 'Yes, but . . .'. The instigator's (existential) *payoff* is 'Parents are never right', the responder's (existential) *payoff* is 'I am unloveworthy'. Each player additionally achieves various 'psychological and social advantages' (see Chapter 6) along the way. ' "Why don't you. . . . . .? 'Yes, but. . . .' " ' may also be viewed as a dialogue between Be Strong and Please Me.]

Th: Yes. [To Alan] Every time I tease you, or anybody else, I smile.

A: I'm sorry to go back to this, but I was interested when you said you can use your Parent. I tend to feel that my tendency is to use my Parent too much in small, petty ways. [Most of Alan's energy is cathected into the *confusion* of his Parent/Adapted Child *contamination*.]

Th: That's what I've been working hard to tell you for the past year. I'm glad you realize it now.

R: I've realized that in an awful lot of ways, when I'm in my Child having fun, I operate — nearly always — on Parent to Child one way or the other, with very little actual Child to Child.

Th: Yes, that's extremely difficult for an only child to do. [Richard is an only child, as is Keith.] But think of the positive side of it. Because of your only-childness you do those Parent to Child and Child to Parent *transactions* extremely well.

R: Right. However, that was a preface to something else. Something I do an awful lot and I wonder why, what it's hiding, is that I'm always sort of joking too much — a bit like my mother. She always used to say, 'I like to make people laugh against their will', and I feel as though I'm having to make people laugh all the time. I can't hold myself back. In a way I think it might be Child to Parent, It's 'Laugh at me. See how funny I am' or. . . . I don't know what it is.

Th: It sounds as though you perceive Mother as having asked you to make *her* laugh against her will. Perhaps the little boy in you, when Mother expressed pride in *her* making other people laugh against their will, the little boy in you psyched out that that's what she really wanted the world to do to her.

R: Mm. I don't like it. 'Cos what comes over after it's all gone by is I feel inauthentic — sometimes. The thing I used to do a lot at university. I'd sort of go into little groups — in the evening when there were lots of coffee parties all over the place — I'd always pop in and do my bit, and before they could even react — they'd all laugh or something — and then I'd be off.

Th: That kind of acting behaviour is often an adaptation that somebody makes positively to difficulties they experience in Child to Child *transactions* — and especially an only child, because it's a kind of positive adaptation to Please Me in that in playing a part you are expressing emotion, but according to some controlling director's definition of what the emotion should be and how it should be expressed. So it's a warm feeling of being in your Child, because it's emotional, and it's giving out to other people's Childs, who applaud you from their Childs, but at the same time you are not called upon to be spontaneous. You are called upon to do it in a certain way, so you're secure in the constraint of the role.

R: Also, another thing that comes from it is that I am secure in a way, but also I can't get out to others. I feel locked in.

Th: Right. It's as if you see other people's Childs there [therapist gestures distance with her arm] and you're here and acting enables you to go half way. It prevents you ever going right there, but it also enables you to move some distance from where you started out. So probably the best actors in the world are positively adapted to Please Me.

K: That's what I meant by the 'irony' in Richard [Keith had, some months ago called Richard's personality 'ironical', but had not been able to articulate further what he meant by this], because the irony is the distance between the real you and the role. It gives you a perspective on the role.

R: I never understood what you meant by the 'irony' until just then.

Th: Martin? [who has not spoken this evening].

Martin: Mm?

Th: When are you going to tell us what you're frightened of?

M: Well I think it's a matter of being vulnerable. It's the thing I most want to express . . . . it's sort of a rejected feeling.

Th: The only difference is that since your Child has responded with more of a Hurry Up than a Be Strong to the same kind of thing, you give us less chance even than Alan to get close to you.

M: Yeah.

Th: It's bad enough having a Be Strong in trying to get close, but with Hurry Up you're lost before you begin even. What can we do about it?

M: Draw me in, I suppose.

Th: How?

M: In the way you've just done.

Th: It feels as though that applies to you and Keith and I feel some responsibility towards Alan, too, because I feel his **Be Strong** is likely to suffer in silence and say 'I don't need anything, I don't need anything. . . .' and go away. So there are three of you here. . . . .

A: The point is that what will happen is that someone will crack and then the others will crack up in sympathy. . . .

M: I don't want nurturing, I want taking apart. I mean I can be fairly vulnerable amongst people I am familiar with, but there's always a shell there. Once I have committed myself to being vulnerable, then that's all right. I don't need nurturing initially. It's just getting through, first.

R: I want to change my job pretty soon and I would like some ideas, some suggestions. I just really don't know.

Th: Do you remember some months ago we talked about jobs for you and we came to the conclusion that some form of being on the stage — not necessarily literally. . . .

R: But with roles, yes. I once thought I'd like to have a go at telephone sales, but it's very high pressure.

Th: Would you like to be a salesman, generally?

R: No, not generally.

Th: But aren't you a salesman at the moment?

R: No, I work in a record shop at the moment.

Th: Don't you serve behind the counter?

R: Yes, but there's no pressure to sell anything.

Th: But you can use that lovely Please Me smile, can't you? My younger daughter's got Please Me and she works in the corner grocery shop on Saturdays, and whenever I walk past I see her going like this [gives a big grin], and what's really terrific about it is that when she comes home on Saturday nights, she's more *authentic* than she's been all week. It's as if she's got all her Please Me out of her system.

R: Fair enough for groceries, but in a record shop you've got to be hip, and it's not hip to be Please Me. On the contrary, ... [everybody laughs]. However. . . .

Th: You're looking for a job now to see you through to a year in September, when you start your law again?

R: Right. Yes. But when I go back to do that one year, I'll have spent as many years in the third year as most people spend doing the whole degree.

Th: But you'll have done a lot else for yourself in the meanwhile as well [meaning personal growth through therapy].

R: I accept that. Has nobody got any ideas?

Th: What would you like to do?

R: I imagine something where, say, I'd have to be in contact with somebody, and then as soon as that was over I'd have something fresh, where there would be many times in the day where I'd have to sort of alter. . . .

Th: What about a messenger?

R: Maybe something like that, where I help people.

M: There's a job advertised in Harrow Sports Centre — a Security Assistant, £70 a week.

R: I'm guessing, but probably it's shift work. . . .

M: Yes, it is.

R: I didn't really want to. . . .

A: Helping people, looking up things for people, ...?

Th: Information officer?

R: That's what I do now, really. 'Where do you get this record?'

A: Or in a job centre, an employment agency, something like that.

R: You know, my local library has a lovely atmosphere.

A: In an employment agency, you reassure people as well. You say, 'Ring me back on Wednesday. . . .'.

Th: It's a bit of a harassing job, though.

R: Yes.

A: Is it?

R: Yes, and it's a commission-only type job.

Th: There are a lot of people employed in the Building Centre — off Tottenham Court Road. It's a place where you go to find out anything you want to know about building materials. And there's a library there.

R: Actually the Building Centre sounds marvellous, and also the library idea. They'd be the complete opposite to my present job.

Th: You'd like somewhere quite peaceful, then?

R: Yes

Th: OK then. [End of session.]

168

Notes of the Session

Martin: He was silent and looked disconsolate for a long time, so I asked, 'When are you going to tell us what you're frightened of Martin?'. He responded by joining in the group dialogue and expressed appreciation for my having 'drawn him in'. He later put it that he *needs* '*to be cracked open*' in order to achieve the capacity for *intimacy* (which he so fears). I agreed to go on 'drawing him in' in future.

Keith: I opened the session by asking Keith to 'give us something of himself', and this led us into the subject of *teasing transactions* (initiated by me and others), which Keith cannot handle and often misconstrues as *Parent to Child discounts*. I gave him information concerning how to recognize the difference, and he agreed to feed this into his Adult (even if his Child is not immediately able to make use of it).

Alan: I raised the issue of 'unfinished business' with the group of last week, but he expressed (Be Strong) unwillingness to open up, at least tonight. However, we did analyse a little further his maladaptive *hyper-sensitivity*, and especially his *script* perception of the nature of teasing — that is, either Father *criticizing* him Parent to Child or big sisters indulgently *patronizing* him. I asked him and Keith to be objectively aware of each others' responses to being teased, thus each using the other to gain insight about himself whilst maintaining 'cool' and analysing the other's responses.

Richard: He wants to change jobs, and asked for the group's help to choose a job he would enjoy. He seems to want a job which is *quieter* than his present one and also offers some variety, through being divided into discrete tasks with different people. We came up with jobs involving helping people and libraries, both of which appealed to him.

Summary

Group therapy (in contrast to individual therapy) provides for the patient a microcosm of the world, in which to achieve his *contract*. It also enables the individual to share with others the universal needs to come to terms with his own helplessness, ageing, and death, and to harmonize 'giving' and 'taking' and 'being' and 'doing'. Claude Steiner's four rules for co-operative living — No Rescuing, No Secrets, No Power-play, and Loving Confrontation — are valuable guidelines for defining an *OK* TA group.

There are no laid down 'rules' for TA therapists concerning the formation of groups or the running of them. However, most TA therapists are fairly conventional with respect to generalizations agreed on by most group therapists of whatever theoretical persuasion. For this writer, these generalizations include: six to eight members in a group; heterogeneous group membership; once-a-week sessions of two hours' duration; groups open to new members when individuals leave; no visitors or observers of groups; group members pay for all sessions, irrespective of absence for any reason.

Rules of conduct for patients, agreed on before they join a group are: no sex or physical violence in the group; resignation requires discussion of reasons for leaving with the group (but no resignations considered within six weeks of joining the group); what takes place between any group member and the therapist is the 'property' of the group.

A transcript of a group therapy session is presented and concluded with the therapist's notes of that session.

Notes and References

1. E. Berne, 'Group therapy' abroad', *Int. J. Group Psychotherapy*, **8**, 466–470, 1958.
2. I first heard these 'four rules for co-operative living' spoken by Claude Steiner at the Second European ITAA Conference in Enschede, Holland, in July 1976.
3. C. Steiner, *Scripts People Live*, Grove Press, 1974.

CHAPTER 13

Conclusion

Human Nature

It is unlikely that the total span of recorded history has been a long enough time for evolution to have wrought any noticeable changes in 'human nature'. Whenever and wherever men have recorded their reflections on the problems inherent in human beings' relationships with each other and with the universe, the same difficulties and perplexities are met with essentially the same solutions and wisdoms over and over again. Notwithstanding the barriers of language, culture, and sociology, the things that bother us most seem to be timeless and universal.

Yet one of the most obvious facets of human nature is the ironical fact that every culture — and probably every individual, too — at some time feels the necessity to wonder if there aren't, in fact, better ways of understanding ourselves than have so far been found. It is as if we believe that if only we think a little harder utopia is achievable. In the parlance of today, this quest itself may be seen as a reflection of our homeostatic disposition, the constant pull-push of arousal and quiescence, which is written into biology. It is our consciousness of this ineluctable tension which sets us apart from all other species of life and which has amongst its spin-offs all of Art, Science, and Philosophy.

Man's Twentieth Century Voice

However, whatever may be the over-riding cosmic forces that determine all things, the history of ideas manifests two disparate and more or less consecutive orientations to understanding, namely holism and atomism. Although neither attitude has ever been entirely absent, the general tenor of human thought seems to have begun holistic and have become atomistic about two and a half thousand years ago, an orientation that prevailed until the present. But much of the marked restlessness and anguish of the collective human spirit right now, in the twentieth century, seems to express our hovering transition into a new era of holism. The apogee of analytical thinking is giving way to the discomposure of our present Age of Uncertainty. Physics seems to have reached the turning point first, expressed in Heisenberg's Uncertainty Principle and Einstein's Theory of Relativity. Biology lags behind a little — it seems to have a little more yet to do in the way of analysis — and Psychology, which only began to be atomistic when most other fields of endeavour were nearly finished with analysis, as an academic discipline is wildly out of step with the current human condition.

Outside academia, Psychology seems to have found its twentieth-century voice by blending itself with Philosophy and Medicine, both of which fields have branches which seem precisely to reflect the compromises between materialism and mystery, determinism and choice which characterize man's present outlook. In Philosophy, Existentialism is the name of the game, in Medicine it is Homeopathy. Psychology that blends itself with these calls itself Humanistic.

Berne's Achievement

Transactional Analysis, as theory, makes sane the previous schizoid fragmentation of Psychology into theories which were either precise and meaningless or profoundly true and inoperative. TA is the bastard child of psychoanalysis and operant conditioning. Psychoanalysis, as mother, gave birth to and has nurtured TA to maturity. However, had there been a birth certificate it would have registered 'father unknown', although the genetic contribution of operant conditioning is indisputable. TA is both 'hard' and 'soft', diagnostic and prescriptive, subjective and objective, holistic and atomistic.

At an applied level, Berne's genius has created a language in which it is possible to communicate very many wisdoms which were previously only available to sophisticated thinkers, but which TA can communicate with concreteness and conviction, even to an eight-year-old! As for therapy, life is too short for us to wait the years that psychoanalysis takes — if, that is, it can of itself cure. Meanwhile, we cannot take time off from our relationships and swear to make no substantial changes in our daily lives. On the contrary, it is the *action* we want and need, to make the unbearable bearable and the bearable joyous, and in this respect the transactional analyst is a thorough-going pragmatist. He does not shrink from giving positive advice (in terms of sound principles) when required, he *strokes stroke*-eliciting behaviour within the group, and reinforces with more *strokes* his patients' reportage of *authentic, stroke*-abundant *transactions* outside the group. Even by this criterion alone, I believe TA enables people vastly to increase their sense of well-being. Through continuous positive feedback, to a large extent the mask does become the face. Hamlet knew this when he urged, 'Assume a virtue, if you have it not. . . ./For use almost can change the stamp of nature,/And master ev'n the devil or throw him out/with wondrous potency'. And combined with all the other tools of TA's conceptual armoury, the TA therapist is demonstrably capable of doing an excellent job of curing people of their psychological ills.

But for all of this that TA offers us it exacts a price — committment to the acceptance of the determinism of our lives and our own responsibility for the fates we chose for ourselves in the first place. For some people this price is too high.

Let Berne have the last word. The last paragraph of *Games People Play* reads

The somber picture . . . . . [of our *scripts*] . . . . in which human life is mainly a process of filling in time until the arrival of death or Santa Claus, with very little choice, if any, of what kind of business one is going to transact during the long wait, is a commonplace but not the final answer. For certain fortunate people there is something which transcends all classifications of behaviour, and that is awareness, something which rises above the programming of the past, and that is spontaneity, and something that is more rewarding than games, and that is intimacy. But all three of these may be frightening and even perilous to the unprepared. Perhaps they are better off as they are, seeking their solutions in popular techniques of social action, such as 'togetherness'. This may mean that there is no hope for the human race, but there is hope for individual members of it.

APPENDIX I

Annual Winners of The Eric Berne Memorial Scientific Award
(See Author Index for textual references to award-winning theory)

1971 Claude Steiner

1972 Stephen Karpman

1973 Jack Dusay

1974 Jacqui and Aaron Schiff

1975 Bob and Mary Goulding

1976 Patricia Crossman

1977 Taibi Kahler

1978 Fanita English

APPENDIX II

Recommended Further Reading

E. Berne (Ed. P. McCormick), *Intuition and Ego States: The Origins of Transactional Analysis*. Transactional Publications, 1977.

Transactional Analysis Bulletin (1962–70). Collected and bound edition available from Transactional Publications.

E. Berne, *Transactional Analysis in Psychotherapy*, Grove Press, 1961.

E. Berne, *Games People Play*, Andre Deutsch, 1966.

E. Berne, *Principles of Group Treatment*, Grove Press, 1966.

E. Berne, *What do you say after you say hello?* Bantam, 1973.

C. Steiner, *Games Alcoholics Play*, Bantam, 1971.

C. Steiner, *Scripts People Live*, Bantam, 1974.

Glossary of Principal Terms

(Cross-references are italicized)

Adapted Child. An *ego state.* The Parent-in-the-Child, designated P_1. Structurally, that part of the *Child* which is adapted to the demands of parents and society. Functionally, expresses *script.*

Adult. An *ego state*, designated A_2. Structurally, contains knowledge and skills. Functionally, collects, processes, and stores data. Is purely objective.

alternatives. The outcome of the effective collaboration of *Adult* and *Child.*

antiscript. An unstable part of the *Adapted Child*, which seeks to evade *script payoffs* by overt rebellion, but which inevitably achieves what it seeks to evade.

authenticity. *Game*-free thought, feeling, or behaviour.

autonomy. Thought, feeling, or behaviour which is aware and *script*-free.

Child. An *ego state*, designated C_2. Comprises the *Natural Child*, C_1, the *Little Professor*, A_1, and the *Adapted Child*, P_1.

compromise. The outcome of the effective collaboration of *Parent* and *Child.*

confusion. The content of the contamination of *Parent* and *Child* or of *Adapted Child* and *Free Child.*

contamination. A maladaptive resolution of an *impasse* between *ego states*, in which the incompatible impulses of the relevant *ego states* are expressed in a single *inauthentic* concept or attitude.

contract. The explicit agreement between therapist and patient to work towards a specified goal for the patient.

counterinjunction. A *message* transmitted by a *Parent* (usually of Mother or Father) into the developing *Parent* of a child.

counterscript. The total collection of *counterinjunctions* and *decisions* made around them.

decision. A committment made in childhood by the *Little Professor* to incorporate a

175

given existential dimension or frame of reference into the *script* or *counterscript*.

delusion. The content of the *contamination* of *Adult and Child*.

discount. The functional manifestation of either a *contamination* or an *exclusion*. A kind of negative *stroke*.

drama triangle. A simple diagram illustrating the roles of Persecutor, Rescuer, and Victim, amongst which people switch when they are playing *games* or are in *script*.

Driver. The beginning position of the process of the *miniscript*. There are five different Drivers: Be Perfect, Be Strong, Please Me, Try Hard, and Hurry Up.

ego state. A state of being manifesting a consistent pattern of feelings and experiences directly related to a corresponding consistent pattern of behaviour.

episcript. A very powerful *injunction* and associated *decision* having an over-riding influence on the general pattern of an individual's life.

exclusion. The dissociation of one or more *ego states* from the functioning personality.

executive ego state. The *ego state* which, at any moment, has the most active energy.

Final Miniscript Payoff. The end of the *miniscript* process, at which point a *script* position is re-experienced and reinforced.

Free Child. The biologically given parts of the *Child*, as opposed to the part which manifests adaptation to parental and societal demands. Usually taken to mean the *Natural Child*, C_1, and the *Little Professor*, A_1. Occasionally taken to refer to C_1 only.

gallows laughter. Laughter which expresses the triumph of the Witch or Ogre when the individual experiences a *script payoff*.

game. A set series of ulterior *transactions* with a well-defined psychological *payoff* for each of the players.

impasse. An unresolved disagreement on some issue between *ego states*.

injunction. An inhibiting *message* transmitted by an *Adapted Child* (usually of Mother or Father) into the developing *Adapted Child* of a child.

intimacy. A candid *Child* to *Child* relationship without ulterior motives, reservations, or exploitation.

judgement. The outcome of the effective collaboration of *Parent* and *Adult*.

Little Professor. An *ego state*. The Adult-in-the-Child, designated A_1. Structurally, that part of the *Free Child* which has insight. Functionally, explores, hypothesizes, and is creative.

message. An overt or covert *transaction* (usually from Mother or Father) making a powerful and lasting imprint on the structure of the *ego states* of the growing child.

miniscript. A sequence of behaviours usually occurring in a matter of seconds or minutes, which culminates in the reinforcement of a *script* position and *decision.*

Natural Child. An *ego state*, designated C_1. Structurally, contains innate feelings and *permissions.* Functionally, expresses spontaneous and *authentic* emotion.

palimpsest. A second version of the original *script* (*protocol*), usually laid down between the ages of six and twelve.

Parent. An *ego state*, designated P_2. Structurally contains values, beliefs, and generalizations. Functionally, controls, protects, and nurtures the Child.

payoff. The re-experiencing of a *script* position or *decision* as the outcome of a *game* or *miniscript.* May also refer to the achievement of a life goal laid down in the *script.*

permission. A *message* transmitted by a *Free Child* (usually of Mother or Father) into the *Free Child* of a child, usually reinforcing some aspect of the *Free Child's* innate capacity for pleasure or joy.

potency. The power in the therapist's *Parent* involved in the process of curing the patient.

prejudice. The content of the *contamination* of *Parent* and *Adult.*

protection. That aspect of the therapist's *Parent* which counteracts the wrath of the patient's Witch or Ogre when the patient disobeys them.

protocol. The original version of the *script*, laid down in the first six years of life. Contrasted with the later version, the *palimpsest.*

racket. An habitually experienced bad feeling. Part of an individual's *script.*

redecision. A new *decision* made by an individual to free himself of an *injunction* or a *script decision.*

script. The sum total of the *messages* and *decisions* incorporated into an individual's *Parent, Adult,* and *Child.* Sometimes used specifically to refer to the *messages* and *decisions* in the *Child* in contrast to the *counterscript messages* in the *Parent.*

script matrix. A diagram delineating *injunctions, counter injunctions, permissions, decisions*, etc., which provides a structural analysis of the whole personality

Stopper. A position in the process of the *miniscript*, at which point the individual experiences a *racket* feeling in response to an *injunction.*

stroke. Any unit of recognition between one person and another. *Strokes* may be positive or negative, conditional or unconditional.

time structuring. The six ways in which people may get, give, or avoid *strokes*: withdrawal, rituals, pastimes, activities, *games*, and *intimacy.*

trading stamps. Racket feelings collected towards a *payoff.*

transaction. What occurs between people when they meet.

Vengeful Child. An optional position in the *miniscript* process in which the individual exhibits *antiscript* behaviour.

trilog. A simple diagram showing how the *ego states* collaborate to form *judgements, alternatives,* and *compromises.*

Author Index

Subject Index

activities (work), *see* time structuring
Adapted Child   12, 32–6, 41, 43–6, 47, 48, 80–1, 88, 175
Adult   1, 3, 11–17, 32–7, 41–2, 47, 49, 117, 175
Affirming Free Child, *see* miniscript
Allower, *see* miniscript
alternatives   175
   see also trilog
antiscript   43, 46, 47, 175
authenticity/inauthenticity   27, 71, 73, 82, 88, 121, 175
autonomy   27, 49–50, 93, 121, 122, 125, 175
awareness   50, 172

behaviour modification (and TA)   28, 92, 116
   see also operant conditioning
blocked flow, *see* trilog

Child   1, 3, 11–17, 32, 35, 47, 49, 117, 175
   see also Adapted Child, Free Child, Natural Child
child development
   functional 31–8
   structural 40–52
compromise 175
   see also trilog
conflict, *see* impasse
confrontation   150–1
confusion   175
   see also contamination
contamination   3, 59–63, 175
counterinjunction   41–2, 47, 48, 175
counterscript   41–2, 46, 47, 175
cure   2, 66–7, 115–16, 120–1

damaged flow, *see* trilog
delusion   175
   see also contamination
despair/desperation, *see* contamination
diagnosis
   of ego states   12–14
   of pathology   65–7, 94–105
   of personality   81–4, 88–90, 92–105
   technique in   93–5
discount   127, 176
drama triangle   xv, 72, 176
Driver   176
   see also miniscript

efficiency   87–8
egogram   32, 39
ego states   xi, xii, xiv–v, 1, 11–17, 24, 31, 40–1, 93, 176
   boundaries and permeability   37–8, 58, 63
   executive   14–15, 176
electrode   43–4
   see also injunctions
episcript   46–7, 176
exclusion   63–5, 176

Final Miniscript Payoff   176
   see also miniscript
flexibility   87–8
flow point, *see* trilog
Free Child   12, 33, 47, 176
free flow, *see* trilog

gallows laughter   131, 176
games   24, 26–7, 45–6, 69–71, 74–5, 80, 123–4, 164, 176
Goer, *see* miniscript

health   27